Genesis II

Other books by Dale Peterson:

A Mad People's History of Madness

Big Things From Little Computers: A Layperson's Guide to Personal Computing

Intelligent Schoolhouse: Readings on Computers and Learning

Genesis II
Creation and Recreation With Computers

Dale Peterson

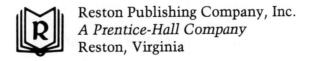

Reston Publishing Company, Inc.
A Prentice-Hall Company
Reston, Virginia

Library of Congress Cataloging in Publication Data
Peterson, Dale.
    Genesis II, creation and recreation with computers.
    Bibliography: p.
    1. Computer art.   2. Arts, Modern—20th century.
I. Title.   II. Title: Genesis 2, creation and recreation
with computers.   III. Title: Genesis two, creation and
recreation with computers.
NX260.P47   1983   700'.973   82–25043
ISBN 0–8359–2434–3
        0–8359–2433–5 pbk.

"Five Poems From the Chinese," by Marie Borroff, from *Computer Poems*, edited by Richard W. Bailey (Drummond Island, Michigan: Potagannissing Press, 1973), p. 3, has been reprinted by permission of Marie Borroff and Potagannissing Press. Two Russian folk tales, from Klein, Aeschlimann, Appelbaum, Balsinger, Curtis, Foster, Kalish, Kamin, Lee, Price, and Salsieder, "Modeling Propp," *Patterns in Oral Literature*, edited by Jason and Segal (The Hague: Mouton, 1977), pp. 141–222, have been reprinted by permission of Sheldon Klein. The Tale-Spin tale by James Meehan, from *The Metanovel: Writing Stories by Computer* (Yale University Department of Computer Science: Research Report #74), pp. 229–231, has been reprinted by permission of James Meehan. "Old Woman," by Louis T. Milic, from *Erato* (Cleveland: The Cleveland State University Poetry Center, 1971), p. 10, has been reprinted by permission of Louis T. Milic. A small amount of the material in the chapter on computer music has been paraphrased from material in an earlier book by the author: *Big Things From Little Computers*, by Dale Peterson, © 1982, pp. 118–120, 123–126. Reprinted by permission of Prentice-Hall, Inc., Englewood Cliffs, N.J. 07632.

© 1983 by Reston Publishing Company, Inc.
A Prentice-Hall Company
Reston, Virginia 22090

10 9 8 7 6 5 4 3 2 1

Printed in the United States of America

For my father

Contents

Remarks and Acknowledgments

I began this book thinking I was writing about "the creative uses of computers." Gradually, I began to realize that most uses of computers are "creative." It thus occurred to me that I had to narrow the topic, and I came to focus on the creative uses of computers in the creative arts. While computers are being used in the arts on an international scale, I felt it necessary to concentrate on computers in the arts in North America. Even that was too large a topic, though, since computers are used in so many, many areas of creative art—in choreography, stage lighting, special effects in film, and so forth. I narrowed the topic further to consider four kinds of creative arts: visual arts, music, literature, and what I call the participatory arts (games).

It is very clear that entire books can and have been written on any one of those four topics. By including all four, then, I have chosen breadth at the expense of depth. I have not been able, for instance, to write about all the important visual artists, or all the important musicians in North America using computers. Instead, in writing about individual artists, I have selected from among the top ranks—according to my own idiosyncratic sense of both accomplishment and representativeness.

The title, *Genesis II*, was acquired early. Certainly, any literal comparisons between the murky origins of the world (from either the Big Bang or the Big Word) and this latest direction of technology may be a little absurd; but I mean no literal comparison. Simply, the original story of *Genesis* tells of a universal creation—a good analogy to open a discussion on the creative possibilities of a tool that seems to have universal applications. Of course, I might have been less grandiose and called the book *Gutenberg II*, or *Printing II*, making some more modest and graspable comparison. Computers and printing are comparable in the sense that both seem to expand human intelligence, while most other technologies have expanded human physical power. But I strongly suspect that the ultimate impact of computer technology is going to be much more profound than the impact of printing.

Several people have helped substantially in the research for this book—giving advice and information, consenting to interviews, referring me elsewhere, and so on. Particularly, I wish to acknowledge the generous help of Professor Richard W. Bailey of the University of Michigan, artists Charles and Colette Bangert, composer David Behrman, Gwen Bell of Digital Museum, George Blank of *Creative Computing*, James Blinn of Jet Propulsion Laboratories, composer John Bischoff, poet Marie Borroff, composer Bill Buxton, composer John Cage, Loren Carpenter of Lucasfilm, artist Harold Cohen, composer John Chowning, Willie Crowther of Xerox PARC, David DiFrancesco of Lucasfilm, games designer John Dunn, artist David Em, scientist J. Martin Graetz, composer Lejaren Hiller, artist Miljenko Horvat, artist Marty Kahn, Scott Kim of Stanford University, Professor Sheldon Klein of the University of Wisconsin, artist William J. Kolomyjec, Professor Arthur Kunst of the University of Wisconsin, David Kusak of Passport Design, Robert Lafore of Interactive Fiction, Professor Kurt Lauckner of the University of Michigan, artist Ray Lauzzana, artist Ruth Leavitt, P. David Lebling of the Massachusetts Institute of Technology, Michael Loceff of Cromemco, Carl Machover of Machover Associates, artist Aaron Marcus, Nelson Max of Lawrence Livermore National Laboratories, composer Mike McNabb, Professor Louis Milic of Cleveland State University, Jim Meehan of Cognitive Systems, composer James Moorer, artist John O'Neill, artist Jim Pallas, artist Duane Palyka, Jamie Parker of Digital Museum, scientist Stephen D. Piner, Professor Joseph Raben of Queens College, artist Emily Reilly, composer David Rosenboom, scientist Stephen Russell, artist Ann Sandifur, artist Lillian Schwartz, Dick Shoup of Aurora Systems, Randall Stickrod of *Computer Graphics World*, composer Laurie Spiegel, Alvy Ray Smith of Lucasfilm, composer John Strawn, artist

John Whitney, Don Woods of Xerox PARC, and Ramon Zamora of ComputerTown, U.S.A.!

In addition, I am extremely indebted to the following people, who have read and commented upon significant portions of the manuscript in various stages of preparation: artist Darcy Gerbarg; John Gordon of the Center for Computer Research in Music and Acoustics at Stanford University; Ken Knowlton of SRI International; Ray Gerard Koskovich of the Department of Art of Stanford University; John MacMillan of Apple Computer and Data 22 Corporation; and Jenny Franchot, Wyn Kelley, Annie Janowitz, Tia Lombardi, and Jack Prostko of Stanford University's Departments of English and of Modern Thought and Literature. I thank them sincerely for their tremendous help and generosity.

Tracy Deliman helped me get started, and provided some of the initial ideas for the book. Thank you, Tracy. My editors at Reston, Nikki Hardin and Linda Zuk, have been extremely patient and helpful; I am grateful. My father encouraged me greatly throughout the writing and production of this book; to him the book is dedicated. Finally, my wife put up with me; I appreciate it tremendously. Thanks, Wyn.

In my research for this book, I have relied particularly on a handful of earlier works. I wish to acknowledge my special dependence on the following: Richard Bailey's "Computer-Assisted Poetry: The Writing Machine is for Everybody," James Burke's *Connections*, Christopher Evans' *The Micro Millennium*, Paul Griffith's *A Concise History of Avant-Garde Music*, Robert Hughes' *The Shock of the New*, John F. Kasson's *Civilizing the Machine*, Allen Strange's *Electronic Music*, John Strawn's "Digital Synthesis," and John Ziman's *The Force of Knowledge*.

Genesis II

Therefore the Lord God sent him forth
from the garden of Eden, to till the ground
from which he was taken. He drove out
the man; and at the east of the garden of
Eden he placed the cherubim, and a flaming sword which turned every way, to
guard the way to the tree of life.
    —The Book of Genesis

Prologue

Adam ate of the fruit of knowledge, and technology began. There
appeared the flaming sword that turned every way, forever block-
ing the path back to Paradise; and, of course, Adam needed a plow to
till the ground. Technology came when innocence left—the sword
as part of the curse, and the plow as Adam's feeble response to the
curse.

1

At a dinner party not long ago, I spoke with a distinguished
elder poet and teacher, with whom I had once shared a feeling for the
writings of D. H. Lawrence. The poet told me he was planning to
move to Nova Scotia and live on a farm. When he asked me what I
was doing, I mentioned that I was writing a book about computers.

"They're up to no good," the poet said.

"Computers?"

"Yes, they're up to no good."

At first, I was taken aback that he spoke of computers as if they
could choose to be good or not good. Then I hastily tried to work up

a defense for the machines. I suggested that in some ways they would simplify our lives. I mentioned some of the many useful things that small, inexpensive personal computers can do, and I compared them to other beloved tools of great usefulness—a guitar, a favorite carpentry tool, a good ten-speed bicycle, and so on.

The conversation soon took a turn, and the subject was closed. But strong opinions interest me, and I resolved to think along those lines: *They're up to no good.* Of course, D. H. Lawrence would have applauded my friend the poet. Lawrence concluded early that most machines were up to no good. His father worked around heavy, dirty mining machinery all his life, digging up coal to make other machines run, and Lawrence hated it. He hated the machines, hated what he saw as the imprint of machines on working men's bodies and souls. I suspect he saw The Machine as one of the great destructive forces of World War I, and I'll never forget the image, in his postwar novel *Lady Chatterley's Lover*, of a war-crippled Lord Chatterley angrily navigating through a field of wildflowers in his motorized wheelchair, chewing up the earth, destroying flowers as he went.

In a phrase certain to make decent people hide their bug spray, poet Ezra Pound once said, "Artists are the antennae of the race." He meant, I think, that artists (visual artists, musical artists, literary artists, and the like) are or ought to be a little more sensitive, and they ought to see a little farther, a little better, than other people—also, that artists possess, among other things, the acumen to understand what's going on in a broad sense, and the responsibility to tell us about it in their art.

I know a young man, approaching his late twenties, who often goes to work in sandals and levis. If his clothes were a little more tattered on the edges, he could pass for an impoverished artist, but he happens to be the founder and vice president of a large, extremely successful computer company. I understand his net worth can be described by a middle-sized digit followed by eight zeros. In a time when many people have been successful in the computer industry, he has been extraordinarily so. In other words, he's the Henry Ford of the 1980s. I once asked him where he thought computers would be taking us in the next thirty years. He leaned back, stretched, touched the bottom of the bookcase above and slightly behind him (as if to gather a little quick wisdom) and said at last, "The next thirty years don't interest me. I have more than enough to do just thinking about the next ten years."

Well, that was an engineer speaking. Ezra Pound's idea of the artist is that he or she is indeed interested in the next thirty years, and more. So what do artists tell us about technology?

2

The distrust of technology articulated by my friend the poet would not have occurred to Leonardo da Vinci. In da Vinci's time, artist and technologist were barely distinguishable. The sum total of knowledge was less than it is now; learning was not particularly compartmentalized; science as we know it did not exist. Engineering and the technological disciplines were crafts, as was art, and the word *artist* was used interchangeably with the word *artisan*, meaning *skilled craftsman*. For da Vinci, visual art was the "Queen of all sciences," and his fame rests almost as much upon his legacy of designs for a remarkable array of gadgets, devices, processes, tools, machines, as it does upon his few painted masterpieces.

Artists over the centuries have habitually depended on technological advances: easels in the twelfth century, oil-based paints around the fourteenth century, lithography at the end of the eighteenth century, premixed paints in tubes in the 1840s, prestretched and primed canvases in the 1850s. J. S. Bach relied on the technology of the pipe organ. Come to think of it, nearly all music relies upon instrument technology. Certainly, when photographic techniques first produced finely detailed, realistic, and permanent images on paper in the nineteenth century, many visual artists felt threatened. Some (the miniaturists of Paris, who specialized in miniature realistic portraits) went out of business. On the other hand, it soon became apparent to others that photography could complement painting. Gustave Courbet and Eugène Delacroix, for example, found they could substitute photographs for live models.

If technology has seemed quick to influence the artistic medium, though, its impact on the message has been more equivocal. Technology produced many immediate benefits for nineteenth-century Europe and America, and *one* prevailing attitude was optimism and hope for the Machine Age. Through science, many people reasoned, mankind might acquire ever increasing intellectual control over the world. Through industry, mankind could hope to achieve greater physical control. This would automatically produce the motion of history known as Progress—the gradual but steady acquisition of greater happiness for more people, leading ultimately to Utopia. From our perspective, looking back at the nineteenth century, we may tend to see the railroads and factories as despoilers of the pastoral garden. But many nineteenth-century thinkers and luminaries argued the reverse. In America, Ralph Waldo Emerson noted that while "Readers of poetry see the factory-village and the railway, and fancy that the poetry of the landscape is broken up by these...the poet sees them fall within the great Order not less than the beehive or the spider's geometrical web." And, in 1848, journalist, soon-to-be poet, Walt Whitman expressed a common aesthetic response of the time when he wrote in the *Brooklyn Daily Eagle* that "there are few more magnificent pieces of handiwork than a powerful steam engine swiftly at work!" Popular visual art in Europe and America (lithographs and wood engravings in periodicals) fed a tremendous public fascination with industry, machinery, and the latest technological developments. The predominant American lithographers of the time, Currier and Ives, published numerous dramatic railroad scenes, while *Harper's Weekly* entertained its readers with scenes from factories, foundries, cotton-mills, and so on.

Perhaps the greatest, certainly the tallest, symbol of nineteenth-century faith in technology was erected in the middle of Paris in 1889. At a height of 1,056 feet, the Eiffel Tower dominated the skyline of Paris, an engineer's steel monument to the coming millennium of technology. By 1900, a number of painters—particularly a group of Italian artists who described themselves as Futurists—began deliberately reflecting this positive feeling about machinery and technology in their subject matter. "We declare that the world's wonder has been enriched by a fresh beauty: the beauty of speed," declared an Italian Futurist manifesto in 1909. "A racing car with its trunk adorned by great exhaust pipes like snakes with an explosive breath...a roaring car that seems to be driving under shrapnel, is more beautiful than the Victory of Samothrace." The Futurists created canvases that glorified a brave new noisy, dynamic, violent world of machines, factories, lights, cities. And French Cubist Fernand Léger echoed this enthusiasm with his own painted visions of the coming Machine Age: often bizarre but sometimes serene interconnections of machine metal and human form, intimating that machinery might ultimately lend its own particular harmony and resonance to human society. In music, Futurist Luigi Russolo decided that the world needed a new music, an art of noises, which would be in tune with modern machines and factories. To that end, Russolo invented a series of *intonarumori*, or noise machines, which he demonstrated in Italy and London before World War I, and in Paris in 1921. All of Russolo's machines were destroyed in World War II, but in the meantime other composers had begun creating Machine Age music. Erik Satie's score for the ballet *Parade* (1916–17), for instance, included parts for automobile horns and a typewriter, as well as traditional musical instruments. George Antheil's *Ballet Mécanique* (1926) called for—along with several pianos and xylophones—two electric doorbells and an airplane propeller.

P. 1. Fernand Léger *Three Women* 1921
Oil on canvas 72 $\frac{1}{4}$ × 99 inches
Collection, The Museum of Modern Art, New York. Mrs. Simon Guggenheim Fund

Part of the public's fascination with machinery in the nineteenth century had to do with a cultivation of the *sublime* in art. Artists and critics claimed that works of art might evoke for the viewer a sense of the sublime by calling forth feelings of human powerlessness before the wondrous grandeur of nature. The Corliss steam engine—almost forty feet high, weighing 680 tons, and generating 2,500 horsepower—dominated the Philadelphia Centennial Exposition of 1876 and provoked the author of at least one exposition guidebook to proclaim that machinery too could evoke the sublime: "Poets see sublimity in the ocean, the mountains, the everlasting heavens; in the tragic elements of passion, madness, fate; we see sublimity in that great fly-wheel, those great walking-beams and cylinders, that crank-shaft, and those connecting rods and piston-rods,—in the magnificent totality of the great Corliss engine."* To one degree or another, though, the experience of the sublime—because it arose from a feeling of awe and powerlessness before a grand, powerful Other—contained a potential for anxiety, a shadow side to the sunny optimism of much nineteenth-century aesthetic response to machinery.

Even without contemplating the harms or potential dangers of technology and a machine society, nineteenth-century *fine arts* (as distinguished from the popular arts) generally treated industrial subjects as unworthy of aesthetic consideration. Paint in tubes may have allowed nineteenth-century artists to go outdoors, but many landscape artists deliberately excluded industrial subjects from their canvases. Railroads appeared in works by Joseph Turner, Claude Monet, Camille Pissarro; factories in Pissarro, Georges Seurat, Vincent Van Gogh; but such appearances occurred long after the actual arrival of railroads and factories. Even then, they remained rare or secondary motifs. Meanwhile, such nineteenth-century novelists as Charles Dickens in England, Stephen Crane and Theodore Dreiser in America, were charting their own dark visions of the netherworld of Victorian urban-industrial existence.

If the Futurists had some following and promise at the turn of the century, World War I crushed most people's simplistic faith in technology. Futurism—habitually shrill, aggressive, and vaguely militaristic in philosophy—gyrated in isolation, eventually surfacing as an inspiration for the official art, architecture, and personal style of fascist Italy. After the War, most European and American artists proclaimed themselves profoundly critical of modern technology and the society with which it resonated. "We are the hollow men," chanted poet T. S. Eliot in 1925, calling forth images of soulless mechanical men living in a desiccated landscape, dancing in an eternal circle of desireless sex and faithless prayer. Two years earlier, Marcel Duchamp had stopped working on his own vision of the hollow men: his masterpiece painting on glass, *The Bride Stripped Bare by Her Bachelors, Even* (otherwise known as *The Large Glass*). Duchamp's *Large Glass* is a gigantic, satirical design for a machine that will perpetrate endless sexual intercourse between a continually undressing mechanical bride and a continually revolving series of pathetic, mechanical bachelors, represented as suspended hollow suits and jackets. According to Duchamp's sardonic pseudoscientific notes (which are part of the work), the basic concept originated with Freud's statement in *The Interpretation of Dreams* (1900): "The imposing mechanism of

---

*See John F. Kasson's *Civilizing the Machine* for a more thorough consideration of the sublime machine. Many of my comments about the nineteenth-century American response to technology come from that source.

P. 2 Marcel Duchamp *The Large Glass,* or *The Bride Stripped Bare by Her Bachelors, Even* 1915–23
Oil and lead wire on glass 109 $\frac{1}{4}$ × 69 $\frac{1}{8}$ inches. Philadelphia Museum of Art. Bequest of Katherine S. Dreier

male sexuality lends itself to symbolization by every sort of indescribably complicated machinery.'' The machinery in *Large Glass*, according to Duchamp's notes, runs on ''Love Gasoline,'' which thrusts the ''feeble cylinders'' of a ''desire motor.'' In tone and feeling, Duchamp's *Large Glass* remains a world apart from da Vinci's marvelous, loving drawings of machines and gadgets.

In the 1920s, Berlin Dadaists Max Ernst, John Heartfield, Hannah Hock, Raoul Hausmann, and George Grosz used the new techniques of photomontage and collage to repeat this and similar themes, producing explicit and disturbing images of machines growing out of men, and vice versa, while later artists created their own hollow men. Bruce Lacey's *Boy, Oh Boy, am I Living!* (1964), for instance, presents a little man constructed entirely out of prosthetics, who smiles a Fuller Brushman's smile and can do nothing but kick one foot.

As Italian fascism illustrated, hollow men with power can become monsters. The image of the hollow, mechanized man first arose with those post-War visionaries Eliot and Duchamp, but the image of the mechanized monster goes back to 1818, when Mary Shelley published her novel about the monster created by Dr. Victor Frankenstein. Certainly the story of Frankenstein reflects some of the early nineteenth-century fascination with electricity and its potential as a new source of power; but it also embodies a vaguely nightmarish warning about science and technology. We have, in Dr. Frankenstein, another Faust, prying forbidden secrets out of nature, and using them for destructive ends. We have, in Frankenstein's monster, a frightening marriage between humanity and technology.

A marriage between humanity and technology means the divorce papers from nature must have finally come in the mail . . . and if ever an obsessive dream appears in art and literature, it has to do with that on-again off-again first marriage. The story begins, of course, with Adam in Paradise, pure Nature, and his peremptory dismissal for insubordination. We are reminded of the Roman poet Virgil's mythical land of Arcadia, which offered escape from the stresses and perversions of the city and human artifice. One American version of this obsessive dream appears in the idyllic story of Huckleberry Finn, floating down a primitive Mississippi River on a raft, carefree and smoking his corncob pipe, surrounded only by the grandeur and beauty of nature . . . until suddenly Huck and his companion Jim are almost drowned by a steamboat that looms ''big'' and ''scary'' and ''monstrous,'' with open furnace doors that look like ''red-hot teeth,'' violently noisy, ''pounding'' out of the darkness:

> She was a big one, and she was coming in a hurry, too, looking
> like a black cloud with rows of glow-worms around it; but all of

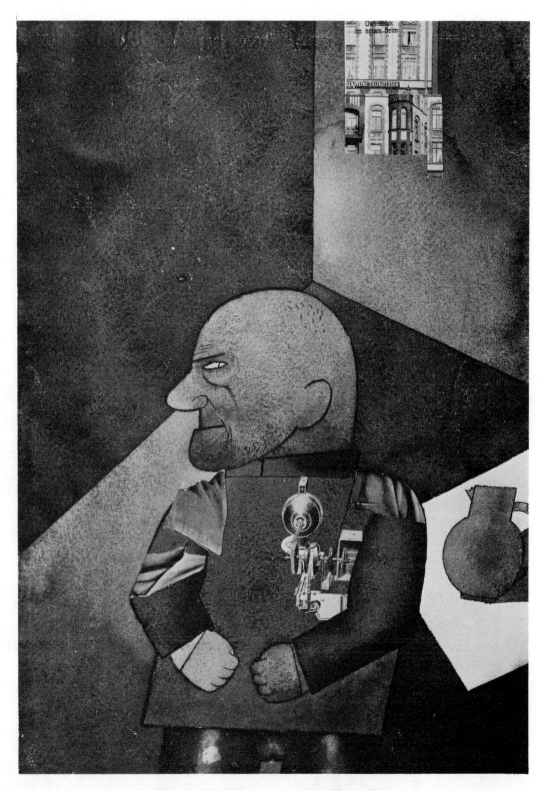

P. 3. George Grosz *The Engineer Heartfield* 1920
Watercolor and collage of pasted postcard and halftone $16\frac{1}{2} \times 12$ inches
Collection, Museum of Modern Art, New York. Gift of A. Conger Goodyear.

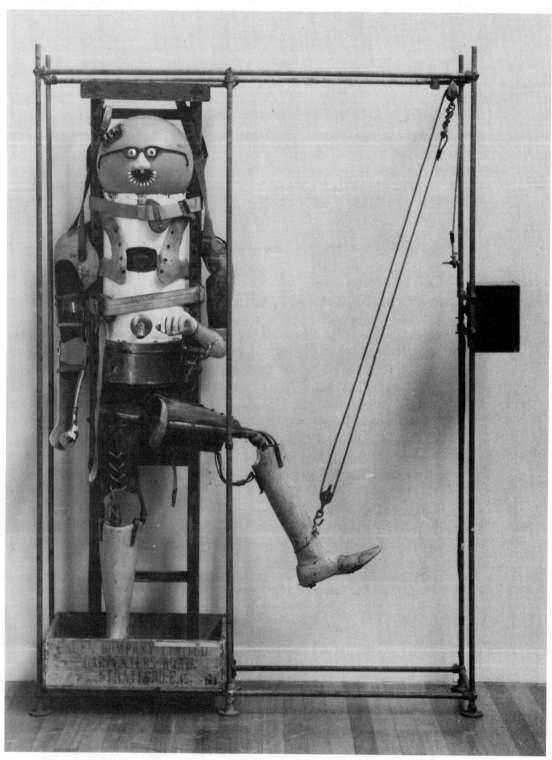

P. 4. Bruce Lacey *Boy, Oh Boy, am I Living!* 1964
78 × 60 × 12 inches. Collection, Tate Gallery, London.

a sudden she bulged out, big and scary, with a long row of wide-open furnace doors shining like red-hot teeth, and her monstrous bows and guards hanging right over us. There was a yell at us, and a jingling of bells to stop the engines, a pow-wow of cussing, and whistling of steam—and as Jim went overboard on one side and I on the other, she come smashing straight through the raft.*

If the machine was sometimes portrayed as a monster, in literature and art, it was a monster that began to take on human form. By 1920, the idea of the machine as monster in human form was embodied in the fascinating, powerful, and sinister image of the robot. Karel Čapek coined the term in that year, and his play about robots, *R.U.R.* (Rossum's Universal Robots), was a grand success in Czechoslovakia.

R.U.R. takes place in a robot factory, and the story goes something like this. In 1922, a physiologist named Rossum discovered on a remote island a substance that looked and behaved like living matter, although it wasn't. After years of experimentation with the stuff, and aided by his nephew, Rossum at last learned to synthesize human-looking robots. The robots lasted only about twenty years before they wore out, but other than that, they were superb workers. Superb particularly because Rossum's engineer nephew designed them to be devoid of any distracting impulses—emotions, for instance, or the urge to play games. During the action of the play, a problem arises because some of the robots are used in warfare. In addition, an irresponsible Dr. Gall gives them the ability to experience pain and feel emotion. As we might expect, once that happens, the robots feel resentment and anger at their human masters. They rebel and use their skills in warfare to take over the world and kill all humans but one.

Up to no good!

With his robots, Čapek introduced the twentieth-century version of the Frankenstein monster, prototype for an extensive

*Mark Twain's expressionistic monster machine that destroys Huck and Jim's peaceful communion with nature is unintentionally reminiscent of the real American steamboat, *Western Engineer*. Launched at Pittsburgh in 1819, *Western Engineer* was designed to resemble a massive, reptilian dragon, with the hope that it would frighten away hostile Indians during exploration of western regions. Joseph Kastner, in *A Species of Eternity*, quotes a newspaper reporter's description of *Western Engineer:* ''The bow of the vessel exhibits the form of a huge serpent, black and scaly rising out of the water from under the boat, his head darted forward, his mouth open vomiting smoke and apparently carrying the boat on his back. From under the boat at its stern issues a stream of foaming water, dashing violently along. All the machinery is hid. The boat is ascending the rapid stream at three miles an hour. Neither the wind nor human hands are seen to help her and to the eyes of ignorance the illusion is complete: that a monster of the deep carries her on his back, smoking with fatigue and lashing the waves with violent exertion.''

science fiction and fright literature to come. During the next several decades, robots in film and literature expressed in fantasy the growing concern that somehow machines were getting out of hand, that they really were up to no good.

By the third quarter of the twentieth century, however, an entire generation of artists knew no other normality than to live and work among buzzing and whizzing devices, to walk city streets surrounded by humming and honking machines. Before then, technological advances of use to artists had appeared every century or every fifty years, but after World War II, such technologies were appearing every few years: acrylic paints, plastics, resins, lasers, holography, computers.

Out of the junkyard of modern technology, after World War II, the so-called *machine artists* built some disarmingly charming machines that may have hinted at the savage irony found in Duchamp's work, but that, overall, delighted in the physical and aesthetic potential of tinkered cogs and wheels. Machine artist Jean Tinguely's gargantuan sculpture *Homage to New York* (consisting of some eighty wheels of bicycles and tricycles, a broken-down player piano, a bathtub, glass bottles, a small weather balloon, an old toy wagon, and various other *objets d'junk*) deliberately slobbered and clobbered itself to death one night in 1960, in the garden of the New York Museum of Modern Art—making a statement about technology or about New York City, perhaps, but also providing marvelous entertainment. During the same decade, Pop artist Andy Warhol, having declared "I want to be a machine," stamped out images characterized by machine-like regularity and repetition—an oil painting, for instance, depicting two hundred almost identical Campbell's soup cans. Pop Art of the 1960s was fine art looking at mass art, but with more mimicry than mockery. The violence and intensity of Duchamp's vision, in the first quarter of the century, were missing. Indeed, Duchamp's vision was irrelevant. Meanwhile, the frightening idea of the robot seemed to degenerate into something both more benevolent and less powerful: people today are most familiar with the helpful if often inept, charming if occasionally unctuous, vaudeville act of C3PO and R2-D2 in the film *Star Wars*.

Can't these artists ever get together in their opinions? Looking for some artistic consensus about technology seems as appropriate as waiting for agreement in the United Nations General Assembly. Artists may be the antennae of the race, as Ezra Pound said, but what good is that if we can't decide what distant and shadowy shapes they're vibrating about? What good is it if artists seem just as confused as the rest of the world?

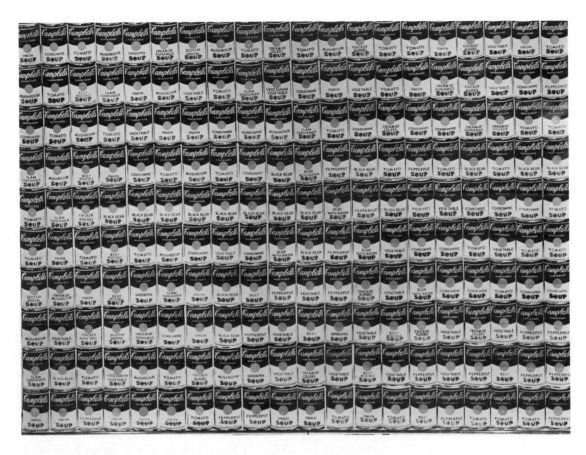

P. 5. Andy Warhol *200 Cans of Campbell's Soup* 1962
Oil on canvas 72 × 100 inches. Photo Courtesy of Leo Castelli Gallery, New York

Some of the confusion may have to do with the dual nature of technology—being both sword and plow. Some of it is certainly related to the differences among the various arts, and to the changes in any single art over time. But much of the confusion arises from our own misunderstanding of what technology is and what it means.

3

Great machines can express great beauty. In 1900, Henry Adams, historian and upstanding offspring of two American presidents, lingered beside a forty-foot dynamo at the Great Exposition in Chicago and decided (as much as it was possible for Adams to make a decision) that the power of the dynamo was somehow equivalent to the moral force that built the great medieval cathedrals. The dynamo inspired such fear and fascination in Adams that one suspects, left to meditate on the matter a while longer, he might have decided that the machine itself was a twentieth-century cathedral. "The planet...seemed less impressive, in its old-fashioned, deliberate, annual or daily revolution," he wrote, "than this huge wheel, revolving within arm's-length at some vertiginous speed, and barely murmuring—scarcely humming an audible warning to stand a hair's-breadth further for respect of power—while it would not wake the baby lying close against its frame. Before the end, one began to pray to it."

But why is it that more than eight decades after Adams wandered the hall of dynamos in the Great Exposition, we still never mistake a machine, even a very beautiful machine, for a work of art? The answer may be obvious. Machines are objects that have been designed to *do*. Art is designed to *be*. *

If art is designed to be, does that mean art exists for art's sake? Does that mean art is functionless, purposeless—that art just sits there? Obviously, the distinction between objects of doing and those of being is not absolute, but more a matter of degree. We might say that art ultimately is intended to do many things: to enlighten, to expand one's awareness and sympathies, to disconcert, to put bees in bonnets, to stimulate the artist's love life, and so on. But finally art's purposes are distant, often obscure, often psychological or spiritual. Whereas a machine's purposes are immediate, obvious, direct, and physical.

Civilization in its physical form is composed of objects made by humans. There are two classes of such objects: (1) those designed to be, and (2) those designed to do.

Objects that are designed to do are often used in the production of objects that are designed to be. Hammer and chisel produce sculpture. Some designed-to-do objects (the steamboat, for example) are dynamic. Others (the ordinary house, for example) are static. They "do" only in a passive fashion. Designed-to-do objects that are dynamic (or potentially dynamic) make up what I call technology. Sometimes the word *technology* is used to suggest the craft or knowledge involved in making such objects, and sometimes it is used—as I am using it—to refer to the objects themselves.

In this context, then, technology means tools and machines. And the purpose of such objects is to expand human powers. We

---

*As historian Kasson suggests, many nineteenth-century American machine engineers slightly obscured this fact with their habits of elaborate ornamentation. The locomotive *America*, winner of a gold medal at the Paris Exposition of 1867, epitomized this tendency. The cab of the locomotive was finished in ash, maple, walnut, mahogany, cherry; the boiler, smokestack, and other metal parts were covered with German silver; the locomotive's name, painted in scrolling script on the tender, was accompanied by a dramatic heroic portrait of General Ulysses Grant.

tend to think of technology as simply that massive collection of tools and machines which happen to be the casual and habitual droppings of science. The words, *technology* and *science*, are often spoken in the same breath, and confused in the same thought. But that happens primarily because we live in an age of science. Clearly technology existed before, and exists independently of, science. I count at least five kinds of technology, originating during five different phases of history.

Hand Technology. Beginning long before recorded history, this technology consists of tools that simply extend the human hand. Examples would be the hammer, arrow, sword, and plow.

Power Technology. Originating around the beginning of recorded history, this technology is distinguished by the simple use of natural forces apart from human strength. Examples would be the ox-drawn plow, the sailing ship, the wind mill, the water mill.

Industrial Technology. This is distinguished by the use of artificial, rather than naturally occurring, forces—steam, controlled explosions of petroleum products, and so on—for power. The beginning of Industrial Technology more or less coincides with the beginning of the Industrial Revolution in Europe, between 1750 and 1850.

Scientific Technology. This technology emerges from the deliberate and intelligent application of scientific knowledge to objects and processes. Clearly, some artifacts of Scientific Technology appeared as early as the beginning of formal scientific method (seventeenth century). But I prefer to mark the beginning of Scientific Technology as, roughly, 1900, when it came to have a distinct impact on people's lives and on their perceptions of themselves and the world.

Information Technology. For the most part, this technology begins in the 1940s, when an increasingly sophisticated knowledge of electronics was applied to the old technology of calculating machines. Mostly, it derives from a single invention: the computer. One *might* say that Information Technology began in the nineteenth century, when some people realized that electricity could not only produce power, but also send signals (thus the technologies of the telegraph and telephone). But not until the arrival of the computer in the 1940s—with its ability to manipulate signals—did Information Technology acquire anywhere near the significance it has today.

There are some interesting things to notice about the above progression. First, with the possible exception of Information Technology, it is clearly a progression from simple to complex and from little to big—from the arrowhead to the atomic bomb. Second, each subsequent stage of the progression involves shorter and shorter time spans, from tens of thousands of years to a few decades. Third, the progression does not involve replacement, but addition. Power Technology never replaced Hand Technology. It was simply another version of technology, coexisting with and making use of what preceded it. In other words, the overall progression is similar to a stairway of five steps, with each step in turn being raised and supported by all preceding steps. Fourth—and this is somewhat related to the third observation—technology is becoming more. That is, we are collecting it. Old technologies seldom fade away—they accumulate. This partly explains why "technologically advanced" countries not only have "advanced" objects, they have more objects. Fifth, the first two technologies appear closer to nature. They are tools and machines that work through natural sources of energy, while the last three depend upon artificially manipulated or synthesized energy.

The last observation may help to explain the arrival of Frankenstein's monster at the beginning of the nineteenth century. Technology has always been intimately related to humans. Technology has sometimes been an enemy and sometimes a friend, sometimes sword and sometimes plow. But in all cases it has been close to humans. Often, it seems almost human: designed, built to fit the organic shape of human hands and to conform to organic human needs. At the same time, technology has always possessed non-human attributes: it is, after all, the inorganic *thing*, the object. This peculiar human/nonhuman (or organic/inorganic) *duality* of technology is, of course, precisely what disturbs us about Frankenstein and a host of other monsters, robots, and aliens from outer space. They have some human qualities. They may have two eyes, a nose, a mouth, but at the same time they are blatantly different, and likely to be indifferent to human needs and feelings. Humanoid features but no human heart. Human and nonhuman. Organic and inorganic.

The strange and potentially disturbing duality of technology, however, was not so very recognizable at first. The hammer (although it extends the reach and force of the human arm) is nonhuman and inorganic . . . but so what? The windmill of what I call Power Technology is nonhuman and inorganic, but then it's also picturesque, and quiet, perhaps a little creaky but not creepy, and it only runs when the wind blows. It depends on nature, and as the moss grows up its sides we begin to forget altogether that it is apart from nature. But the steam engine of Industrial Technology is

P. 6. The Robot Alpha at the London Radio Exhibition of 1932.
BBC Hulton Picture Library.

different. Moss never grows on it. It is bigger, more powerful than anything that came before. It has nothing to do with the coursing of rivers or the vagaries of winds. It runs on strange and powerful energies that have never been seen before, and it alters nature and civilization at a speed and with a force never before imagined.

With the coming of Industrial Technology, tools and machines lost their old connection with the organic world of naturally-occurring power: tools and machines were noisier, more violent, less peacefully intertwined with the natural world. Suddenly, there seemed the possibility that technology could, like some monster in rough human form, take on a life of its own and run out of control—servant destroying master. In early industrial Europe vast numbers of farmers and farm workers and other members of a peasant economy migrated to crowded, disease-ridden cities to work in the factories. Urban populations multiplied disastrously, and though European societies eventually may have become better off in some general sense, the people who worked in the shadows of the giant machines and sweated next to the burning coal that made them run, were miserable and usually died young. Mary Shelley created the image of Frankenstein's monster at this time, and we were blessed with literature's first technologically incubated monster.*

---

*It may appear paradoxical at first that when electricity is made to seem most hostile to humans, it is given quasi-human form (in the Frankenstein monster). It may appear paradoxical that when the steamboat in *Huckleberry Finn* seems most antithetical to a human connection with nature, it is described with certain organic attributes. But it is precisely this apparent paradox that makes the machine as monster so compelling and ultimately disturbing an idea. The human/nonhuman duality of Frankenstein quite parallels the human/nonhuman (or organic/inorganic) duality of machines in general—a paradoxical quality that became more extreme and more apparent in the nineteenth century. Why is this duality disturbing? I think it is disturbing both for logical and psychological reasons. Logical: That which is likely to be most threatening to mankind is that which has some human connection; those elements of the universe that are entirely unconnected to human life are likely to be profoundly and pleasantly indifferent. Psychological: Professor Mori, director of the robotics department of the Tokyo Institute of Technology speaks of an *uncanny valley* when describing the human sense of familiar comfort with robotic forms. Robots can be built along entirely functional lines, having little external resemblance to human form, or they can be made to mimic human form quite closely. Professor Mori notes that people observing robots experience an increasingly pleasing sense of familiarity the closer robots come to human form—up to a point. At a certain point, though, the sense of comforting familiarity plummets; the robot begins to seem disturbingly *uncanny*. Yet a robot that entirely resembles human form no longer evokes the uncanny reaction. Thus, it is the time of cognitive dissonance, when the human observer is trying to decide whether the robot is human or not, that causes the disturbance, the uncanny valley. A robot displayed at the Osaka World's Fair in 1970 was built to look human, and included the mechanisms to imitate twenty-nine facial muscles engaged in a smile. When the robot was programmed to smile in a normal way at a normal speed, the result was pleasant. When the speed of the smile was significantly diminished, however, so that it began to look both near-human and yet distinctly not human, the uncanny result was frightening. See Reichardt's *Robots* for a more thorough discussion of Mori's theory.

Pre-scientific technologists learn their skills through tradition. Clockmakers learn their craft from other clockmakers and from the tradition of clockmaking. Similarly, primitive arrowmakers did what their fathers did before them, and their fathers before them, back into forgetting.

When pre-scientific technologies change, they change somewhat predictably. They grow in a fashion similar to Darwin's scheme of evolution, beginning simply, and gradually growing into more complex forms. Changes usually come through simple trial and error experimentation. Occasionally, changes are brought about by inventors and discoverers—individuals or very small groups of people who suddenly, with some creative or intuitive leap or discovery and through traditional knowledge of the craft, devise a way to improve or change the technology. But usually the improvement is minor, the change gradual, because the technologist works from traditional knowledge. To say that change is gradual, though, is not to underrate its possible impact. As in Darwinian evolution, there are moments when a plateau is reached, and some gradual change that has been underway suddenly makes a profound difference. At that point, historians take out their pencils and write—for technology, because it expands the power of individuals, influences the course of history.

The development of the Hand (and later Industrial) Technology of printing is generally associated with techniques introduced in the fifteenth century by Johann Gansfleisch, a goldsmith living in Mainz, Germany. Gansfleisch, or Gutenberg, as he preferred to be known (*gansfleisch* means *goose flesh*), didn't really invent printing, of course. Well before his time, calendars, playing cards, and occasional illustrations, capital letters, or even whole pages in books had been ''printed'' by stamping on parchment or paper inked patterns from laboriously carved blocks of wood. But carving individual blocks of wood for a portion or a page of a book was not much more efficient than the standard method for reproducing books during the Middle Ages: battalions of scribes scribbling away with quills on parchment.

Gutenberg's idea was that books could be printed easily by using wholly interchangeable letter types, made of metal, that could be squeezed together into one whole unit, forming a whole block. Printing would involve staining the front of the block with ink and pressing it against a sheet of paper, thereby producing a single printed page. As soon as the required number of pages were printed from that one block, the individual types could be separated and reformed for another page. Carved wooden letters wouldn't work for this because the pieces had to be durable enough to withstand repeated applications on the press. The letters also had to be more uniform than hand carving could make them. They had to be of precisely uniform depth so that each letter would strike the paper with equal pressure. They had to be uniform in width and length so that they could be squeezed together into a block and stay squeezed.

Gutenberg knew he had to cast his types out of metal, and of course coins had been cast for ages. But typically coin minting involved using a separate mold for each coin. The coin was cast inside the mold and the mold had to be broken. This process simply was not accurate enough for producing type, and so Gutenberg instead made molds consisting of three separate parts which could be held together temporarily by an iron spring. Once any letter was cast, the mold could simply be opened up, ready for another letter. What kind of metal would be used? Lead was too soft. Many metals would shrink in the transition from their molten to solid states, and shrinkage would probably have made it impossible to produce uniform type sizes. Gutenberg, through trial-and-error experimentation and probably with some help from his father—who as an employee of a mint was well-versed in the craft of working with soft metals—arrived at a combination of tin, antimony, and lead that was durable and unshrinkable. Of course, the molds themselves had to be standardized, and probably his partner, Johann Fust, a goldsmith, assisted directly at this point, providing the steel hallmark punch used in goldsmithing, as well as other traditional tools and techniques.

Like some new and highly successful mutation or hybrid that has evolved biologically, Gutenberg's alterations in printing technology were so obviously superior that they swept the field. We date the use of movable type in Germany at 1454. By 1465 it had appeared in Italy, and within a few years it was being used in Switzerland, France, Holland, Belgium, Austria, Hungary, and Spain. It reached England in 1476, Denmark in 1482, Sweden in 1483, and Portugal by 1487. Printing with movable type proved to be a highly successful way to produce books at a time when books were in great demand . . . but my point is this: in inventing the process, Gutenberg depended upon the traditional technologies of minting, metalworking, and jeweling to fulfill his idea. He made use of earlier versions of a screw press, used in papermaking and grape and olive pressing, and of the traditions of printing by woodblock. Impressive though it was, Gutenberg's invention arose from a new combination of old crafts. Like all other pre-scientific technologies, it evolved from the traditional techniques that preceded it.

Science—the systematic study of the physical world—began in the seventeenth century in western Europe. Prior to that time, with remarkably few exceptions, education meant the unexamined transmission from one generation to another of the accumulated cogitations of the ancients. In the seventeenth century, however, a small number of people suggested a new way of acquiring knowledge about the world. Francis Bacon in England suggested that much could be learned by isolating segments of the natural world, toying with them, and watching carefully: experimentation and observation. "Nature, like a witness, reveals her secrets when put to torture," is the way he described the method, and he popularized it in an extended fable, *The New Atlantis*, published in 1626. New Atlantis was an imaginary island in the South Seas where a number of inquisitive and far-sighted men tried to understand certain occurrences in nature by conducting experiments, observing the results, and generalizing from them. Largely through Bacon's inspiration, groups of educated men with time on their hands formed societies dedicated to this new style of learning: the Royal Society in England (1662), for instance, and the Académie des Sciences in France (1666).

This was the beginning of scientific thought. In the seventeenth century, only a hundred or so individuals could really be considered practitioners of this new method of learning, and they were almost all amateurs, gentlemen *savants* (as they were called). But their technique seemed to be a particularly effective way of learning about, and learning how to manipulate, nature.

In minor ways, science had an almost immediate effect on technology. The telescope was invented in a "traditional" (prescientific) fashion by a Dutch lens grinder, Hans Lippershay, in 1608. The craft of grinding glass into lenses to make spectacles had existed for about three hundred years. One day Lippershay discovered accidentally that by putting lenses at both ends of a tube, and then putting the tube up to his eye, he had a particularly spectacular spectacle. He called his device a *looker*, and thought it would be useful in war. Galileo got hold of one, improved it a little, and then used it himself to challenge prevailing ideas about the solar system. This early telescope, however, produced blurred images with various colors around the edges. Then, in 1671, Isaac Newton thought he had discovered the reason why. As a scientific experiment, Newton had placed a glass prism in front of a beam of light and observed a rainbow of colors on an opposing wall. He concluded that normal light was really composed of several bands of color that, for some reason (later understood to be varying wave lengths), tended to disperse when passed through a lens or prism. Newton quickly applied this new piece of experimentally acquired information to the traditional technology of the telescope, designing and building one that magnified images by reflecting (instead of refracting) light with curved mirrors. The result was an image free of chromatic aberration.

One remarkable thing about this new way of acquiring knowledge, this scientific method, was the way it expanded. The number of new practitioners doubled approximately every fifteen years, expanding in size by a factor of 100 every century—which means that for every person practicing science in 1670, there were one million (100 times itself 3 times) in 1970. Additionally, scientific knowledge itself, by its very nature, expanded: it built upon itself, second principles were derived from first principles. Traditional philosophy, in comparison, is not expansive. Philosophical systems are born, take hold, and then are replaced, but they do not expand indefinitely.

By the nineteenth century, accumulated scientific information and theory began splitting, largely out of sheer mass, into various specialities or disciplines. We can get some sense of this development by enumerating the founding of various learned societies in England: the Geological Society in 1807, the Royal Astronomical Society in 1820, the Zoological Society in 1826, the Entomological Society in 1833, the Chemical Society in 1841, the Physical Society in 1874, and the Physiological Society in 1876. The nineteenth century also saw gradual introduction of scientific courses in the universities, and an increasing employment of active scientists in the academic community as professors. There was little impetus, however, to apply the knowledge of science to the problems of industry or technology, except perhaps in Germany. If we assume that the Industrial Revolution and some "scientific revolution" took place at the same time, we ought to recognize that they took place separately. The Industrial Revolution in England was powered by the steam engine. With the sole exception of James Watt, however, steam engine technologists had almost no knowledge of, or interest in developments in science. "Until the middle of the nineteenth century," according to science historian John Ziman, "the steam engine did far more for pure science than science did for the technique of power engineering: it was not until near the end of that century that rational thermodynamic design could improve on experience, trial and error, and intuitive invention in this field of technology." In other words, with some notable exceptions, the University and the Factory remained disconnected, self-sufficient islands.*

By the twentieth century, however, western European scientific knowledge and theory about the workings of nature had apparently reached a critical mass. A tremendous transfer from knowing to doing, from thinking to tinkering, began. The relationship of science to technology became what we are familiar with today, and I consider the turn of this century to mark the beginning of Scientific Technology.

What distinguishes Scientific Technology from the technolo-

---

*Many of the ideas expressed here about science and technology are taken from John Ziman's *The Force of Knowledge*.

gies that preceded it? By definition, Scientific Technology arises from the direct application of science to technology. In addition, innovations in Scientific Technology—because they emerge less from generally understood traditions of technology than from a rapidly expanding scientific knowledge—are likely to be more sudden and to have greater impact than innovations in pre-scientific technology. Finally, because scientific knowledge pierces deeply through the visible surfaces of nature, Scientific Technology is likely to seem more incomprehensible, and potentially more threatening, than pre-scientific technologies. Water power, steam power, and atomic power all ultimately gather their energies from nature. But water power makes use of a nature that is visible to the human eye and has always been apparent. The origin of atomic power is much less visible, and its connection to nature much less apparent.

Around the end of the nineteenth century, most European farmers fertilized their land with sodium nitrate, imported from Chile in large chunks, then crushed to a powder and spread on the fields. Although the deposits in Chile had once seemed virtually endless, by 1900 they were approaching depletion. European chemists began searching for alternative sources of fertilizer, and in 1909, Fritz Haber, a young German chemist with a penchant for both pure research and industrial application, solved the problem by discovering an economical process for synthesizing ammonia, which was then easily converted to sodium nitrate. A painful European dependence upon some unreliable resource from South America was ended: science had been applied to technology in a dramatic fashion.

Fritz Haber was bald and sometimes smoked fat cigars. He carried two business cards—the one he chose depended upon the occasion. One card said, ''Fritz Haber.'' The other said, ''Professor, Dr. Phil., Dr. Ing., E.H., Dr. D. Landw., E.H., Fritz Haber, Nobel Prize winner...Director of the Kaiser Wilhelm Institute for Physical Chemistry and Electrochemistry.'' Actually, his second card was modest considering what it might have listed: Honorary Professor of the University of Berlin, Knight of the Iron Cross, Knight of the Kaiser House Order of Hohenzollern Swords, Member of the Order of the Crown Third Class, Honorary Fellow of the Bayer Academy of Science in Munich, also of the Prussian and Gottingen Academies, President of the German Chemical Society in 1923, Recipient of the Bunsen Society Gold Medal, of the Wilhelm Eimer Medal, and the Goethe Medal. Largely because of his discovery of an economical technology for synthesizing nitrogen, Fritz Haber became the most prominent chemist in a country renowned for its chemists. He remained a national hero until he was dismissed in the early 1930s for possessing an inferior heredity—along with a third of Germany's Nobel Prize winners.

Haber's discovery, by the way, became important in fields other than farmers'. In 1914 Germany declared war against the rest of Europe. Sodium nitrate plus sulphuric acid makes nitric acid, which, when applied to cotton, makes gun cotton—very useful on the battlefield. At the start of the War, Britain blockaded Germany's natural source of sodium nitrate, the Chilean mines, and Germany found herself entirely dependent upon the Haber process.

On April 22, 1915, applied chemistry entered the war a second time. Several divisions of German troops were locked in a stalemate with French and Canadian troops at Ypres, France. Except for occasional artillery exchanges, that particular day was pleasant. It was spring, the air was warm, the sky clear and sunny, and a gentle breeze blew from the east. For most of the afternoon both sides of the line were quiet, and no doubt some of the soldiers in the trenches were trying to catch a bit of sun. At about five o'clock in the afternoon, however, the German artillery began booming, and suddenly some British observers noticed a large greenish-yellow cloud billowing up and sweeping slowly with the breeze toward French and Canadian trenches, gradually turning into a pale white mist. The cloud consisted of chlorine gas, 168 tons worth. The French and Canadians who were soon enveloped by it first noticed the pungent smell, then an irritation to the eyes, then to the throat. They began choking, running, stuffing shirts in their mouths, and burrowing into the earth. Almost an entire division suffocated to death, and in all, French and Canadians suffered twenty thousand casualties and five thousand deaths, while the Germans quickly took four thousand yards of ground. Meanwhile, back at the Kaiser Wilhelm Institute for Physical Chemistry and Electrochemistry, who was puffing on a cigar and continuing his studies on the effects of various poison gases on laboratory animals? Captain Fritz Haber of the German Army, soon to be director of the German Chemical Warfare Service.

Up to no good!

The Germans tried chlorine gas two days later against a Canadian division at Ypres, but the Canadians were prepared enough to protect themselves with rags dipped in water. They held their position. On the other side of the Channel, the British called in their own chemists: professors Haldane, Baker, and Water, who realized that the Germans were using chlorine gas and recommended respirators made of cotton pads soaked in hyposulphite and carbonate of soda. By May 15, 1915, the first of 250,000 such respirators arrived at the trenches. Soon thereafter, the British began manufacturing full *hypo helmets*, covering a soldier's entire head with a flannel bag that had been impregnated with hyposulphite of soda. The helmet included eye-pieces made of mica, later of celluloid.

The British began using chemical weapons themselves, and during the course of the war, British, French, and German research chemists, often elevated in rank to generals, tested more than three thousand substances for their toxic effect—including phosgene, arsine, hydrocyanic acid, and mustard gas. Europeans tossed some 125,000 tons of about a dozen poison chemicals at each other. One account of the war suggests that gas was a minor weapon, that it may have caused less than five percent of the total 21.5 million casualties. But the abhorrence this new weapon aroused was profound. Haber's 1918 Nobel Prize was vigorously protested—a unique event in the history of the award. He was labeled "morally unfit," and was vilified for years after the war in newspapers and sometimes in professional journals. Haber himself never quite understood this reaction. For him gas was just another weapon, and people had become upset about it simply because it was new. "New weapons break [the soldier's] morale because they are something new, something he has not experienced, and therefore something that he fears. We were used to shell fire. The artillery did not do much harm to morale, but the smell of gas upset everybody."

Of course guns could kill you just as dead as gas. Guns could hurt, too. So why the distaste? I suggest that the revulsion against poison gas as a weapon had something to do with the nature of this new kind of technology, Scientific Technology. Guns were familiar tools of warfare, part of a long tradition of explosive armaments that evolved from the introduction of gunpower to Europe in the thirteenth century, the first clumsy cannons or bombards, and the arquebus of the fourteenth century, to the sixteenth century musket, up to the rifle and Gatling gun. They are, of course, nonhuman as all technology is; but at the same time they have always seemed somehow close to human. After all, they typically fit in your hand or against your shoulder. The trigger is curved to fit your trigger finger. The mechanism is understandable, and ultimately death by gun is likely to be more or less as pretty as death by sword. Gas, on the other hand, was far more devastating: five thousand deaths in one swoop at Ypres. Gas was a nasty surprise: the attack in Ypres didn't arise out of a long tradition of poison gas technology, but rather from a tradition of science in the laboratory suddenly applied to the world outside. Gas remained the ultimate weapon in the age of Scientific Technology for several years, until theoretical physicists showed us how to apply $E = MC^2$ to a hundred thousand Japanese civilians and their chromosomes.

At last we begin to understand the complexities of people's feelings about "technology." In the first place, there is more than one kind of technology. The artist who uses computers and tries to justify this partnership with a machine by referring to the technology of mixing oils, or of putting paint in tubes, and then suggesting that artists have always used the technology around them, is not explaining things entirely. The use by Courbet and Delacroix of the camera has nothing whatever to do with Grosz's *The Engineer Heartfield.* For Cervantes to poke fun at Don Quixote's funny poking at mills; and for novelist George Eliot to put onto paper some of the nicest things ever written about a mill, in *The Mill on the Floss;* while poet-prophet William Blake writes of "dark Satanic Mills" is, we see at last, no contradiction. Quixote's mills were powered by wind, Eliot's mill was powered by water, while Blake's ran on burning coal. People who insist they "hate technology," might really only hate Scientific Technology, and they are likely to hate it for its own particular and distinctive qualities: its unprecedented power and potential for violence, the suddenness of its innovations, its apparent distance from nature and humanity.

4

Earlier, I compared the progression of the various technologies to a set of stairs. With the comparison I hoped to emphasize that new technologies don't replace older ones, but rather build on them, use them as a foundation, and coexist with them. Information Technology is recent. I list it as beginning in 1940. But its precedents go far back in time: Information Technology in its most obvious form, the computer, exists today partly because some people applied the science and emerging technology of electronics—moving controlled bunches of electrical charges in provocative ways through interesting circuits—to the old technology of counting machines.

The earliest counting device, the abacus, seems a little like a direct mechanical representation of hands and fingers. It is a rack consisting of wires on which beads are strung. There may be just about any number of beads per wire, but let's assume there are nine beads per wire. Counting with fingers is often inefficient, partly because we have only two hands: arrive at a number beyond 10, and we either have to go to the toes, or remember that one hand is already full and start over again. The abacus is more efficient than finger counting, then, first because it frees the hands. Second, the abacus can easily hold more beads than we have fingers and toes. Third, the abacus operator uses a different and more efficient system than most finger counters do. The system is simple, and most of us are familiar with it. It involves the idea of valued columns, columns in which the numerical value of the bead increases from right to left. For example, in an abacus with five columns (that is, five wires) each of which has nine beads, each bead in the far right column will have a value of 1, each bead in the next column will have a value of 10, each bead in the column next to that will have a value of 100, and so on. To count up to 100 by old-fashioned finger counting requires either a good memory, or one hundred fingers. To count to 100 with an abacus such as the one described above, though, all we need is nine beads each in the first two columns and a single bead to slide down to the bottom of the third column (or wire), upon reaching 100.

In spite of the efficiency of the abacus, which was widely used for three or four thousand years, and in spite of the adoption in Europe of the convenient Arabic system of numerical notation (in place of the clumsy Roman system), most people still didn't like doing ordinary mathematics. The motivation for building a better number machine persisted.

Leonardo da Vinci made sketches of a new form of counting machine: it would be powered by a hand-turned crank, and it might have up to thirteen wheels, each with ten cogs. The gearing would be such that any wheel would have to advance ten times before the wheel to its immediate left would advance once. Thus it would operate in principle somewhat like an abacus with nine beads: that is, after reaching the tenth unit the operator activated the next column.

Da Vinci's notebooks disappeared for a long time, but the basic idea was simple and reasonable enough. In 1642, at the age of eighteen, Blaise Pascal constructed just such a machine, which he called the Pascaline. His father was a tax collector in France, and Pascal thought that the Pascaline would be an excellent way to reduce the routine mathematical chores involved in his father's occupation. The Pascaline consisted of six sets of wheels and meshing gears, and as with da Vinci's concept, each wheel represented a column in the decimal system. The full system of wheels and gears was housed in a nicely crafted wooden box. The box had six little windows on the top, and one could look in and see the numbers as they appeared for each of the six columns. The entire machine was powered by turning a crank, and to add two numbers the operator simply cranked in one, then cranked in the other. The machine displayed the total in the windows. To subtract, the operator reversed the direction of the crank. Multiplying was just a matter of adding one number as many times as the second number dictated. Division was a little trickier, but essentially was just the reverse of multiplication.

A few years later, in 1673, the German mathematician Gottfried Wilhelm von Leibnitz looked at Pascal's box, and decided he could make a better one. Pascal's machine multiplied by repeated addition, but Leibnitz added a special cog with teeth of increasing length that did multiplication in a single stroke. Leibnitz's design was repeated basically unchanged in mechanical and electro-mechanical arithmetic machines manufactured well into this century.

Ultimately, however, Leibnitz's device could only perform the four types of calculation used in simple arithmetic. One or two people tinkered with more complicated math machines, but it was not until the nineteenth century that Charles Babbage in England conceived of a machine that would theoretically carry out all mathematical tasks.

In Babbage's time, a primary occupation of professional mathematicians was the production of numerical tables, such as logarithmic tables, by rote application of numbers to some algebraic formula. It seemed obvious that anything done by rote, a standard method, might be done by a machine, and while still a student at Cambridge, Babbage began to dream of such a machine. Eventually he designed and built a working model of what he called his Difference Engine, which was to solve one particular type of mathematical equation by grinding it out with a hand crank, through a hodgepodge of shafts, wheels and gears. After each part of the equation was complete, a bell would ring. The machine would be reset for the next part, and cranked again. Babbage's prototype worked. He demonstrated it before the Royal Astronomical Society, which quickly encouraged him with a gold medal, while the British government encouraged him to the tune of £15,000.

Thus heartened, Babbage set up shop on his estate, hired professional machinists to help, and proceeded with the construction of a full-scale, hand-cranked, brass and pewter Difference Engine. But the engine was never completed, remaining forever un-crankable because machining technology of the day was not precise enough. After thirteen years of work on the Difference Engine, Babbage did the only reasonable thing he could. He scrapped it and began working on a calculating machine that was far more grandiose. This he called his Analytic Engine, and he believed it would be the first universal calculator, one able to carry out any mathematical task required.

Babbage never finished this second machine either, though his son finally built a model of it. But the Analytic Engine is of interest to us because it was almost identical in concept to the modern computer. It had a *memory*, which was at the center of the Engine, and which consisted of a complex series of interlocking cogged shafts similar to the cogged wheels of the Pascaline. The machine was to turn these shafts and store intermediate results of mathematical work in progress simply by letting the cogged wheels rest. The stored numerical values could be picked up and entered back into the mathematical process at any later time. The Engine also had a *processor* (Babbage called it a "mill"), which consisted of several different and independent units that were designed to perform all the different steps of arithmetic. Additionally, there was a system for an overall coordination of the sequences of the parts of the mill. The Engine would go from one process to another, from one part of the mill to another, by means of what we might call a *program input*, an encoded punch card, the idea for which Babbage cleverly borrowed from contemporary weaving technology.* At the other end of the machine, Babbage was going to attach an *output device*, a small printer, capable of printing any sequence of numerical results that the machine achieved.

It may sound like an impossible Rube Goldberg construction, but Babbage's Analytical Engine might have worked. It failed for the same reason that his Difference Engine failed—imprecise machining. The parts didn't cohere quite smoothly enough. Nonetheless, his work is of more than passing interest, largely due to the efforts of the beautiful and brilliant Lady Ada, Countess of Lovelace (who was, incidentally, the poet Lord Byron's daughter). Lovelace may have been the only person who fully understood Babbage's works. She remained his friend, even partner in the Analytic Engine business for several years until the end of her life (she was thirty-six when she died). She encouraged him, corrected his errors, but most important, she wrote about the work—and her writings passed Babbage's principles down to a later generation of number-engine tinkerers.

Later in the century, in the United States, another inventor applied some of the emerging knowledge of electricity and electromagnetism to the idea of a counting machine, and produced the first automated census tabulator, which was used to complete the 1890 U.S. census. The inventor's name was Herman Hollerith, and his device was designed to make use of punched cards the size of dollar bills, which—in deliberate imitation of the cards in the automated Jacquard loom—encoded significant numerical information (age, sex, dates of birth, and so on) with holes. When placed in a special box, each card either stopped the descent of metal wires, where there were no holes, or—where there were holes—allowed the wires to pass through into a bed of mercury. The wires that passed through completed electrical circuits, which activated electromagnets; these drove mechanical counters that kept track of all the various statistics of the census. In 1896, Hollerith formed the Tabulating Machine Company to produce more of his machines, and by 1924 the company had acquired its present name, Interna-

---

*The production of woven patterns on a loom requires the lifting of different sequences of warp threads before each pass of the shuttle. Previously, this had been done manually, by assistants reading a chart. But Joseph Jacquard in 1805 began encoding the patterns into sequences of punched holes on cards. The warp threads would be attached to rods which, when rested against the punched cards, either passed through or were held in place, according to the arrangement of holes.

tional Business Machines, or IBM. Today IBM is more or less synonymous with computers, but Hollerith's Tabulating Machine Company manufactured nothing of the sort. Mostly it made more counting machines, and later applied electricity and electromagnetism to calculators based on the old Leibnitz design . . . until the 1940s.

Modern interest in electricity began in 1675 when a French astronomer, Jean Picard sauntered back from his observatory one evening and, casually swinging his barometer, noticed a glow inside the thing. Shaking the barometer, he found he could increase the glow. He called it the ''glow of life.'' This peculiar accident inspired several experiments, and in 1705, Francis Hauksbee demonstrated before the English Royal Society that the glow of life was most intense inside barometers that contained partial vacuums. Hauksbee believed the glow was caused by friction between the mercury and the glass of the barometer, but by 1706 he produced similar effects by first creating a partial vacuum inside a glass globe containing no mercury, and then spinning the globe and pressing his hand against it lightly as it spun. He also noticed some other qualities of this glow of life (which we would call *static electricity*): a slight crackling sound that reminded him of lightning, and also an attraction for light objects such as feathers, threads, and flakes of metal.

These first provocative demonstrations led to a craze of experiments and demonstrations. In 1752, Ben Franklin foolishly flew a kite in a thunderstorm and concluded that lightning and ''electrical matter'' were made of the same stuff. Later in the century, James Graham built a Temple of Health in London where, for a fee, childless couples were able to make love in a bed erected next to a Hauksbee machine producing static electricity. In Europe, Anton Mesmer began hypnotizing people and claiming he had discovered an animal-electromagnetic field that influenced health and disease. By 1800, in Italy, Alessandro Volta discovered that by interlaying pieces of copper and zinc and placing them in weak acid, he could produce a continuous flow of electricity. This was the *voltaic pile*, the first battery.

During the nineteenth century, most practical applications of electricity were based on its ability to create magnetic fields. Strong magnetic fields, produced by large currents of electricity, could move large objects: most particularly, armatures of electric motors. Electricity began replacing steam as a dominant source of power. But because they could easily be controlled (stop the electricity and you stop the magnetism), smaller electromagnetic fields were used to move smaller objects in closely controlled ways, and electricity became a way of transmitting information: short and long pulses of electricity became the dots and dashes of Morse code on the telegraph. In certain circumstances, electricity also produced light—as demonstrated by the carbon-tipped arc lamp in mid-century, and by Thomas Edison's carbonized filament in a partial vacuum, ready for public consumption by 1879.

By and large, these nineteenth-century practical applications of electricity occurred with little input from scientific laboratories. Most inventors used large currents of electricity, and manipulated them in imprecise ways. In the laboratory, though, some scientists had begun looking at electricity on a much smaller scale. Wilhelm Conrad Röntgen in Germany and J. J. Thompson in England were carrying out experiments with electrical charges in gas at low pressures. Röntgen discovered X rays, and Thompson demonstrated the existence of what appeared to be particles—he called them "corpuscles"—that were far lighter than the lightest known atoms. Later these entities were called *electrons*, and we recognize them today as the particles that, when caused to move *en masse*, produce electrical energy. Meanwhile, during Edison's development of the electric light, an interesting thing had happened: Edison and his researchers noticed a bluish glow around the glow of the filament itself, inside the glass bulb. This came to be known as "the Edison effect," and research scientist J. J. Thompson concluded that it was caused by a flow of electrons in a reverse direction to the main current.

Further research and experimentation led to a number of theories about the behavior of electrons in a vacuum, and ultimately to a number of ideas about controlling them. Sir John Ambrose Fleming, scientific advisor to Edison's company in Britain, suggested that a certain type of circuit within a vacuum tube could be used to transform radio waves (which produced a back-and-forth motion of electrons) into a single-direction, weak-and-strong signal. This type of change in electron flow is called *rectification*. When another researcher discovered a way to take this rectified flow and *amplify* it (make it into a stronger signal), the development of broadcast radio became possible. Soon, other types of circuits in vacuums were developed, providing other ways of controlling an electron flow. Vacuum tubes were invented that could cause a single direction to *oscillate* (fluctuate regularly). Other vacuum tubes could change the frequencies of a signal, while still other tubes could be used for switching a current on or off.

In short, nineteenth-century laboratory work led, by the early twentieth century, to an expanding ability to manipulate electricity in refined ways for control and information rather than power. This was the emerging science and technology of *electronics*.

Computers as we know them appeared in the 1940s mainly through a sudden combination of: (1) the new technology of electronics, (2) the old technology of counting machines, and (3) the old idea of *binary numbers*.

Our most commonly used counting system is, of course, the decimal system. Including zero, there are ten symbols (representing ten values) used in the decimal system. Each column in the decimal system can use or "hold" up to ten symbols before a new column begins. The binary system, by contrast, contains only two symbols, and each column holds only those two symbols before a new column begins. Usually the two binary symbols are 1 and 0—although, of course, the same values could be represented by almost any kind of symbol, just as, in decimal, 0 through 9 could be represented by the letters A through J, or apples through bananas. In a manner similar to the progression of decimal numbers, simple binary counting might go as shown in the table on page 33.

There are some obvious disadvantages to binary counting. For one thing, if you're used to the decimal system, it seems a little confusing and awkward to be dealing with 2s, 4s, 8s, 16s columns, and so on. For another thing, it requires more writing, and takes up more space on the page. About the only advantage of a binary system is that it requires fewer original symbols. You only need the two symbols, 1 and 0, and, really, they can be represented by many other symbols. Recall that the Pascaline, and the Leibnitz calculator, and even Babbage's Analytic Engine represented numbers by a series of geared wheels each of which had ten values, ten stops; after reaching the tenth stop, each wheel would activate the next wheel to the left—quite analogous to regular counting. And "memory" took place when the wheels stopped turning. Well, regular counting, the decimal system, is a perfectly reasonable way to arrange a mechanical calculator that works with gears and wheels. But the nice thing about a binary system, which requires only two values, is that one can use electricity. Instead of 1 and 0, the symbols can be *on* and *off*, which happen to be easy signals to produce with electrical pulses.

Probably the first person to think (briefly) *electronics* and *binary* while at the same time thinking *number machine* was Konrad Zuse, an engineering student at the University of Berlin who in 1936 built a electromechanical binary number machine in the middle of his parents' living room. Zuse's machine, like the Babbage machine, was designed in theory to carry out any conceivable mathematical task. Although he was probably unaware of the nineteenth-century automated Jacquard loom, Zuse used holes punched in film to enter information into his device. The little machine employed electromagnetically operated relay switches to do its binary calculations. And, lo and behold, it actually worked: the relays clicked rapidly away, and the results appeared in binary code on a series of little light bulbs.

Meanwhile, in his spare time Zuse tried out for the part of *King Kong* in an amateur dramatization of the movie, but lost the part to

100s	10s	1s		128s	64s	32s	16s	8s	4s	2s	1s
0	0	0		0	0	0	0	0	0	0	0
0	0	1		0	0	0	0	0	0	0	1
0	0	2		0	0	0	0	0	0	1	0
0	0	3		0	0	0	0	0	0	1	1
0	0	4		0	0	0	0	0	1	0	0
0	0	5		0	0	0	0	0	1	0	1
0	0	6		0	0	0	0	0	1	1	0
0	0	7		0	0	0	0	0	1	1	1
0	0	8		0	0	0	0	1	0	0	0
0	0	9		0	0	0	0	1	0	0	1
0	1	0		0	0	0	0	1	0	1	0
0	1	1		0	0	0	0	1	0	1	1
0	1	2		0	0	0	0	1	1	0	0
0	1	3		0	0	0	0	1	1	0	1
0	1	4		0	0	0	0	1	1	1	0
0	1	5		0	0	0	0	1	1	1	1
0	1	6		0	0	0	1	0	0	0	0
1	2	5		0	1	1	1	1	1	0	1
1	2	6		0	1	1	1	1	1	1	0
1	2	7		0	1	1	1	1	1	1	1
1	2	8		1	0	0	0	0	0	0	0
1	2	9		1	0	0	0	0	0	0	1
1	3	0		1	0	0	0	0	0	1	0

P. 7. Comparison of binary and decimal numbers. Note that binary uses two symbols, while decimal uses ten.

one Helmut Schreyer, an electrical engineering student. Schreyer became interested in Zuse's contraption, and quickly recognized that fully electronic components would make it far faster and more efficient. The electromagnetic relays Zuse had been using were capable of switching on and off several times a second, but electronic vacuum tubes could perform the same tasks thousands of times a second. Schreyer wrote a dissertation about the idea, and Zuse considered it. But tubes were hard to get, and also not very reliable. By 1940, Zuse and Schreyer had decided that their calculating machine, if used as a code-maker and -breaker, could help Germany win the war, but Hitler had decreed that all scientific work be directed toward immediately achievable goals. The Nazis expressed no further interest, and Zuse was forced to suspend work. All of his machines were destroyed during the Allied invasion of Berlin except one, which Zuse managed to carry away and hide in an apple barrel in Switzerland.

Zuse later claimed that he was not aware of the work of Babbage when he began building his machine. But at about the same time that Zuse moved into his parents' living room in Berlin, Howard Aiken, a Harvard professor of mathematics, had begun looking into the writings of and about Babbage. Aiken soon decided that Babbage's Analytic Engine could be built, using more modern equipment. He approached the president of IBM and persuaded him that such an idea was possible, and probably profitable. IBM lent Aiken a million dollars to prove it, and Aiken's machine—known as the Automatic Sequence Controlled Calculator, or the Mark I, for short—was finished in the early 1940s. The thing was housed in a glass and steel box eight feet high and fifty-five feet long. Navy officers operated it, and it was said to perform an amazing six calculations per second. It was also noisy, mainly because Aiken believed, as Zuse had before him, that electromagnetic relay switches would be the most efficient innards.

Meanwhile, in both England and America, and mostly because of the war, scientists and engineers were beginning to design and construct similar machines that used, for the first time, electronic vacuum tubes as primary switching units. The English built a series of such devices, known as the Colossus series, specifically for the purpose of deciphering German codes. The Americans began with a machine called the ENIAC, which was supposed to calculate ballistics tables for new weapons.

The ENIAC, completed under the direction of John Mauchly and J. Presper Eckert early in 1946, filled an entire room, weighed several tons, used nineteen thousand vacuum tubes, and required massive amounts of electricity to operate—but it was capable of making about five thousand calculations a second. Every few hours, one of those thousands of vacuum tubes could be expected to burn out, but other than that, the machine was splendid. Actually, it had one additional shortcoming. *Data* in the form of electronic on and off signals would be entered, and the machine would process the data through predefined sequences. In theory, the machine could do any mathematical task—it could process data through *any* sequence of instructions. But in fact, the machine was wired to carry out only one mathematical task at a time. In order to alter the sequence of mathematical processes, one had to rip out existing circuits and then build and solder in new circuits. That problem was soon solved, however, when the mathematician John Von Neumann suggested that the computer be designed in such a way that instructions about mathematical sequences could be sent into the machine in the same form as the data: *electronic signals.* Such instructions came to be called *programs;* and because they existed (once inside the machine) in the "soft" form of electronic signals, instead of the "hard" form of wiring, such programs came to be known collectively as *software.*

Certainly at that moment, the computer looked like one more specimen of twentieth-century Scientific Technology. It was huge. It was expensive. It was nasty. Only scientists and engineers could get near it. And anyone who recognized the characteristic trends of Scientific Technology would have predicted that the machine would only get bigger and nastier. Instead, wonder of wonders, it became smaller and nicer.*

Squinting through our retrospectroscope, we see that smaller happened inevitably, owing to the very nature of the machine. Before the computer, nearly all of technology was directed toward increasing human power in the physical world. Where physical power is important, bigger is better, as any football fan will attest. Where intellectual power is concerned, and most chess fans will agree, size is not so important. Actually, in the case of computers, size came to be quite important—in the negative.

Computers work because electric charges can be made to travel in groups of pulse and non-pulse (or on and off). The groups of pulse and non-pulse (on and off) represent 1 and 0 in the binary number system. Thus, a string of carefully fluctuated charges somewhat resembling this

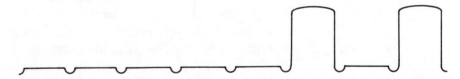

represents the binary number 00000101, or the decimal number 5. The individual units of pulse and non-pulse, which are often considered individual units of information, are called *bits.* They are small bits of information. The overall collection of bits (in this case there are eight bits) is often called a *word.* The word 00000101 might be used to represent the number 5, as I just mentioned, but

---

*See Christopher Evans' *The Micro Millennium*, or Harry Wulforst's *Breakthrough to the Computer Age*, for a more detailed history of computers.

then the number 5 might be used to represent something else—the letter E, for example.

Given the developing technology of electronics, it was relatively easy to process these pulse groups through *logic circuits* (which can carry out various simple mathematical operations, such as addition and subtraction) and to place the results into memory whenever appropriate, simply by using various kinds of vacuum tubes. Electricity travels through wires at roughly half the speed of light, some 90,000 miles per second, and at those speeds one might think that for all practical purposes a computer the size of a large room would be just about as fast as a computer the size of a bathtub.* But the basic circuitry inside any computer is very complex, and in any task of computing, the groups of electronic pulses may be traveling up and down, back and forth, into memory and out again, and just about all over the place. The old ENIAC contained five hundred miles of circuitry—so you can begin to understand how computer size is indeed related to processing speed and efficiency.**

Smaller meant faster, which meant better and more efficient, and if there was in fact any possible way to make computers smaller, it was bound to happen. At the time of the ENIAC, the major limiting factor was the size of the vacuum tubes. They were the size of monkeys' fists. Of course the charges traveling inside were smaller than atoms, but the tubes themselves seemed to be about as small as they were ever going to get. It might have been possible to spend some unknown billions of dollars to figure out how to make them smaller—and I have no doubt that such a project would have been undertaken—but in the meantime three scientists at Bell Telephone Laboratories discovered an entirely new way to manipulate electronic charges.

Certain materials commonly found in nature will react to electronic charge in more than one way. These materials are sometimes called *semiconductors.* In one state, they are *insulators* of electricity: they stop the motion of electrons. But in some circumstances—for instance, after being hit by a pulse of electrons—they become just the opposite. They become *conductors* of electricity. They encourage the motion of electrons. Of course, I am describing a material that can function as a switch. It can be on or off, depending on what previous signals it has received. Arranged properly, pieces of semiconducting material could carry out all the circuit switching previously done by vacuum tubes. Also, because they were solid, single pieces of material, they proved to be much

---

*The speed of electricity depends upon the nature of its conductor; it varies from 0.3 to 0.9 times the speed of light.

**Shorter circuitry is not the only reason that smaller equals faster in computers. Smaller switching components can flip to new states (of on or off) more rapidly; they have less "inertia" than larger ones.

more reliable than tubes: they didn't break so easily, and they tended not to wear out. But the greatest advantage of these little pieces of semiconductor—they were called *transistors*—was that they could be smaller than vacuum tubes. A lot smaller. And not long after transistors hit the market at the end of the 1940s, computers suddenly became smaller. Smaller, as I have already noted, meant faster and more efficient. It also meant cheaper, since the computers required less material to build, took up less floor space, and required less energy.

Because some people like to save money, small continued to be beautiful, and scientists and engineers went to work on the transistors and circuits, hoping to make them smaller yet. The first transistors were about the size of peanuts, but before long people discovered that they could be as small as fleas and still work perfectly well. Another concern had been the waste of all that spaghetti of wiring leading from one transistor to another. Engineers removed all the wiring and simply stamped, or printed, the circuits right out on boards. Instead of spaghetti, you had hieroglyphics. The transistors could be soldered right onto the *printed circuit board*, wherever in the circuit they were needed. That was simple enough, and a great improvement. Electrons don't require much space to wiggle, and people began to realize that printed circuits could be reduced in size again, and again, and again. As the 1950s came to a close, computers were small enough and cheap enough that large corporations could afford to own or lease them.

The printed circuit boards and the transistors had some things in common. Both depended on interesting combinations of conduction and nonconduction. Thus, someone recognized that it might be possible to print, or etch, the circuits onto a board of semiconducting material right along with the transistors. Whole logic units, with circuitry and twenty to one hundred individual components (previously individual transistors) now were etched together right onto a single semiconducting chip small enough to fit two abreast on anyone's thumbnail. Computers were growing smaller, cheaper, faster. Now it was possible to construct a computer equal in capacity to the large-room-sized ENIAC, and fit it inside a refrigerator. As the techniques for producing integrated circuits advanced, thousands of transistor components were soon being etched on chips. Then tens of thousands. By the middle of the 1970s the entire processing circuitry of a computer could be placed on a single chip, and suddenly, remarkably, unexpectedly, it became possible for amateurs to buy a few chips and build an entire computer. In 1975, people began selling computer kits for a few hundred dollars, and soon after the first personal computers appeared on the market.

At the same time, many people used the miniature components to build large computers (though never as large as they had been in the 1940s), which became increasingly sophisticated and powerful.* But bit for bit and word for word, the personal computers are a particularly good illustration of the miniaturization process because—though only a few times more powerful in memory and processing ability than the old ENIAC—they are several thousand times smaller and cheaper. As Evans suggests in his excellent book, *The Micro Millennium*, a similar alteration of cost and efficiency in the automobile industry would give us Rolls Royces costing under five dollars each and getting three million miles to the gallon. One of them might be the size of a tennis ball, or a golf ball, but you could climb inside and enjoy just as comfortable a ride as ever.

5

Because so many astounding things are emerging from Scientific Technology all the time, it may seem inappropriate to single out the computer and suggest that it deserves a special category of its own—Information Technology. What other "era of technology," as I have described it, has been based upon a single invention, or even a handful of inventions?** What distinguishes Information Technology from the Scientific Technology out of which it emerged?

First of all, the computer is not really a single machine. It is not so much an invention as it is a cultural phenomenon. We can, of course, trace the history of computers through the Hand Technology of counting machines and into the Scientific Technology of electronics. We can describe the important people involved, and the significant events, just we can for any other individual invention. But between the 1940s and the present, a mere four decades, millions of people have been inventing and reinventing the computer. The computer is protean, and it was designed to be so. That's the function of programs and programming: to reinvent the machine in an instant, to make it into a new machine again and again. New program equals new machine!

Earlier, I described a trend that is apparent in the four earlier technologies: passing from the simple to the complex. In some ways this is also characteristic of Information Technology. Many of the processes associated with producing computers have increased in

---

*While early large computers could perform several hundred mathematical calculations a second, today's supercomputers can carry out 100 million calculations a second.

**A much more ambitious delineation of Information Technology would also consider in detail such other technologies as television, radio, satellite-based communications, and so on. All these arise from early twentieth-century developments in electronics, and all expand human intellectual capacity. The computer, however, is the crucial and core technology.

complexity. But computers themselves are becoming simpler. They are physically simpler—several thousand times smaller, with several thousand times fewer moving parts. Most important, however, massive improvements in software have made them remarkably simpler to operate. It used to be that one had to be a highly trained programmer with enough professional status to acquire security clearance just to touch one of the machines. To get one running might require several complex steps in programming input, and once it was running, just to make it perform simple calculations required an expert understanding of the computer's on-off innards and logic. But those days are gone. Now virtually every computer contains, as part of its standard working software, *programming languages* that translate relatively simple commands punched by a human operator on the keyboard into the relatively complex instructions required by the interior of the machine. This trend, from complex to simple, is continuing. And for common computer uses, one no longer needs to be able to program at all, since so many programs are on the market (existing on the surfaces of magnetic disks or tapes) ready to be put into the computer with a single motion of the hand. Additionally, computer scientists are continuing to develop what they call the "human interface." Among other things, this means the creation of programming languages that perform increasingly automatic translations for the computer, and therefore require less and less human translation. The ultimate goal may be the construction of various *natural languages*, that is, programming languages close enough to ordinary human discourse that people with no knowledge of programming at all would be able to instruct the computer to carry out complex and open-ended tasks.

Earlier, I suggested that an overall trend of the four earlier technologies was toward some increasing alienation from nature and humanity. Information Technology may be moving in the reverse direction. The image of the cold, gray computer operated by cold, gray men is more an artifact of the 1950s than of today. Largely because of astounding decreases in cost and size, and increased sophistication of programming languages, elementary school children are looking inside computers and learning to program them. Those nasty days when people thought that only bespectacled and ectomorphic geniuses, condescendingly called "computer whizzes," could handle computers—those days are gone forever. The housewife down the street is likely to have her own personal computer, which she uses to store recipes, records, and household accounts. Your local secretarial service probably has a computer with a piece of word processing software tucked inside, while your local farmer may be planning fertilizer mixes or keeping track of livestock feeding with a small computer.

All technology, by definition, expands human power. Information Technology is one of the first, however, to expand intellectual power in any significant way. Possibly only the development of printing has had any comparable effect.

Information Technology is also the first mass technology based on motion on such a tiny scale that the distinction between matter and energy blurs. This partly accounts for its efficiency, and its essentially nonpolluting nature. Electrons are put into motion relatively easily. Once in motion, electrons encounter relatively little friction: thus computers are likely not to wear out or break at the same rate as machines more strictly dependent upon mechanical motion.

But are computers *up to no good*?

The bumper-sticker slogan, "Guns don't kill people, people kill people," implies that the nature of any particular piece of technology has no effect on the people who possess it. It suggests that just as many homicides would occur in the world if several million people carried Cuisinarts instead of pistols. Like most single-sentence slogans, this one appeals more to emotion than to reason. The best that can be said for it is that it tells a limited truth.

Various pieces of technology *do* affect human behavior. A gun is designed to transform the passing impulse—momentary anger, or fear—into an irreversible decision. It can change the slightest twitch of a finger into an act of the highest violence and the greatest permanence.

In the same decade that computers appeared, two writers published warnings about the new technology that are still well remembered today. Norbert Wiener, in *Cybernetics*, warned of a new Industrial Revolution which is "bound to devalue the human brain, at least in its simpler and more routine decisions." George Orwell, in his futuristic novel *1984* warned that totalitarian governments would use Information Technology (he never directly referred to computers) to destroy privacy and exert ultimate controls over individual thought and action.

Although both fears are entirely relevant to our time, Wiener concerned himself primarily with the issues of automation and robotics, while Orwell primarily thought Information Technology would continue in the same direction as other developments from Scientific Technology. Neither author foresaw what vast expansions of human possibility would arise from this new technology. Neither anticipated that computers would reach into areas of scientific and artistic creativity. Neither expected that small computers would become so common and so inexpensive that everyone's child would learn to program them. Orwell specifically foresaw a totalitarian state that came to power preaching socialistic or Marxist dogma—deliberately and cynically monopolizing information to maintain its own regime. Of course, such societies exist today, although not all of them justify their existences and crimes with socialist slogans. Orwell foresaw astutely that even more basic than the power of guns is the power of the word. He predicted that monolithic societies, governed directly by a cruel elite, would first attempt to monopolize information. He did not foresee, however, that the most significant tool of information, the computer, might by its very nature facilitate, even require a two-way flow of information—and thus ultimately decentralize power.

The computer is, by all accounts, an incredible machine. Is it *up to no good?*

As with most complex questions, the answer is complex. Computers are part sword and part plow, and no one yet knows the proportions. They can make smart bombs smarter. They can make mean people meaner, and powerful governments more powerful. On the other hand, they can transfer the experience of experts to the acts of non-experts. They can expand scientific and medical knowledge and creativity. They can give power to and expand the competence of ordinary people.

People often think of the computer in terms of one or two or three specific applications, but it is a universal machine, with universal applications. Computers have given visual artists new colors, shapes, ideas, visions. Computers have given musicians new sounds and new power over sound; writers, a new control over the conspiracy of language; gamesters, new challenges. Computers are expanding the external boundaries of the arts; simultaneously, they are penetrating boundaries that once divided the arts. The visual arts can resemble music. Music can resemble poetry. Fiction begins to resemble games. Games incorporate music and light.

The computer can be either sword or plow. This book is about the computer as plow, as a benevolent machine, as a tool of creation.

And God said, "Let there be light"; and
there was light. And God saw that the
light was good; and God separated the
light from the darkness.
    —The Book of Genesis

Chapter 1

Creation
in
Light

First was light created, suggesting a primacy of the visual sense.

1

M. C. Escher's lithograph *Reptiles* can be taken as a statement
about the relationship between art and reality. "Real" reptiles seem
to crawl out from a sheet of paper on which appears a perfectly in-
terlaced, or tesselated, group of "drawn" reptiles. It is also a statement about some relationship between art and Art, as well as reality
and Reality. There is the "reality" that appears in the lithograph:
convincingly realistic objects depicted in full perspective, perfectly
shaded, perfectly detailed, urging us at some level to pretend for at
least a moment that the lithograph is "reality." But there is a drawing inside the lithograph, and if we entered the lithograph would we
then, from the reality inside there, be seduced—as the reptiles

1. 1. M.C. Escher *Reptiles* 1943.
© Beeldrecht, Amsterdam/ VAGA, New York. Collection Haags Gemeentemuseum—The Hague, 1981. Reproduction courtesy of Vorpal Gallery, New York, San Francisco, Laguna Beach.

are—into entering the pencil-and-paper "drawing"? One could talk forever about the various levels of meaning and antimeaning, confusion and surprise in Escher's piece. It is a self-mocking work of art, a Zen riddle, a paradox and a paradiddle. To use philosopher Douglas Hofstadter's idea and term, *Reptiles* is a self-referring *strange loop* that suggests an infinity lurking within seemingly finite forms, that destroys the artifice of category by looping out of and then back into category (for instance, art appearing to loop out of and into art).

Most intriguingly, the lithograph suggests or even embodies a never-ending battle between the creations of God and the creations of man: that is, between organic form and artificial form, between nature and art.

At some level, of course, the two creations (organic and artificial, or nature and art) are one, and this may be one of the points made by the loop, if a loop can make a point. "God created nature, including man, who created art" means that God created art. At another level, we recognize that the two creations are two: they are different, two parallel versions of the Genesis story.

It may be impossible to state precisely how nature and art are different, but at least we can gather, from looking at *Reptiles*, how we often perceive the difference. At the bottom left of the lithograph we see a representation of an organic creation: the cacti. At the bottom right we see a representation of an artificial creation: the corked bottle and glass. Even if we had never before seen either, we most likely would know that the cacti were organic and the bottle and glass were artificial. How? The cacti, although simpler and more symmetrical than most multicelled organisms, still appear to be much less simple and (because they have grown to be tilted in the pot) less symmetrical than the bottle and glass. In a similar way, the reptiles, as they progress in their loop from seemingly "artificial" to seemingly "organic," progress from simple to complex, and from perfectly symmetrical to noticeably less symmetrical (actually, the "organic" reptiles, as they crawl along, move in and out of symmetry).

The reptilian loop may remind you of grade school lessons in drawing and perspective: you start with simple geometry to capture good form, and then you add detail and complexity and occasional asymmetry to make your outlined form seem realistic. Or, going to the other side of the loop, it may remind you of a style of early twentieth-century art known as Cubism: you start with a complex and asymmetrical image of nature as it is and intuit the geometric form "behind" it. In either case, we see that Escher's lithograph may not be about the differences between nature and art so much as it is about the similarities, as suggested by the strange loop interconnecting them.

Escher created *Reptiles* in 1943, almost before computers existed, and distinctly before computers were used to create visual images. Yet his work illustrates nicely some of the problems of using computers to create pictures.

If the screen of any particular computer could be divided into a million dots, and you wanted to draw a complex picture on the screen, or have the computer draw the picture, how would you go about it? In nature, the force that creates life is able to produce forms that are highly complex and capable of moving in and out of symmetry, because it has all the time in the world. If you wanted to make a picture on your million-dot computer screen, you might do so by giving the computer a million instructions, one for each dot of light on the screen. You might be able to create a pleasing image that way, but do you have the time? What you have to do, in other words, is think about the qualities of the computer and figure out some shortcuts.

The computer was originally designed to be a super-mathematics machine, so perhaps one shortcut might be to use its number-crunching abilities to your advantage. Euclid described a group of shapes (circles, squares, triangles, rectangles, so on) that were interesting mostly because they could be described mathematically.

By reading the works of Euclid or your high school geometry textbook, you might be able to formulate a series of simple instructions that would force the computer to go through the complex act of drawing a Euclidean shape—for instance, a circle—on its screen.

Before you can give the computer any instructions, however, you have to figure out a way for it to "understand" what your instructions are referring to on the screen. In other words, you have to label each of the million dots or elements on the screen. You might number the elements from 1 to 1 million; but looking at the screen, you notice that the dots are arranged in a regular grid—of 1000 rows divided into 1000 columns—so you decide to give each dot a number according to its horizontal and vertical location. This means that the element at the upper left of the screen is described as 1, 1, while the element at the lower right is described as 1000, 1000.

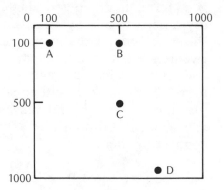

1. 2. Numbering system for computer screen with a million picture elements

Point A = 100,100
Point B = 500,100
Point C = 500,500
Point D = 700,983

Having decided to use that system, you discover that everything is vastly simplified. To ask the computer to draw a circle, you might simply instruct it to start with point 500, 500 in the very center of the screen and draw a curved "line," which is really composed of all the points found at the same distance (let that distance be equal to a quarter width of the screen, or 250 picture elements) away from the center point. The computer follows your instructions and—voila!—you have a circle exactly as you wanted it. Its center is in the center of the screen, and its radius covers a quarter of the screen. If you want the inside of the circle to be a different color or shade of gray from the rest of the screen, you simply instruct the computer to color in, or shade in, every point between the center of the circle and the outer circumference.

But the circle looks flat, unreal, Euclidean. What if you want it to look like a ball or globe? What if you want to give it the illusion of depth, of three dimensions? Notice in Escher's lithograph that you first recognize that the reptiles are emerging from two dimensions into the illusion of three because of the shading—and the shading seems to be affected by the position of an imagined light source.

Perhaps you could add some shading to the circle on the computer screen, to give the appearance of three dimensions, to make the circle look like a ball or globe. How? You could give several hundred thousand instructions to the computer, specifying the precise shading or degree of intensity for each of the dots or elements inside of the circle on the screen, but you can't spare the several years needed for that. You decide again to think about shortcuts.

Eventually you arrive at a clever solution. The program to draw a circle is already written, so to have the computer draw 2 circles, 200, or even 2,000 circles should be very easy. Why not start with that same point in the center of the screen (point 500, 500), and have the computer draw a series of concentric circles, starting with the smallest possible one (a width of 2 dots or elements), and working outward, increasing the width of your circle by a value of 2 each time until you reach 500 (double the radius)? If you do this, and (as you're gradually expanding the width) if you gradually decrease the intensity for each circle, you'll finally have the illusion of a shaded globe—much like the globe below, which was drawn precisely in this way.

1. 3. Michael Loceff *Sphere*
By permission of Michael Loceff and Cromemco

That was a clever solution, and the computer seemed particularly suited to carry it out. Notice that you only had to give the computer one basic instruction: how to draw the circle. After that, all you had to do was instruct the computer to do the same thing again and again and again, each time changing only two details about the circle—width and intensity. That kind of automatic repetition, often called *iteration*, is one activity the computer performs superbly. That kind of program is often called a *loop* (because it loops).

The problem with such a shortcut, however, is that the globe is highlighted and shaded as if the light source were located directly in front. What if you wanted to highlight and shade the globe with a hypothetical light source in front of it but off to the left? No longer would the illusion created by concentric circles work. One solution might be to describe to the computer a globe that really does have three dimensions. Of course, your screen is always going to remain in two dimensions, but you could define the "globe" on it *in terms of* three dimensions.

How does one define a globe on the flat screen in terms of three dimensions? Instead of assigning two numbers for each of the picture elements (representing height and width), assign three (for height, width, and depth). Simple principles of geometry will enable you to write the program for defining a sphere with all three values. The computer will use the first two values to locate the picture on the screen, and will use the third number to calculate intensity, based upon calculated distance from the hypothetical light source. This may turn out to be a more complex program, but once the basic program is written you have it forever—and you might even want to use the computer's iterative powers to draw several globes at one time. A pretty picture? Yes. Not only that, but you might use the program to draw a model of a molecule, using a series of interlocking globes to represent atoms. For example, consider the model of a segment of DNA in Color Plate 1A.

Notice that this model is composed of a series of interlocking globes of five different colors and sizes. The five different colors represent five different kinds of atoms in DNA. The different sizes are based upon actual size ratios of those five different atoms. The complex arrangements and positions of the globes are based upon what we know of the actual arrangements and positions of atoms in a real DNA molecule.

That the atoms of this model of a molecule appear opaque might not at first glance be surprising, but it should be. If you had described all the globes to the computer in all three dimensions, the computer would have automatically drawn all this information about the globes, front and back. The result, a transparent model of a molecule, could be attractive, but perhaps a little confusing. How was the model made to appear opaque? Opaque means that we are not able to see the back sides of an object—here, it means the computer has been instructed not to draw them. In other words, you need to give it more instructions.

Remember that you told the computer to carry out the shading by calculating the distance of each picture element from a hypothetical light source? You might use a similar technique to make the image opaque—describe to the computer an imaginary point where a hypothetical viewer's eyes will be and then calculate what should be seen and what shouldn't. Erase everything that shouldn't be seen.

Why go to all this trouble to make a computer draw a DNA molecule in the first place? For one thing, seeing what a molecule looks like can be a superb learning experience. Because the computer has that three-dimensional model of the molecule in memory, given a few commands it can show you another view of it, and another, and another. You can look at the model from any angle, any perspective. You can twist it, turn it, and what is perhaps more important, you can enter the model of another molecule onto the screen, twist and turn it randomly. Perhaps you'll discover an interesting "fit" between the two models. Perhaps you'll discover a potential bonding, a potential chemical reaction between the two. In other words, computer-assisted molecular modeling is likely to be not only an excellent teaching device, but also an extremely useful tool in biochemical research and genetic engineering.

2

Almost without exception, the computers of the 1940s were used to perpetrate complex mathematical calculations. When the calculations were done, all that was left to do was display the results. Since outputs typically consisted of some final numbers, displaying them did not require dazzling visual effects. The numbers could be displayed across a row of little lights, which would be either on or off, signifying some value in the binary system of numbers. Alternatively, the numbers could be punched out on paper tape, or binary numbers could be sent to a typewriter that was specially designed to translate binary signals into typewritten decimal numbers on paper.

At the same time that some people were developing the first electronic computers, other people were using the new science and technology of electronics to develop picture machines. These picture machines, otherwise known as television, relied on a new kind of electronic vacuum tube created by Vladimir Zworykin in 1928. Since he had recently emigrated to America from Russia, when it came time to name his invention, Zworykin recalled the term for holy image in the Russian Orthodox Church, *icon*, and named his device an *iconoscope*.

The iconoscope consisted of a vacuum tube containing a thin film of mica, which was coated with a light-sensitive metal. An image or "icon" was cast onto the face of the metal-coated film in much the same way that images are cast onto film in an ordinary photographic camera—through a lens. The nature of the metallic coating on the mica film was such that the varying intensities of light falling on its face produced varying intensities of electron activity, or charge. In other words, the device converted a visual "icon" into a corresponding electronic "icon."

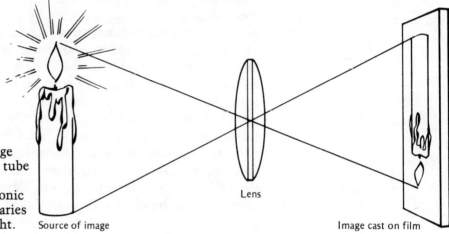

1. 4. An iconoscope: an image cast onto the film inside the tube produces a corresponding "image" or "icon" of electronic charge. Intensity of charge varies directly with intensity of light.

Source of image

Lens

Image cast on film

An image cast onto film in a photographic camera is of little consequence until the film has been taken out of the camera and processed. Similarly, the image or icon of varying electronic charge inside the iconoscope was of little consequence so long as it remained in its first form, on the metal-coated film of mica. In order for it to be transferred or transmitted out of the iconoscope, the icon had to be converted into a linear form.

The problem is comparable to having a beautiful drawing inside a locked room, and wishing to pass the drawing to a friend in another room on the other side of one wall. The only passage between the rooms is a very small vent, much too small for the picture to pass through. What can you do? One obvious solution would be to cut the picture into thin strips of paper, pass the strips through the small opening one at a time, and let the friend paste together the strips until the full drawing has been reassembled in the next room. Well, the same kind of process was necessary to transfer the image from Zworykin's iconoscope to the outside. The metallic sheet of electronic charge, the electronic icon, could not be transmitted all at once. To be passed out of the iconoscope and transmitted elsewhere, it had to be converted into linear form by some methodical scanning process. This was done with an additional device called a *scanner*. One may think of the scanner as similar to a squirt gun: it was placed a small distance away from the metal-coated film, and it "squirted" onto the electronic icon a regular beam of electronic charge. Of course, the beam had to move across or stroke the film in some regular fashion, just as we scan a printed page regularly when we read. Electrons are highly sensitive to magnetic fields, so it was relatively simple to wrap an electromagnetic device around the scanner and cause the beam of charge to be deflected very methodically, stroking the icon from left to right, top to bottom. As that regular beam from the scanner stroked the icon, it completed a circuit that reproduced, in linear form, the pattern of varying charge on the icon.

That was the first television camera.

The linear, electronic information "read" by the scanning device was useful because it could easily be transmitted over wires or even across space in the form of waves. At the other end was a device for receiving the waves, amplifying them, and then putting them together, or converting them back to the original image. This was done by another, similar electron gun scanner inside another vacuum tube, stroking in the same pattern and at the same speed, firing the same varying intensities of voltage at the back of a screen coated with phosphor. The phosphor very briefly glowed in an intensity directly related to the intensity of the electron flow striking it, producing a final image or icon in light.

That was the first television set.

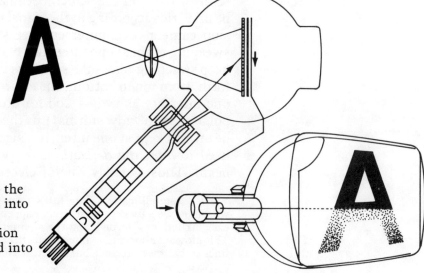

1. 5. Television: a scanner alters the electronic icon inside the camera into linear form; the linear electronic information is sent to the television receiver, where it is reconstituted into a picture on the screen.

In today's standard television, the electron gun strokes a series of 525 lines, all of which are coordinated into an image pattern taken from the original image inside the camera. An entirely new image, from line 1 to line 525, is generated every thirtieth of a second—fast enough to create the illusion of motion.* Recalling the earlier example of passing a drawing from one room to another through a small hole by cutting the drawing into thin strips, we might now think of the process as passing thirty drawings a second through a small hole by cutting each drawing into 525 strips, passing everything through in precise order, with the friend reassembling everything in the same order and at the same speed.

For color, separate the original image into three primary color images, send through the air or over the cable electronic voltage information about all three color-separate images. At the other end, run it into a television receiver that has three electron guns firing onto a phosphor screen that will respond with the three primary colors; the viewer perceives them as mixed into the more complex, secondary colors.

Television and computers have much in common. They both appeared at the same time in history because they both arose from the same developments in technology—primarily in electronics. You might say television is a near and dear relative of the computer. They both have the same blood type. So it was perhaps inevitable that some people in the late 1940s and early 1950s began attaching televisions to computers. Once the television tube was attached to a computer, however, computer engineers faced an important new problem: how to place the computer's information onto the screen.

One way this was done is particularly ingenious. The tube of the ordinary television set is able to display lighter and darker patterns of light on the screen because the intensity of the sweeping beam varies according to the signals coming from the remote television camera. Computer engineers decided, however, to fix that sweeping beam at one intensity. Naturally, if it had been allowed to keep sweeping across the screen as before, in parallel lines, back and forth, from top to bottom, the entire screen would be illuminated at one intensity as well—good for nothing but producing pictures of polar bears in snow storms. But the engineers recognized that if the beam was kept at one intensity, signals from the computer could be used *to alter the deflection*, or sweeping pattern of the electron beam. Thus a steady line of electronic charge being transformed

---

*This is a simplification. If the full screen were altered only thirty times a second, we would see a flicker. What really happens is that half the 525 lines are changed each sixtieth of a second, and the alternating half are changed the next sixtieth. This provides almost the same visual effect as one would get from changing all 525 lines sixty times a second, but it requires less information, and therefore is less expensive.

into a glow on the screen could be moved wherever the computer was instructed to move it—up, down, right, left, diagonally, in a circle, and so on. "Draw a straight line from A to B," some programmer might instruct the computer, and the computer would cause the electromagnetic deflector inside the television tube to move the beam from A to B. "Draw a line from A to B but make it curved so that it resembles the letter C"—and the deflector moves the electron beam so that it draws a letter C on the phosphor screen. Such a display system was called a *vector* system, from the Latin verb meaning *to carry*.

By the early 1960s, a few people began coordinating television tubes with computers in a second way, called a *raster* system (coming from the Latin word, *rastrum*, meaning *to scrape, rake, or shave*). It more closely resembled the original television system. The electromagnetic deflector was left to work much as it had with television, raking or sweeping methodically across the screen, in parallel lines, top to bottom.

The problem was how to *vary the intensity* of the beam in a way that would produce some desired pattern (at that time, mostly letters, numbers, and simple graphs) on the screen. The ordinary television camera varies intensities easily and automatically by simply imitating the varied intensities of the electronic icon on the metal-coated film inside the camera. But the computer can't produce smoothly varying voltages. All it can do is provide discrete pulses of voltage, high and low pulses, or on and off signals. The solution was to produce an image on the screen that was a grid, smaller but much like a grid of light bulbs one might see in New York's Times Square—and a picture would be produced by making

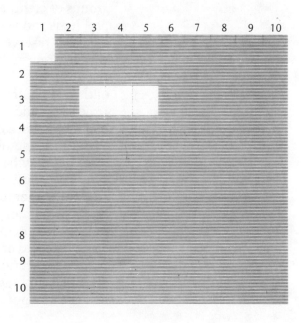

1. 6. A simplified raster screen system, in which picture elements (pixels) 1,1; 3,3; 4,3; and 5,3 are on, while all the others are off.

some elements in the grid on and others off. The grid was really all those horizontal lines on the screen simply cut into vertical sections. There might be around 250 horizontal lines each divided into 250 pieces, providing a total of 250 times 250, or 62,500 separate sections, or *picture elements* (or *pixels*, for short). Such raster systems are the most common systems for producing images on a computer screen today, and the smallest computers of today may indeed have a little over sixty thousand pixels on the screen. More sophisticated computers might have a million or more.

Certainly it was relatively simple for the computer to make each one of the pixels either on or off, white or black. But what about shades of gray, or color? Since in the computer on and off signals usually travel in groups (called *words*), it quickly became obvious that instead of assigning a single signal to each picture element, one might assign it a group of signals, or a word. What happens then? The individual signal can only represent on or off, 1 or 0—but a group of eight signals can represent some larger number, actually anything from 0 to 255. So if you assign a word to each pixel, with a value of 0 to 255, you can then translate those 256 values into 256 intensities of voltage firing from the electron gun. You can also use those 256 different values to vary the intensities of three color-separated electron guns, if you prefer color. And in some of the large and sophisticated computer systems of today, if the words consist of sixteen individual bits or even thirty-two or more, the number of possible gray and color values can range in the millions.

Even a small computer that places its on and off signals into groups of eight, and has only 62,500 pixels on the screen, runs into problems, however. If it has a 62,500 pixel screen, the computer needs to reserve a corresponding 62,500 places in memory. But if the electron gun is sweeping across the screen sixty times a second, the computer has to send all the contents of that memory—each of the values of each pixel—out to the gun in perfect sequence, sixty times a second. That's a lot. And if you want more than one image, or a moving image, the computer also has to change the contents of the grid in memory continually, but without disturbing anything else that may be residing in memory (such as a program).

The point is, coordinating these various demanding uses of computer memory is extremely difficult—unless one takes a fat hunk of memory circuitry and sets it aside, away from the computer's central memory, using it for nothing other than to maintain a stable record of an electronic icon to be sent out to the screen. This particular section of memory circuitry might be compared to a shock absorber, or a buffer: it is placed between the television tube and the computer's ordinary memory primarily to simplify things.

At first, this "buffer" of memory was simply a rotating electromagnetic disk, apart from the main computer. By the late 1960s and early 1970s, however, memory circuits became inexpensive enough that the buffer could be built out of circuits precisely like all the other memory circuits inside the computer: little chips of silicon containing thousands of microscopic elements that could easily be switched on or off and maintain that memory of on or off much in the way that an ordinary light switch "remembers" it is on until someone turns it off. This new, separate, and special-purpose hunk of memory was called a *frame buffer* and it is virtually always used in the raster systems of today.

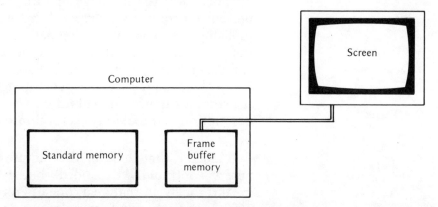

1. 7. The frame buffer maintains a stable memory of what is to be placed on the screen; it is isolated from other memory chips in the computer to simplify circuitry.

That's how a television set was attached to a computer. No longer would anyone have to observe the little rows of light bulbs flashing binary signals. Instead, ordinary decimal numbers and letters appeared on the television screen.

One of the first computers with a television-like display screen was the Massachusetts Institute of Technology's experimental, custom-built Whirlwind, which appeared in the early 1950s. One of Whirlwind's first programs, known as the *Bouncing Ball*, was simply a demonstration with no particular purpose other than to show the interesting things a computer could do on a screen. *Bouncing Ball* might be considered the grandfather of some of today's computer games, such as *Pong* and *Breakout*. What you saw on the screen was a ball that bounced, according to the physics of any normal bouncing ball. It bounced up and down on the screen, losing height with each bounce, until it dribbled out and at last fell through a "hole" in the bottom of the screen.

On a December 1951 show in his regular television series, *See It Now*, Edward R. Murrow interviewed Professor Jay Forrester of

MIT, and Forrester demonstrated some of the capabilities of the Whirlwind. Murrow was in New York. Forrester was in Cambridge. They spoke by telephone, while television cameras in New York and Cambridge recorded the events. First Forrester ran the *Bouncing Ball* program. Murrow was suitably impressed. Next Murrow telephoned someone at the Pentagon in Washington, D.C., who had some mathematical information about a hypothetical rocket. Professor Forrester put all the information into the computer, and lo, the computer drew graphs of the hypothetical rocket's trajectory, speed, and fuel consumption.

The interview concluded with Forrester saying something like, "The boys in the lab have had fun putting together a Christmas present for you," whereupon Whirlwind played *Jingle Bells*. But probably the most interesting part of the interview occurred when the rocket trajectory appeared on the screen. What it demonstrated was that (1) computer graphics might be used in practical ways, and (2) an obvious practical use of computer graphics was in transforming complex mathematical information (such as the mathematical description of a rocket trajectory) into a simple picture.

During that decade, the picture-making capacities of computers continually expanded—but 1963 marks a revolutionary breakthrough. In that year, one of Professor Forrester's students at MIT, Ivan Sutherland, completed a doctoral dissertation in which he described his *Sketchpad* system for producing computer graphics.

Before Sutherland began his work on *Sketchpad*, engineers had designed an ingenious little device, called a *light pen*, that enabled a person to "draw" lines directly on the computer screen. The light pen consisted of a light-sensitive (photoelectric) cell placed inside a piece of plastic and metal about the size and shape of a regular fountain pen. A person using the light pen placed it directly against the computer screen, and the computer would follow where the pen touched the screen by sending out scattered tracking spots of light, and then noting whether or not the photoelectric cell registered light. Because it was able to track the presence and movement of the light pen on the surface of the screen, the computer could then produce a steady line of light that trailed the pen's movement precisely.

Sutherland recognized that, using the light pen as a primary tool, he could devise some additional hardware and programs that would make the computer an excellent device for carrying out some tasks in engineering drawing. For example, he automated the drawing of straight lines: the user could touch two points on the screen with the light pen, and then after a simple manual command (pressing a button or flipping a switch), the computer would automatically produce a perfectly straight line between the two points. If the user wished to move the line, or lengthen it, redefining the end points was the only necessary act.

Sketchpad automated much of the drawing of simple figures: parallel lines and perpendicular lines could be produced by first drawing them roughly with the light pen, and then instructing the computer to perfect the rough sketches. To draw a square, the user merely needed to draw a rough quadrilateral with the light pen, and then instruct the computer to make all four sides equal in length and one side perpendicular to an adjacent side. The square could be moved or rotated to any position on the screen. The square could be defined in any size by instructing the computer to make one side a particular length: since all four sides had already been defined to the computer as equal in length, the entire figure would automatically expand to the new size. *Sketchpad* enabled a user to repeat automatically any figure: a simple figure drawn once could be reproduced any number of times on the screen. *Sketchpad* drew perfect circles; and it could define one figure according to another. Thus, an equilateral hexagon could be produced by defining a circle, drawing with the light pen a rough hexagon inside the circle so that all six corners touched its circumference, defining all six sides as equal in length, and then instructing the computer to erase the circle.

Although he began *Sketchpad* with the tools of engineering drawing in mind, Sutherland eventually realized that he had invented a tool with capacities markedly different from those of conventional drafting tools. "An idea that was difficult for the author to grasp," he wrote, "was that there is *no* state of the system which could be called 'drawing.' Conventionally, of course, drawing is an active process that leaves a trail of carbon on the paper. With a computer sketch, however, any line segment is straight and can be relocated by moving its points. . . . The major feature that distinguishes a *Sketchpad* drawing from a paper and pencil drawing is the user's ability to specify to *Sketchpad* mathematical conditions on already drawn parts which will be automatically satisfied by the computer."

Because *Sketchpad* was a computer-based system, any drawing could be saved in memory, and stored in a large library of magnetic tapes. Thus, engineering draftsmen needed to draw an individual figure only once: thereafter, the figure could be called up from memory and used as part of any larger drawing. Figures could be experimented with in a way that was before impossible. Changing part of a larger figure, for instance, would automatically alter the appearance of the whole figure. And, computer graphics could function as a way of modeling the real world. Pictures could include, in a dynamic fashion, information about what the pictures represented. For example, an electrical circuit could be designed on the screen, and then tested, while still on the screen. Another example: a picture of a bridge truss structure could be used to test the stresses caused by different loads placed on top of the bridge.

Sutherland went on to form a computer graphics company, Evans and Sutherland, and his early work at MIT went on to revolutionize computer graphics—which soon became an important tool for engineers, architects, and designers. Today American businesses are expanding their investment in computer graphics systems at more than fifty percent a year. Why? For businesses, computer graphics can transform an overload of confusing numerical information into immediately understandable pictures—pie charts and bar graphs, for example. Many industries use computer graphics in design, testing, and even in manufacturing. A computer graphics system might be used to design an automobile or jet plane, for instance, and then, on the basis of principles first suggested by Sutherland, test the model for wind resistance. A graphics system might be used to lay out the complex circuitry of a computer chip, test it, and then drive the laser that etches the final chip. Color Plates 1B and 1C provide examples of the kinds of images engineers and designers might be staring at on today's computer screens.

3

I have been describing some potentially wonderful artist's tools, but the people who owned and leased the computers of the 1950s and 1960s didn't see it that way. Computers were simply too expensive, precious, and complex to let artists near them. Actually, even scientists, engineers, and programmers had trouble getting near them. Most computers were kept in special rooms and run by specially trained people known as *operators*. The operator's duty was to operate the computer, and he (seldom she) maintained a position akin to that of a high priest assigned to protect the temple. Scientists might suggest a program, programmers might write it, but only the operator would schedule the running of it, only the operator would actually feed it into the machine.

As computers became less expensive and more accessible in the 1960s, a few scientists and engineers during off-hours and spare moments experimented with the graphics capabilities of their computers, using simple mathematical instructions to produce interesting images. The image would appear on the screen and, if they liked it, and wanted a copy to take home to the kids, they might instruct the computer to draw one on a device known as a *plotter*, which consisted of a pen mounted on a rack, driven by electric motors and coordinated by the computer to draw on paper. Figure 1.8, although done recently on a small computer, shows the kind of pleasing image that a large computer and plotter might have produced back then, from a relatively simple mathematical equation.

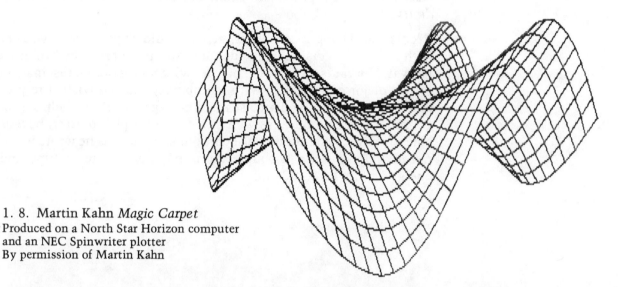

$$f(x,y)=xy(x^2-y^2)/8(x^2+y^2)$$

1. 8. Martin Kahn *Magic Carpet*
Produced on a North Star Horizon computer
and an NEC Spinwriter plotter
By permission of Martin Kahn

In the early 1960s, a few artists now and then sneaked into the "temple." Some of them were married to computer scientists. Some were deliberately sought out by computer scientists and given access to computers just to see what would happen. And a few happened to have some artistic training together with enough scientific credentials to get near a computer. All of this activity, however, was a gradual and informal osmosis.

In 1965, three mathematicians organized the first exhibit of computer-generated visual art at the Studio Gallery of the University of Stuttgart. Other small exhibits were held, both in Europe and America, and in 1968, at the Institute of Contemporary Arts in London, a major exhibition of computer art—including graphics, music, sculpture, and poetry—opened under the title of *Cybernetic Serendipity*. *Cybernetic Serendipity* may have been a turning point: artists who previously had been working in isolation discovered each other, other artists discovered computers, and some critics discovered the artists who were using computers. The catalog of the 1968 show was published as a book, the first on the subject of computers and art, entitled *Cybernetic Serendipity*, edited by Jasia Reichardt. By the mid-1970s a second book on the subject appeared, Ruth Leavitt's *Artist and Computer*, which introduced to the public most of the important artists using computers at that time.

What were the advantages of this new artist's tool? Other than the extra attention almost anyone can acquire by jumping on the bandwagon of some new idea or technology, what did these artists hope to gain by dropping their paintbrushes and other traditional image-making devices and sitting down in front of a computer? At least four things: *precision, iteration, transformation,* and *serendipity.*

Precision. Using a computer, artists could hope to achieve very high levels of precision. Consider, for example, *Eratos,* by Miljenko Horvat. Horvat is a Canadian painter with no particular fascination for, or major competence with, computers. But he wished to produce some complex and precise matrix images. With the help of programmer Serge Poulard, as well as a computer plus plotter, he was able to produce one such image without spending, as he wrote in *Artist and Computer,* "a couple thousand times more in time and energy," than he could afford.

1. 9. Miljenko Horvat *Eratos* 1974
Electrostatic drawing
By permission of Miljenko Horvat

Iteration. Artists also found it congenial to take advantage of the computer's capacity for iteration. Iteration, or repetition, is accomplished by writing a programming loop, which instructs the computer to go through a task and then repeat it, making some standard change with each repetition. Horvat's *Eratos* provides a good

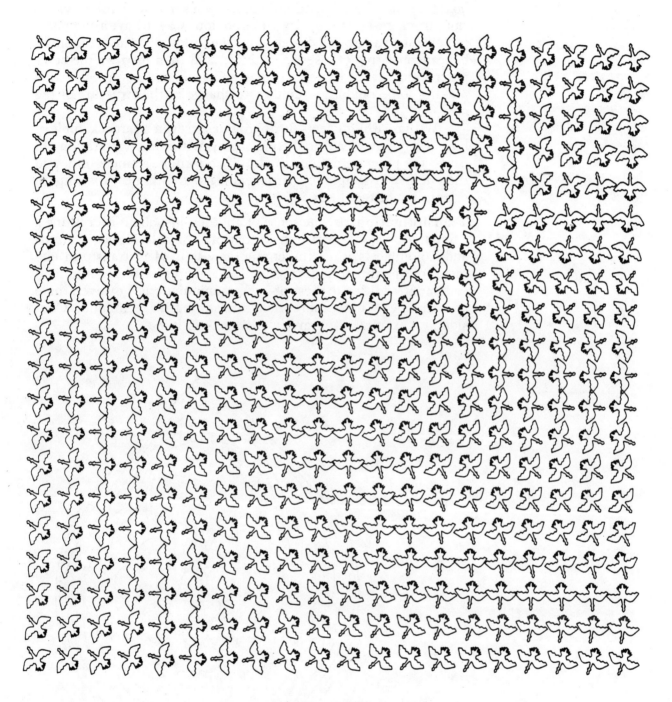

1. 10. William J. Kolomyjec *Birds*
By permission of William J. Kolomyjec
Copyright © 1980 Kolomputer Design

example of how helpful iteration can be: examining the matrix closely one sees that it is made up of a group of smaller matrices, or boxes, identical to each other in many ways, but with minor variations from one box to the next. The obvious way to have a computer produce such an overall design would be to describe one of the small boxes (consisting of a series of lines), and then instruct the computer to repeat the same box again and again and again, each time making some random or deliberate change in the structure of the box.

William Kolomyjec's *Birds* provides an even clearer example of how a computer can produce imagery with simple iteration. In *Birds*, the program defines the outlined form of a single bird, and then defines a simple repetition, along with simple variations in orientation of that form.

Transformation. In one sense or another, just about everything a computer does involves transformations. In both Horvat's *Eratos* and Kolomyjec's *Birds* the computer was used to transform elements of a picture in some methodical and progressive, or iterative, fashion. In addition to these obvious manipulations, however, there are a number of other more tricky transformative techniques. Consider, for example, Kolomyjec's *Water Into Wine*.

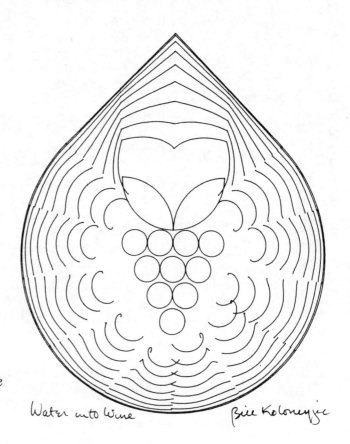

1. 11. William J. Kolomyjec *Water Into Wine*
By permission of William J. Kolomyjec
Copyright © 1980 Kolomputer Design

Kolomyjec began *Water Into Wine* with two basic images—one the shape of a grape cluster (composed of some circles and partial circles on the inside), and, on the outside, the shape of a drop of water. Basically, the artist's program instructs the computer to begin with one image and transform that gradually into the other, stopping at a few places along the way to draw a picture of partial transformations. More precisely, this is done in the following way. Since any image located on the screen (or drawn by the plotter) exists in the computer's memory as a series of points on a numbered grid, we can presume that Kolomyjec began with a numbered description of several of the points along the simple lines of the grape cluster. Next, he considered some corresponding points (points directly outward like the outer ends of spokes) on the raindrop. Obviously the distance between each of the defined points on the grape cluster and each of their corresponding points on the raindrop is greater or less, depending on the starting and ending points. The computer can calculate *that* distance by simple arithmetic, and then calculate where to draw the expanding, transformative "ripples" simply by dividing the distance with small numbers.

Serendipity. The term *serendipity* was coined by British author Horace Walpole in 1754 with the publication of his story about three princes from a place called Serendip, who experienced a series of lucky accidents. Serendipity thus suggests lucky accident, and it was first applied to art by computer at the 1968 *Cybernetic Serendipity* exhibit in London. The title of the exhibit is catchy, a playful pirouette of polysyllables. Beyond that, it seems provocatively paradoxical. *Cybernetic* suggests automation and mechanical control—seemingly the reverse of accident, lucky or otherwise. Thus, cybernetic serendipity suggests some new idea of the machine, some pleasant and perhaps delightfully dynamic combination of control and happenstance.

Artists using computers have, in fact, been particularly susceptible to serendipitous forces. Computers allow more experimentation than most other media. An artist might erase an unacceptable portion of a pencil on paper sketch once or twice, or even three times, without making too much of a mess. But an artist using a computer can change features and details endlessly, and save each version on a magnetic disk or tape, purposefully remaining open to some exchange between mastery of technique and accident—waiting like a cat for, and then pouncing on, the unsuspecting little mouse of serendipity. Also, the computer plus program plus peripheral devices (such as the screen or the plotter) can be more complicated, more likely to produce unexpected results, than a paint brush. Additionally, computers can be programmed to produce deliberate randomness—as in Kolomyjec's *Boxes I*. The pro-

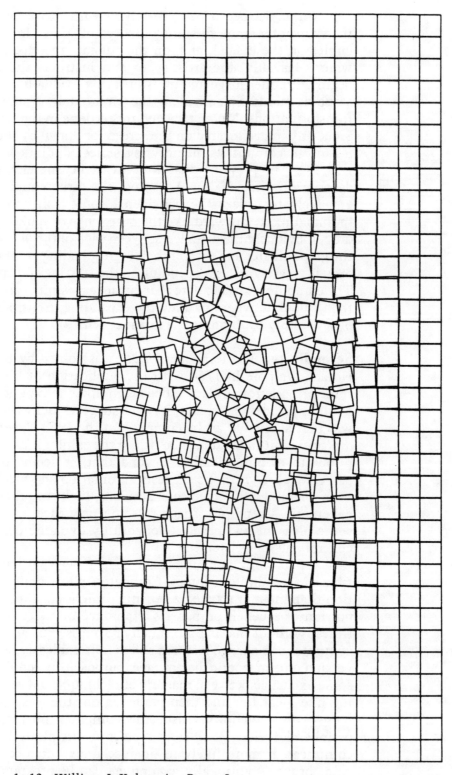

1. 12. William J. Kolomyjec *Boxes I*
By permission of William J. Kolomyjec. Copyright © 1980 Kolomputer Design

gram for this image began with the description of a perfectly ordered matrix of boxes. The distance from the center of each box to the center of the full design was computed, and the distance values for each box were multiplied by values taken from a list of random numbers. The resulting values were then used to determine the degree of disorder (rotation and displacement) for each box: the result is a matrix of boxes that are disordered partly by random choice, and partly according to distance from the center.

Precision, iteration, transformation, and serendipity—all four qualities have also been of some concern in noncomputer art. One thinks of Andy Warhol's obsessive iteration of soup cans and Marilyn Monroes. Particularly, though, one thinks of serendipity.

Nineteenth-century visual art was largely an art of control, and much of the training of the visual artist consisted of acquiring skills of control. Every line and brushstroke had its perfect place, every dot (especially for the pointillists) had its final position—according to the most refined understanding of traditional perspective, optics, and aesthetics. But twentieth-century visual art promoted an increasing openness to the production of virtually every kind of visual event. On the one hand, this led to a highly structured, almost mathematical art, as practiced by painters like Piet Mondrian. On the other hand, it led to the new element of serendipity: the idea that randomness and accident could be significant, even crucial elements in a visual art. After World War I, for instance, Dadaist Jean Arp tore up pieces of colored paper, sprinkled them randomly across another piece of paper, and glued them down where they had landed. Other Dadaists began creating collages and sculptures from objects serendipitously found in the street, or junkyard. Marcel Duchamp described his masterpeice painting *Large Glass* as ''complete'' only after the glass had been shattered accidentally during transportation and he glued it back together (in 1936): he decided he liked the pattern of cracks. In the late 1940s, Jackson Pollock began flinging paint across large canvases, letting splashes and drips pattern themselves according to chance and the physics of flying paint, while in the 1950s, Robert Rauschenberg, rejuvenating the Dadaist taste for found objects, acquired interesting or peculiar objects from his walks around the streets of New York, and transubstantiated them into whimsical, witty, sometimes ironic sculptures.

Precision, iteration, transformation, serendipity—those are some of the qualities that artists found when they began using computers in the late 1960s and early 1970s. Colette and Charles Bangert's *Large Landscape II* illustrates all four qualities.

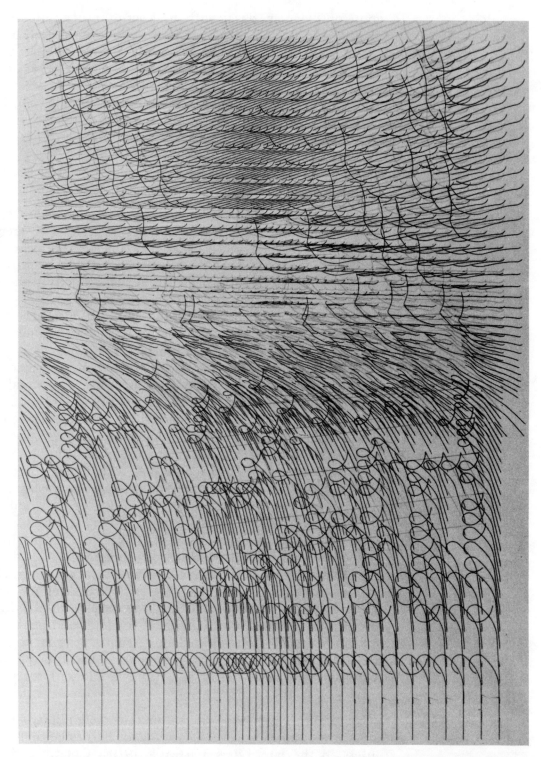

1. 13. Colette and Charles Bangert *Large Landscape II: Ochre and Black*, 1970
Computer-plotted drawing, ink on paper 33 × 32 inches. Done using a Honeywell 635 digital computer and a Benson-Lehner Draft-O-Matic plotter at the University of Kansas. By permission of Colette and Charles Bangert

Here we have what appears to be a landscape. The curved lines and repetitions of lines resemble a grand Kansas vista—grass, or wind-waved wheat in a field, and wispy cirrus clouds receding toward the horizon.

The entire scene was drawn by a decrepit old plotter—laboriously, over a period of several hours—in two passes, one in yellow ink, the second in black ink. The scene depends upon the iteration of some basic curves (moving in rows from left to right and bottom to top); looking closely, one might presume that the curve has gone through a simple transformation from the shepherd's crook at the bottom left corner to the limp "j" at the top right. The idea of a simple transformation makes sense, but then what about the squashed curves in the center, at the "horizon"? They don't appear to be a logical middle point of the transformation. They are, indeed—because there was an additional force at work in the program.

As the plotter drew out its curves, according to the instructions from the iteration and transformation parts of the program, the computer formed a rough map, in memory, of where curves had occurred. The plotter continued drawing curves moving left to right along a row, then moving over to begin the next row—but this additional part of the program instructed it never to draw a curve over any curve that had been mapped into memory. Thus, whenever the pen approached the memory of a previous curved line, it stopped, then started over again. The result was a certain serendipitous unpredictability. First the shepherd's crook started falling out of its orderly rows. And as the plotter plodded along, information about previous curves got thicker and thicker, more and more crowded in the memory map, at last forcing the curve into the squashed appearance you see halfway up the drawing, at the "horizon." Of course, those squashed curves (as they were recorded in the computer's memory) began to give room (because they were squashed) for the curves of additional rows to stretch out again—so the program began returning to its regular transformations, approaching the limp "j" of the upper right.

That was serendipitous. And one recognizes that the serendipity did not arise from some straightforward injection of randomness into the program (through, for instance, a table of random numbers). Rather, it resulted from a small battle between two parts of the program, a complex and dynamic exchange.

Notice also how the top half of the black plot in *Large Landscape II* seems slightly inclined to the right, as if it had been broken off and glued back unevenly, like a cracked Rosetta stone. Here is the artifact of an additional serendipity. During the second pass with the black pen, the plotter broke down. "When that happened," artist Charles Bangert told me, "I started to cry. 'Don't cry,' Colette said. 'Start it up again.' I said, 'Look, this is not something you start up again.' She said, 'What the heck, start it up anyway.' So I did, and it produced the effect you see, that break and skewing of the black plot. And ever since then I've known that we live within the history of twentieth-century art: we have accidents.''

Not all the images generated in the 1970s were in black and white, and run out on a plotter. But many of them were. Color was not particularly common until the end of the decade. And the question continued: How do you generate *stills*? What do you do with that soft and transient, electronically generated image on the screen, how do you make it stand still, transform it into an image that can be hung on a wall or reproduced in a book? The plotter was one device commonly used to solve that problem, producing black and white images, or drawing in color—plotters pushing several pens at once, with several colors of ink.

By the 1980s, photographic techniques became refined enough for artists to produce quite accurate reproductions of colored screen images, and enlarge them to the size of ordinary oil paintings. Now it is also possible to transfer screen images to videotape and videodisk. Transferring computer screen images to video seems a logical step because, for one thing, you can use the same screen. One problem with video reproduction, however, is that colors tend to degenerate during the transfer—the computer produces separate signals for red, green, and blue and then puts them into digital form, whereas a video system collapses all the separate color signals into a single composite signal and then puts that single signal out in analog form.* In addition, if you plan to have animation (moving graphics) instead of stills, a direct transfer to video may be impossible because of limitations in computing speeds. If the animation is relatively simple, the computer can indeed generate a *real-time* moving image. But the computer is more likely to take a second, or a minute, or even several minutes to generate a single image. This means that the artist is forced to use a movie camera, shooting only one frame at a time, to record animation.

Perhaps the most important changes of the 1970s were due to enormous improvements in computer hardware and software. What was previously done only on large computers could now be done on

---

*The computer always has to encode its information into little discrete pieces, usually represented by numbers: information in this form is described as *digital*. Most other information machines (the television, telephone, and videorecorder, for instance) convey information in a way that imitates, or is *analogous to*, a pattern occurring in nature. For instance, the telephone system simply imitates with electrical waves the sound waves made by a human voice; television directly transfers fluctuating patterns of light into fluctuating electronic patterns; video stores similar fluctuations on magnetic tape. Information in this second form is called *analog*.

small computers. On the large computers, processing speeds, screen resolution, and memory all increased drastically. The number of available colors also increased, so that now some computer systems offer artists millions of colors and hues to choose from.

Earlier I described the frame buffer as that piece of memory in the computer especially set aside to collect and hold information about what is to appear on the screen. Needless to say, the efficiency of frame buffers increased, too. What's more, engineers found that frame buffers could be "stacked"—so two, or three, or four can be put into the computer. In this way, the computer and its programmer can easily and methodically deal with several different aspects of a single image. Holding some coloring and shape information in one frame buffer and information about three-dimensional depth and shading in another, for example, proves to be simpler than attempting to put all that information into a single big frame buffer.

Toward the end of the 1970s, some artists and programmers learned to produce images that approached photographic realism. Of course, producing any image on a computer screen is problematic, because one needs to define each dot or pixel on the screen. Producing simple line drawings or even slightly complicated geometrical shapes is not such a problem because the computer happens to be very good at doing the simple mathematics needed to define Euclidean shapes. But what about a piece of fruit? Or a human form? Or a realistic landscape? What about a human face? To see the kinds of realistic scenes being produced today, turn to Color Plates 1D, 2A, 2B, and 2C.

It may be obvious how the still life in Color Plate 2A was produced. All the realistic objects in the scene were defined to the computer as collections of simple geometric shapes, described three-dimensionally—and the simple shapes were patched together in such a way that they resemble the slightly more geometrically complex shapes of the scene. Some subprograms were used to add the shading, shadows, and highlights. Notice how the orange in this scene is really just a sphere, slightly flattened on the bottom, colored orange, with some bumpy surface features added? The bumps were placed there by a technique known as *texture-mapping*. The subprogram for this describes a picture of bumps on a flattened surface. The resulting information on texture is then inserted into the definition of the sphere, thus "mapping" the bumps onto the sphere.

One of the originators of texture-mapping, James Blinn, is responsible for the image depicted in Color Plate 1D. Blinn was a graduate student at the University of Utah when he began exploring ideas of texture-mapping. Upon graduation, Blinn took a job at Jet

Propulsion Laboratories in Pasadena, California. At his new job, he saw a computer simulation of what NASA's Voyager space probe was likely to photograph as it flew by various planets. The simulations were just simple line drawings. Blinn mentioned that he thought he might be able to put surfaces on the computer-drawn planets, and asked permission to try it. An administrator of NASA saw the resulting computer-generated animation at a meeting and decided it would be superb for public information purposes: Blinn was asked to do all the NASA "flyby" simulations.

The two scenes in Color Plates 2B and 2C are almost indistinguishable from real photographs of actual mountain scenes, yet they were done entirely with a computer program written by Loren Carpenter. Carpenter began his mountain scenes by defining with a few points the rough dimensions of a mountain he wanted drawn. These were three-dimensional representations, so each point was specified by three numbers—representing latitude, longitude, and altitude—for the rough outline of his mountains. Putting a lake or ocean into the scene was easy to do because Carpenter could just instruct the computer to draw a flat blue surface covering every point below some specific value of altitude. But portraying the rocks, trees, and snow, was more complex. He had to specify the colors, and then create the crinkled surfaces. Nonetheless, the crinkled surfaces of the rocks, snow, and trees, could all be drawn by means of one basic programming technique; Carpenter had only to define the degree of crinkle.

The crinkle was produced in the following way. Carpenter defined by numbered points the mountains and valleys he wanted. Next, a "construction program" was applied to all the points, which produced a series of interconnected triangles. If shading were added then, the triangles would have looked like large, rough, triangular plates. But the drawing program broke these large triangles down into smaller and smaller triangles—and at each break there was a great deal of unpredictable displacement and rotation, so that as the triangles became smaller, they looked less like triangles and more like crinkled surfaces. The breaking up of the triangles finally stopped when they reached a certain size, defined by Carpenter's program. The different sizes determined the different textures for rocks, trees, and snow. Color was added, and a shading and highlighting subprogram finally provided the three-dimensional appearance.

Why should artists use computers to produce realistic images at all when a camera can do it so accurately and easily? For one thing, the techniques learned in producing realistic scenes can then be used to produce interesting images of any type. For another, the camera can only define, or reproduce, something that was really there, whereas the computer (like the paintbrush) can describe something that never existed. Jim Blinn's flyby simulations, for instance, are valuable to NASA because he is able to produce realistic three-dimensional animations of what, given all present knowledge, a planet *ought* to look like from the perspective of a space probe, well before the probe arrives at that point to take a photograph. Further, Blinn is able to assemble all partial knowledge, including blurred or partial photographs, insert them into his texture maps and eventually produce pictures that are far more accurate than any single photograph. Another example: once Loren Carpenter has generated a mountain scene with three-dimensional information, he can easily move the scene around on the screen. It's easy to enlarge the scene, or make it smaller. It's easy to change the scene, and see what it would look like from another perspective, from around a corner. In other words, Carpenter has all the tools at hand to create a movie from the point of view of someone flying a hangglider into and around those craggy heights, thus creating scenes that few would be foolish enough to try to film in real life. Indeed, Carpenter has created just such an animation. It's called *Le Vol Libre*, and I recommend it highly.

Most computer-using artists are moving beyond realistic representations, though, producing images that take particular advantage of some of the unique capabilities of the computer.

4

Lillian Schwartz, long recognized for her innovative uses of modern technology to create new art forms, is best known for her pioneering achievements in introducing computers to the art world. Her work is collected and exhibited in major museums around the world. Some critics characterize it as displaying more experimentation and versatility in the use of modern technology than the work of any other artist in this century. She has received numerous awards, particularly for her brilliant innovations in film, video, and graphics. Part of her justification for using computers has to do with the fact that they mark our age: "I happen to use computers or lasers or whatever our technology provides," she states. "While I can paint a picture by using such traditional techniques as an undercoat and glazing, I choose to work with the technology of our time to make a statement about the world in which I live."

Schwartz graduated in 1947 from the College of Nursing and Health of the University of Cincinnati. She began her career as a nurse in the United States Navy Cadet Nurse Corps, but always found time to paint and sculpt. She left nursing, studied watercolor in Japan in 1949, and by the early 1950s a number of her works were exhibited at the National Academy, by the American Watercolor Society. As a nurse, she had often protected broken limbs with plaster cast materials, and sometimes used those same materials for sculpting. As an artist, she continued sculpting—often using materials and technology she had become familiar with in nursing.

In 1968, her sculpture, *Proxima Centauri*, was selected by the Museum of Modern Art in New York to be included in *The Machine* exhibit. *Proxima Centauri* is a black "minimal" box with a translucent dome on top and a slide projector inside that casts abstract images onto the dome. A "proximity detector" (an internal sonar device) responds to the approach of viewers, causing the dome to recede into the base, whereupon viewers can see the projected images more clearly. When viewers walk away, a red glow comes over the box, and the dome moves up again. *Proxima Centauri* was quite successful; the original is now in Stockholm's Moderna Museet. It had nothing to do with computers, of course, but in that 1968 exhibit two scientists, Leon Harmon and Ken Knowlton, were exhibiting a computer-generated image they had worked on. They met Schwartz and asked her to give them the input of a professional artist, to create with them programs for the production of new visual images. Thus began Lillian Schwartz's extended, fruitful collaboration with Knowlton, Harmon, and eventually other scientists.

Most computer screens consist of several hundred to several thousand lines of electronically generated light. Because the computer is digital, relying upon discrete, on and off signals, each line is divided into hundreds or thousands of discrete segments, producing on the screen a grid of light. When the *resolution* (the number of picture elements in the grid) is relatively low, those elements become quite visible on the screen. The screen looks as if it were made up of a series of dots. When the resolution is really low, the dots begin to look like small squares. Lines, except when they are perfectly vertical or perfectly horizontal straight lines, have little "stair steps" in them. Figures come out bumpy around the edges. Even in very high resolution systems, such *aliasing* of the image often becomes apparent. Lillian Schwartz recognized that this effect on the computer screen paralleled the meticulous placing of dots of color on canvas that the French pointillists deliberately sought at the turn of the century. Thus she decided to experiment with what she called "technological pointillism." An early graphic deliberately created with this technique can be seen in Color Plate 3A.

Schwartz began this pleasing, stylized image by sketching it out on graph paper. She drew a picture composed of regular squares possessing different degrees of lightness and darkness, differing values of gray. Meanwhile (and with a program written by Ken Knowlton), she had put into a computer's memory a large series of little "boxes," which were really square, precisely defined patterns or "mazes" made up of black dots. Some of these patterns had more dots and thus were darker than others, and she categorized the patterns according to the number of black dots—in other words, according to the degree of darkness, or gray value. With those dot patterns in the computer's memory, Schwartz then sat at the keyboard, graphed drawing in hand, and defined that drawing to the computer by punching in a numbered gray value for each square on the graph paper. As soon as a gray value was punched in, the computer called up a pattern of dots associated with the value and put that pattern onto the screen. Thus Schwartz gradually transferred her hand-drawn picture onto the screen.

Why? What good did it do? For one thing, each of the box patterns appearing on the screen was much more detailed and precisely defined than were the hand-drawn squares on the graph paper. For another, Schwartz had given the computer more than one pattern of dots per gray value, and the computer was programmed to choose from those patterns at random. The artist might, of course, have tried to do all of that by hand, but in her words: "To meticulously replace all those gray values with the maze patterns would have been an horrendous job. Using the computer provokes me to think of ways of creating that were impossible before." Once the final image was completed, it was photographed, enlarged, and, with well-known silkscreening techniques, colored and reproduced.

Schwartz found the full process tedious, however. She found she could spend a full day merely typing in gray values. So the next step was to automate the process. She used a device that would optically scan a picture and automatically assign gray values to as many squares in a grid as the computer could define. The original picture itself did not have to be in a grid form, of course. The computer would quickly scan any image and define it, in memory, as a series of differing numerical values. Only when the computer converted those values into dotted patterns on the screen did one see the grid of differing gray values.

Not only did this scanner and other computer-based techniques automate all the keying in of gray values by hand, but it also enabled Schwartz to use images (often photographic) from the real world, instead of keying into the computer image values taken from a drawing on graph paper. Whereas a human looking at a photograph might be sorely perplexed at the task of determining values of darkness and lightness for each portion, the computer-based scanner simply made optical readings—its programs gave gray values and called up corresponding maze patterns automatically. The final image could then be printed on microfilm, enlarged, and at last given color and permanence through silkscreening. In this way, Plate 3B, *Nude*, was produced.

Nude began as a photograph of a real nude. Certainly the

original photograph was fine, a pleasing study in human form and mood. As a photograph, however, it may not have been terribly distinguishable from thousands of other, similar studies. But once scanned and digitized, once technologically pointillized, it became something quite different, and unique. What was the effect Schwartz was trying to achieve by moving away from the original photographic image? "Photography is an art form in itself, of course. But it can be used with the computer to create a new kind of visual imagery, and that's what I wanted. I believe that much of art is translating into another form, creating new shapes—new ideas—making something that we haven't seen before."

Schwartz continues to use technological pointillism along with a wide range of other techniques which often make use of computers (and sometimes do not). Color Plate 3C is taken from her more recent animation, *Metathesis*. This animation begins, at the program level, with a mathematical equation developed by John Chambers that produces colored forms. By changing values in the equation, the artist instructs the computer to sweep abstract, highly vivid, colored shapes into and out of form on the screen. The final work was filmed directly from the screen, a frame at a time. Schwartz then coordinated the images with a computer-generated sound tract produced by Joe Olive.

Works by Ruth Leavitt, painter, printmaker, and sculptor, are displayed in public and private collections in Japan, England, Belgium, France, Italy, Holland, Scotland, Canada, and the United States. She is the editor and compiler of one of the few significant books about computers in the arts, *Artist and Computer* (1976). Typically, Leavitt works with strong color and geometric pattern, using a computer to experiment and create through an *interactive* process she calls "plastic deformation."

Describing the process as *interactive* means that Leavitt uses her computer directly as a tool. The program she uses (written by her husband, computer scientist Jay Leavitt) allows her to produce colored geometric forms on the screen. Then, with some very simple control devices and commands on the keyboard, she can manipulate those colors and forms on the screen at will, working much as a sculptor might work with clay, trying one thing, trying another, looking for some final combination of color and form that somehow, serendipitously, is what she wanted all along. Leavitt's term "plastic deformation" suggests the way in which she manipulates geometry: she begins with a geometric design, which she then stretches in a way that might be compared to stretching an image printed on a sheet of rubber. "I'm trying to combine order and disorder. I'll begin with the order of a Constructivist kind of art—similar to what Mondrian does—and then I use the program to make it more lyrical, less Constructivist. In the end, I'm just trying to produce artwork, that's my whole purpose, and it just so happens that the computer is a terrific tool."

Visual artists using computers have the problem of figuring out what to do once they have produced an image on the screen, since the screen image itself has no permanence. Leavitt has often used the computer screen simply for preliminary designs, testing out form and color, at last using that design as a model for painting acrylic on canvas; for printmaking; or for creating sculptures in wood, plaster, plexiglass, or bronze. Many other computer-using artists who are manipulating and transforming images on the screen hope to arrive at some destination, some final image that will be of interest. In Ruth Leavitt's case, this may be true as well, but her programs make the process itself visually interesting. In other words, her work seems particularly suited to animation.

Color Plates 4A and 4B are stills taken from her animation on videotape entitled *From Blue to Yellow*. As these stills suggest, her images characteristically possess a certain gem-like quality, fascinating the observer with simple color and faceted form. At the same time, they seem fluid, carefully distorted visions in color and geometry. It is as if one were looking at well-cut precious stones under curved crystal. These images show why she speaks of plastic deformation, why she often refers to the idea of stretching an image. Perhaps we can begin to see why she persists in using a computer: such images might have taken months of planning and execution through more traditional methods, whereas she is able to produce them almost instantly.

Leavitt's work suggests that the computer is likely to have as much effect on contemporary painting as photography had on the painting of a century ago. Suddenly, the visual artist is no longer forced to remain content with static images, with ideas that, once carried out, are fixed and frozen on canvas. The computer-using artist is able to take an initial image-idea and mold it, stretch it, squeeze it, all the while examining the process. Suddenly, flat image-making has taken on some of the aspects of sculpting with clay.

Ruth Leavitt believes that, because of the newness and the strangeness of the computer, a lot of people are reluctant to accept it as an artist's tool. "But it is not replacing anything," she insists. "It merely adds another dimension to art. There were people who objected to cameras, and people who objected to easel painting, who felt that painting should only be done in frescoes on the wall. In my own experience, scientific people who had access to the machine were reluctant to give me access, feeling that it was a scientific tool. Then a lot of my artist friends, my colleagues, felt that it was a sterile type of thing to do. And so I used to go around proselytizing, and I really must say I've lost a lot of that. Not only is it not necessary, I'm just tired of it. At this point, I think we need just to get down to using the thing, instead of saying, 'This could be terrific.' "

David Em acquired a traditional training in painting at the Pennsylvania Academy of Fine Arts. But it quickly became apparent, at least to him, that he had a strong interest in using contemporary technologies in his art. First it was plastics, then video. Finally, in 1975 he witnessed a computer being used to generate visual imagery at a research laboratory owned by Xerox. He describes that turning point: "I couldn't believe it! It was exactly what I was looking for and had dreamed of and everyone had said, 'Oh, it's impossible.' What I was looking for was picture element control. I wanted to control every dot on the TV screen, and here was a computer that did it, and not only did it but could do all these other things too." Em began searching for a congenial computer graphics environment, traveling all over the country, gravitating first to Jet Propulsion Laboratories and later to West Coast University, both in Southern California.

David Em's images are marked by a strong regularity, a cold and almost alien quality. Sharp edges combine with a fascinating feeling of depth and space. Indeed, his images conjure alien places from outer space; and we should not be surprised to learn that David Em works in close collaboration with James Blinn, the person who creates the NASA flyby simulations at Jet Propulsion Laboratories.

Em himself is neither a programmer nor a computer scientist. As he describes it: "I am very, very nontechnical. I am not a programmer. I don't program. I'm not interested in programming. When I'm working with the machine I'm dealing exclusively with creative and compositional issues. I sit down at the computer and work with it in much the same way I might work with a painting. I see where it takes me and I work with the medium. I don't necessarily know what the given end is going to be when I sit down to pick up from the day before." He is an artist, applying what he knows and intuits about color and form to programs that Blinn has designed particularly for simulating scenes in space. Some of the results you can see in Color Plates 5A, 5B, and 5C.

What powers of creation does David Em acquire from James Blinn's programs? Blinn has written a program to generate some three-dimensional shapes, and then map various textures on them. Blinn uses these to produce planets and moons on the screen; Em uses them to create exotically textured spheres, doughnuts, cones, pyramids. Another program written by Blinn allows David Em to draw freehand, using an electronic pen on a tablet. Other programs allow Em to do simple two-dimensional things, such as produce mirror images—taking what's on the left half of the screen, for instance, and generating a perfectly symmetrical reverse image of that on the right half. Other programs can be used to take sections of an image and move them around on the screen, tilt them in three dimensions, or put them in perspective. Em uses another program to take two entirely different images and blend them together, either by blurring them together or by a matting process in which some pixels on the screen are taken from one image and other pixels come from the other. Altogether he is able to call upon a large collection of image-generating software tools of that kind, limited primarily by whatever particular tasks Blinn has been approaching.

How does it feel to be an artist with no technical background working in the confines of a large, important research laboratory? "Right now if you really want to do state-of-the-art computer graphics, you need these machines that are expensive, require a lot of maintenance and a lot of systems and technical people, and have to be kept cool all the time. Additionally, the machines only exist in corporate or governmental situations because nobody else can afford them, so you're now interfacing not only with all the problems and situations related to the machine's life, but to the bureaucratic and political life of some corporation as well. And the artist is neither fish nor fowl. The artist doesn't really fit into any of this, and has to create a space for himself or herself. You need a certain amount of gift of gab to interface with the management types, to tell the president of the company, or the public information officer, 'Gee, I'm doing this stuff and isn't it great.' In addition, you have to have patience. When you're painting, the worst thing that's going to happen is you might run out of a color of paint. When you're working in computer graphics, though, the whole tool could disappear. Also the machines have to be kept cool, so it's about 63 degrees where I work. I nearly froze to death last night. I have a muffler and little gloves with tips cut off the fingers because it's so cold. That's very alien to me. I like to be warm and feel good when I work. So you have to adapt yourself, if you're an artist and you want to work with the very best machines available."

Darcy Gerbarg is a professional artist, formally educated in the fine arts as a painter, a ten-year veteran of the New York art scene. She now paints almost exclusively on a computer screen, and creates final still pieces (suitable for the walls of museums, galleries, and the like) with several techniques, including very precise and expensive photography and enlargement of screen images. Her works have appeared in a number of gallery shows, and on the covers of *Computer Design* and *Computer Graphics World* magazines. She has also helped organize, and been curator of, the High Arts Technology Exhibition appearing at both the SIGGRAPH

1981 Conference in Dallas and Computer Culture '81 in Toronto. Currently, she teaches at New York University's School of the Arts.

While many other artists using computers are creating transformations of recognizably geometrical shapes, Gerbarg's work is notable for its absence of Euclidean form, for its asymmetry, abstraction, and a great sensitivity to color and line and space (see Color Plates 6A, 6B and 6C). At the moment, she may be the only professional artist relying almost entirely upon that combination of hardware and prepackaged software known as a *paint system*.

If other computer-using artists can be said to be painting largely with their programs, we ought to describe Darcy Gerbarg as painting directly on her screen. In fact, if you were to see her at work, that's almost what you would see. You would see her, sitting in front of a computer—the keyboard to one side, the screen perhaps slightly off to the right, and directly in front a piece of flat plastic and metal about the size of a large drawing tablet. She hardly uses the keyboard at all. She loads a program into the computer, and types only about two commands on the keyboard. She takes something that looks like a ball point pen and passes it across the tablet: nothing at all appears on the tablet—no marks, no lines—but up on the screen lines begin to appear. Some interesting things soon become apparent. Although Gerbarg continues to use the same stylus (which looks like a ball point pen) we notice that, by touching certain small squares on the edge of the tablet, she can change the colors of the lines that appear on the screen. Soon we realize that she can change the size and quality of the lines as well. That is, after she touches a marked square on the edge of the tablet, the line on the screen becomes broader, as if she had picked up a wider paint brush. Other simple commands of that sort cause the quality of the stroke to become "heavier" or "lighter" (cause some varied percentage of the pixels in the stroke to be activated), as if she were varying the amount of paint on a brush.

So far Gerbarg might as well be painting with a real brush on canvas, but suddenly we begin to see the computer's particular magic. She draws an asymmetrical figure with a thin "brush-stroke," then touches the inside of that figure and, instantly, the entire figure is filled in with one color. She makes a couple of simple commands on the tablet and, instantly, a portion of the picture on the screen is moved from one position to another, while the rest of the picture remains the same. Next, she makes that one portion larger. Next, she doubles and reverses it into a mirror image. She draws some other lines, tries out some other doubling or quadrupling transformations, and now she has an interesting painting on the screen, composed of lines and symmetrical and asymmetrical figures—but she is still not satisfied. So next she changes colors wholesale. She makes a single command on the edge of the tablet, then touches one area in the drawing portion of the tablet, and instantly its corresponding color on the screen changes from pale blue to magenta. Another two strokes, and all the lines of one color (olive) change to a bright, garish green. Next, she changes the colors of some of the lines to seaweed green, and others to the brown of dead leaves. Finally, after putting in and taking out lines and forms, after changing colors and moving shapes, she begins to like what she sees on the screen. A couple of strokes on the keyboard and that image is stored in permanent memory, on a disk. She might come back to it or she might later decide to erase it, but for now she'll keep it in storage. And she goes back to work, changing the screen image further, playing with it, experimenting.

That's a paint system. It is a combination of software and hardware that allows anyone to put pictures directly onto the screen (using a *graphics tablet* and circuit-completing *stylus)*, and it works mainly because the grid of memory in the frame buffer corresponds directly to the grid of light and color on the screen. Frame buffers were first used in computer graphics systems at the beginning of the 1970s, and, as I noted earlier, they are simply special units of memory set aside to store and organize information about a screen picture until that information is ready to be sent out to the screen. At first, of course, there were only a few frame buffers in existence. Because circuits were still very expensive, frame buffers were custom-made and used experimentally. At about that time, an engineer named Dick Shoup arrived at a computer research laboratory in California and was given permission to do what he wanted. He built a frame buffer, attached it to a computer, and started to think about something so obvious and simple that many other people were left wondering why they didn't think of it first. "It seemed to me perfectly natural," he says, "that an artist with a pen of some kind should be able to draw directly into a frame buffer, and have it displayed on the screen." And thus, he built some special frame buffer hardware, attached a circuit-completing graphics tablet and stylus, and wrote the software that would connect the circuit inside the tablet to the memory grid of the frame buffer.* The result was that anyone could create a complex drawing with the stylus on the tablet, and watch the drawing appear on the screen. The sketch of Woody Allen below is an example of what one might have drawn.

---

*The graphics tablet and stylus had been around for some time, and were used, like the light pen described earlier, to draw line figures on vector system screens. But vector displays flickered; and without frame buffer memory, neither vector nor raster displays could maintain the integrity and stability of highly complex screen images. Obviously, the pioneering work of Ivan Sutherland had a tremendous influence on this later kind of "sketchpad," the *paint system.*

1. 14. Emily Reilly *Portrait of Woody Allen*
Reproduced by permission of Emily Reilly.

A simple addition to the software allowed anyone to change those line strokes into brush strokes—where the width and intensity and color of the lines could be changed at will. And, as hardware and software improved over the decade, so did the sophistication of such paint systems. Resolution improved drastically. Many more colors became possible. Various simple transformative powers were added—the ability to move images, double and reverse them, alter colors, and so on.

Today, one can attach a graphics tablet and stylus to an inexpensive personal computer, load in paint system software, and do much more sophisticated things than Shoup might have imagined. But to acquire the resolution and responsiveness and color command that a serious fine artist needs, Gerbarg thinks it is still necessary to seek out the biggest and best and most expensive graphics computers, owned by institutions and large corporations. As she says, "I think it's important that art using computers not happen as some artsy little curiosity off some place in the twilight zone, and that's what's been happening. Who do artists compare themselves with, if not Cézanne, Rembrandt, Matisse . . . the big leagues? It's that simple. And few people faced up to that in this field because until recently the technology just hasn't been there. Until a few years ago the technology was sort of in the stick-figure and charcoal stage of development."

Duane Palyka is one of those rare people who straddle the two cultures of art and science. He was the only student in the history of Carnegie-Mellon University to receive both the Bachelor of Science degree in mathematics and the Bachelor of Fine Arts degree in painting at the same time. He earned an MFA in painting from the University of Utah while working as a research associate and systems programmer in Utah's computer science department. Currently he is a senior staff member at one of the few places in the world where artistic vision and computer cunning are looked upon with equal seriousness: the computer graphics laboratory of the New York Institute of Technology. Perhaps more than any other contemporary artist, Palyka's work shows this dual mastery: his work is particularly characterized by the use of the computer at the program level to produce striking and evocative images. The programmed manipulations and transformations evidence high analytical skills and logical prestidigitation, while the images themselves seem vastly illogical, as if floating up from deepest dreams.

In several of his images (including Color Plates 7A and 7B), Palyka begins with a three-dimensional rendering of a female form. The program for that original rendering was done by Ed Catmull, who studied a live model and then defined its form to the computer as a group of patched-together geometrical shapes. That the figure is defined in three dimensions means that Palyka, or anyone else, can show it from any angle, and similarly shade or highlight it with a hypothetical light source coming from any direction. In *Pinwheel 1*, Palyka has clothed the form with texture-mapping, then rotated it on a central axis and captured the image at various points in the rotation.

Palyka's *Picasso 2* began with four of those figures. He clothed them with various texture maps, but during the process a "bug" crept into the program, causing a random sparkle in the texture. He decided the sparkle was serendipitous, and left it in. Next, he complicated some of the figures by displaying some hidden sides—and I should explain how. When a figure is defined in three dimensions to the computer, all sides of the figure are stored somewhere in memory. This means that when the figure is displayed on the two-dimensional screen, a subprogram calculates—given a defined point of view—what normally would be seen and what wouldn't. The program then erases the "hidden" part of the figure by assigning it an illumination value of zero percent and giving the exposed part an illumination value of one hundred percent. Since the computer still contains information about those hidden sides, however, it is possible to make the figure "transparent" by giving the normally exposed part an illumination value of, say, fifty percent, and giving the normally hidden portion a value of fifty percent. The result, in *Picasso 2* is an increased and fascinating complexity in some of the human-shaped figures. Finally, Palyka decided to "explode" the second human figure from the left—to see what serendipity would bring. He achieved the explosion by a simple mathematical instruction, inserted into the original definition of the female figure, causing its constituent geometrical parts to fly outward. *Picasso 2* is an appropriate title for the image. I find it to be as visually fascinating as some of Picasso's productions. In addition, the techniques are similar to those Picasso used with his early Cubist nudes, as he experimented with form and texture—stretching, twisting, ignoring traditional rules of perspective, discarding ordinary expectations of seeing.

In *Space-Carrots* (Color Plate 7C), Palyka has drawn a picture by defining and repeating some unusual shapes, giving shading and shadows to some and not to others. It's an interesting study in apparent three dimensions, an incomprehensible dream allegory of alligators and eggs. To create the next image, *Space-Carrots on Soid* (Color Plate 7D), Palyka eliminated the shading and shadow instructions from *Space-Carrots*, and stored that deshaded, deshadowed image in one section of the program. Then, in another part of the program, he defined an ellipsoid, an "egg." He returned to the first image and texture-mapped that onto the egg: thus, *Space-Carrots on Soid*.

"What I do," Palyka says, "is something of a painterly process with computer programming. I write a program, or change someone else's program, or both, and see what happens. See how it affects the images. Then I either change it, or go along in the same direction. So it's more or less like treating the program as if it were an interactive canvas, producing images. In other words, it's as if I paint on the program."

Harold Cohen is a painter by training, a professor of art at the University of California at San Diego, and an internationally recognized artist, who for well over a decade has been designing computer programs to do much of his painting for him. Cohen is one of the few computer-using visual artists who does not rely upon the computer's screen to produce his images—which, by the way, are often mural-sized. Cohen's art lies deep inside the programs he has written. He may be more akin to a composer of music than a performer: he composes programs, and then watches (with some amusement and pleasure) as his computer carries out a serendipitous performance.

Performances usually take place in a large room within an art museum, and here is how one might appear. It is quiet in the way that museums are quiet: shuffling of feet, low talking, the occasional laughter and talk and whispered complaints of children. On the edge of a large room stands Harold Cohen and a crowd of onlookers. On two of the walls hangs a continuous, brightly colored, delightfully patterned mural, perhaps fifty feet long and twelve feet high. Some of the people in the room are directing questions to Cohen. Others are sitting, standing, watching, while in the center of the room a small mechanical device about the size, shape, and speed of a turtle crawls and turns and slowly wiggles about on a huge, wall-sized sheet of paper. The turtle carries some kind of fat pen under its belly, and as it moves, it leaves a trail of black lines. At two of the corners of the sheet of paper there are small sonar devices, while the turtle itself remains attached by a long, suspended umbilical cord to a computer placed back to one side.*

---

*Though it is mildly amusing and distinctly convenient to describe the mechanical "turtle" in animate terms, we do well to remember that it is merely an output device (equipped with feedback mechanisms), no more capable of initiating action than the computer screen. All the action is really in the program.

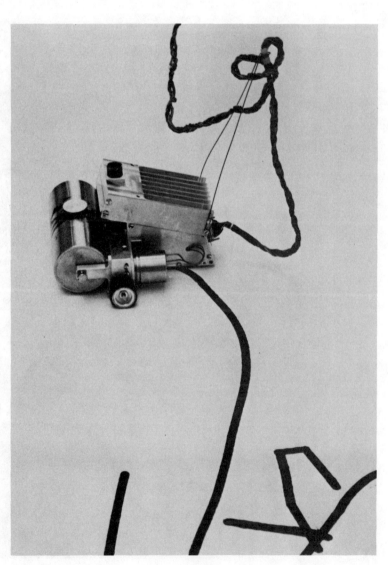

1. 15. Computer-controlled "turtle" drawing at the *Harold Cohen: Drawing* exhibit
San Francisco Museum of Art
Photograph by Becky Cohen

The mural grows. The turtle gradually covers the paper, often working on individual figures before lifting its pen and moving on to another spot, creating a series of abstract designs, asymmetrical closed and open figures—some looking like fish, or stones, or clouds, sometimes filled in by lines resembling gills on fish, or cracks in stone. When the work is at last finished, Cohen begins another. Later, in the quiet of his studio, he may choose to color the design with paint and brush.

1. 16. Harold Cohen at work on 'Spring'
From *Four Seasonal Narratives*, a mural cycle for Digital Equipment Corporation. Artist, Harold Cohen. Photograph by Becky Cohen

Some of Cohen's work resides in the performance itself.* It is worth noting that museum-goers probably spend an average of a few seconds looking at individual paintings hanging on walls, but will spend a half hour, or an hour, fascinated, watching one of the performances by Cohen and his computer-driven turtle. The finished products themselves are surprisingly evocative, pleasing images, usually projecting some primitive and joyful qualities (see Color Plate 8A). Viewers spontaneously tend to interpret them, to define them in terms of known forms and scenes (as I did briefly when I compared the shapes to fish, stones, and clouds), but Cohen's program "intends" nothing of the sort. The program produces solely abstract shapes, images.

If the images are indeed attractive or evocative, one ought to ask, Why? and, How? Cohen answers: "I've called upon my own knowledge of image-making gathered from many years as a painter, and then placed that knowledge into the program as a long list of instructions about drawing, in the form of 'If–Then' statements." In other words, the program contains no predesigned images, waiting to be put on paper. There is no injected randomness. There are no particular tricks. The program represents Cohen's attempt, after observing his own habits, to define formally, with rules (If–Then statements), what a human artist does during the process of drawing. Sifting through these rules, according to established hierarchies within the program, the computer steers the turtle by sending separate commands to the mechanisms controlling the turtle's wheels. If both wheels are turning at the same speed, the turtle will go in a straight line. Differing speeds make it go in curved lines.

If the turtle were merely a spot on a screen, moving and trailing a line, the computer could easily maintain a memory of where it had been, and what image it was creating. Since the mechanical turtle moves on paper, however, the wheels slip frequently, so the turtle's ever changing location is defined to the computer by sonar devices at two corners of the paper. Given what the turtle has just done and where it has just been, the If–Then statements of the program define what it is to do next. What sort of If–Then statements? An example: "If the turtle has just drawn a meandering line, and it is now within a certain distance of where it started, then instruct it to close the figure by going back to where it started." With large lists of such programmed instructions, Cohen's computer directs the turtle to be

---

*In this way, it is clearly related to a major development in the visual arts of the last two decades—Happenings and Performance Art, which are improvisational or scripted theater pieces by visual artists, usually presented in nontheatrical settings. The performance is the major concern; objects produced are merely documents of the actions. Cohen's work is also related to the development, in the 1970s, of Process Art, where the public views a visual work in process (the artist might come into the gallery each day and rearrange or add parts to a sculpture, for instance).

"interested" in such issues as spatial distribution and figure integrity (the turtle carefully avoids drawing one figure on top of another). The program defines for the turtle the difference between figure and ground. The program is able to instruct the turtle in matters of shading. The program defines reasonably well the difference between "insideness" and "outsideness."

The computer does not store any prepackaged shapes mimicked from some artist. There is no overall "intelligence" directing the program. The program is more like a series of hierarchically distributed experts, each of whom knows some things about a particular aspect of picture making. Thus, an "expert" is written into the program—Cohen calls it "The Realtor"—whose function is to find open space on the paper. The spatial distribution part of the program may say, "I need this much space before the turtle can proceed," and the Realtor goes out and finds it, and instructs the turtle how to get there.

Many artists who use computers like to insist that the computer is only a tool to them. They do so partly because they are used to calming public fears and concerns in the face of computer mystique. And many computer-using artists do indeed have a direct control over what images they produce on screens: the computer is indeed a mere tool. In Cohen's case, though, such an insistence is less appropriate. He has defined the rules for picture making, but the results are unpredictable, even uncontrollable: the rules combine and interact in some highly complex and dynamic fashion. In Cohen's words, "Some people who want to back off say, 'Well, after all, the computer is just a tool.' And the answer is, 'It may be just a tool, but it's not what you mean by tool, because what you mean is something with a handle at one end and a use at the other, like a hammer.' Without getting extravagant about it, this 'tool' is more like an 'assistant' to me. When you go into a museum and see a Rubens painting with his name at the bottom, the probability is that Rubens painted three heads and one hand, and all the rest was done by his students and assistants. By the time you've got a machine that can perform like that, a machine that contains knowledge, the word 'tool' has become less appropriate."

5

I have focused attention on some prominent American artists who are using computers primarily to help them produce two-dimensional images: stills and animations. But computers are being used in the visual arts on an international scale to produce not only animations and two-dimensional stills, but choreography, light shows, weaving, and sculpture—including traditional sculpture, as well as kinetic, and even "intelligent" sculpture.

By the early 1970s, for example, artist Robert Mallary was using a computer to help design sculpture. The program he wrote displayed images of various combinations of three-dimensional shapes on the computer screen. With simple controls he could move the images around, rotate them, examine them. Once he found a three-dimensional form he liked, Mallary was able to use the computer and program to draw out with a plotter more complete specifications for the piece. One work he completed in this fashion was an abstract shape in marble. Since the marble came in slabs rather than one large piece, Mallary used his computer to draw specifications for the cut of each slab. Using the plotted drawings, he then cut each slab, laminated the resulting slabs together, and cut and polished the final piece until it was smooth.

Other sculptors have attached computers directly to various kinds of milling machines that can automatically carve three-dimensional shapes. The artist has to create the program, of course, and then has to arrive at some final design. But much or all of the actual work of sculpting can be going on while the artist eats a sandwich. David Dameron has created a number of such automatically milled sculptures. Dameron's milling machine is basically a drill bit on an arm that can be directed to move up and down and back and forth by computer control (the computer is a small, home-made device). The drill bit is able to reach all sides of the material being worked on (large pieces of wax) because the material is placed on a rotating pedestal. The computer, which is given some specifications for the final piece, coordinates the motions of the drill bit with the rotations of the material.

Other sculptors are more interested in using computers in their works to give them some level of intelligence or responsiveness. (Harold Cohen's work in many ways resembles this self-directing, or *cybernetic* use of a computer.) Edward Ihnatowicz, over a period of three years, built a fascinating cybernetic sculpture, called *The Senster*, which he let loose in 1971 at a technology exhibit in Eindhoven, Holland. *The Senster* looked like a strange zoological specimen built from an erector set, but it was huge, fifteen feet long. It had two hefty, stationary "legs" that were joined to an articulated "torso" capable (with the assistance of electrohydraulics) of moving and bending, and a small "head" with "eyes" and "ears" consisting of microphones and radar devices. In exhibit, *The Senster* was protected by a barrier from direct contact by viewers, but a computer, the microphones and radar devices allowed it to respond much as a spiny, spindly zoo animal would to visitors and viewers—slowly, deliberately moving its curious face and body toward low-level sound and motion, rearing back from violent motion or sudden sound.

In Spokane's Metro Mall, Ann Sandifur has built a dynamic sculpture called *Cosmography*. *Cosmography* is a compound curve in ferroconcrete, forty feet long, five feet wide at the widest, and eighteen feet high at its highest. The ferroconcrete structure is covered and contoured with rock and about a ton of porcelain clay. Parts of the surface bristle with light-emitting fiber optics, which are computer controlled. Across and down the surface of this little mountain continually flow rivers and rivulets of colored sand, five colors in all. The sand is channeled and collected at various places around the bottom of the sculpture and then cycled eighteen feet up to the top with a hidden bucket elevator. The flow of the sand can be directly influenced by the computer: when sand reaches the top, it is distributed to a piping network that has small stepping motors and valves. The computer can activate motors, close and open valves, and keep track of flows of sand at various points by means of photo sensors.

At one end of the piece, Sandifur has placed a custom-made, computer-controlled music generating system. The music system includes a keyboard, in case anyone wants to compose music directly, but with help from the computer, music can be programmed for continuous play, or telephoned in from another computer music system. Naturally, various tones from the music system produce vibrations in the ferroconcrete surface of the sculpture. Since the five colors of sand are distributed in five different grain sizes, the vibrations from the music not only influence the quality and rate of sand flow, they also sort the sand into its separate colors during the progress of flow. But the music keyboard does more than define music. It is also a primary input to the computer, able to control all aspects of *Cosmography*. Keystrikes on the music keyboard can control the flow of sand, the operation of the fiber optics, overhead theatrical lights—and generate music simultaneously. In addition, the keyboard controls photographic images: several slide projectors are mounted in the ceiling of the Metro Mall, and, by using tilting and panning mirrors, the artist is able to move the images across the surface of the sculpture. Slide selection, brightness, size, and orientation of the images can all be controlled at the music keyboard. In addition to the photo sensors mounted in the sculpture (which monitor the flow of sand), sensors mounted on the roof of the Metro Mall monitor environmental events, such as the intensity of sunlight and how it varies over time. These sensor inputs are able to control processes in *Cosmography* just as keystrikes on the music keyboard do.

Controlling inputs (keystrikes on the music keyboard or sensor readings) can be recorded and played back in a variety of ways. The artist can play back a composition or any portion of it. The artist can select the playback speed, which can be faster or slower than the recorded speed. It is also possible for the artist to select the method of playback: a musical composition can be played back through the overhead lights, thus creating a musical composition executed in light. Or, the artist can play a composition through a combination of processes, such as music and light together.

The resulting effects are a peculiar and wonderful combination of latent high-tech dominated by an appearance of organicism: a magic mountain created with custom modification of parts taken from two small, inexpensive computers, along with the inexpensive music generator. But perhaps the story of Ann Sandifur and her *Cosmography* belongs in the next chapter, on *Creation in Sound*.

More than a decade ago, English painter John O'Neill retired from the official art world. He decided that what went on in museums and galleries was narrow, esoteric, and profoundly disconnected from the lives of ordinary people. He decided that the art object was not important in itself, but only as it affected people, and that it had to reach people in media they could relate to, in a language they could understand, and at a price they could afford. He began to think that art was meant to be a catalyst for perception and awareness in people: "Material is 'art' if it can excite and stimulate observers or users to a new perception, or throw them out of an established mode of perception." Through the artist, heightened layers of awareness and perception might find their ways into products available to people.

He abandoned both signature and the limiting of editions as false ways of acquiring "value" in the parochial art world, and created the trademark signature Admacadiam (meaning, in his private, symbolic vocabulary, "catalyst"), under which all further catalyst art would be marketed. It became obvious to O'Neill that mass media would be his vehicle, and the approach would lie in "consumerism." In his words, "I decided what I was doing was for people, and that meant turning somehow to the consumer mass market—but not in a parsimonious way, or a pandering way. Not to produce pretty junk. I decided I would produce small things, handleable things, take-home things, affordable things. That meant, at first, postcards and playing cards and board games."

He produced an art exhibit by mail, designing postcards that were, in themselves, beautiful—but when mailed as a series to any point on the globe could be assembled to create one large, coherent work. He created packages of playing cards, with startlingly original images based upon a study of the history of tarot and esoteric religions. He created visual board games, based upon single themes but working without the traditional effluvia of games, such as dice and written messages on cards, working instead through a conflict and resolution of images.

Admacadiam still produces postcards, playing cards, and decals, but it has begun producing video games. O'Neill himself may, for the moment, be best known as the artist for Atari's *E.T.* game—a landmark in small computer graphics. But O'Neill's most serious efforts are reserved for creating image games under the signature of Admacadiam. The Admacadiam *Flyghts of Fancie* series are game simulations of aspects of living (dreaming, loving, traveling, and so on) expressed in graphics and sound. Each game is designed to take the player through several successive layers of interaction with the computer that are analogous to aspects of living, and that together express a complete part of life. The games are structured in ways that lead players from the obvious to the less obvious, proceeding from one layer of image and event to the next, according to a player's skill and perception. The games might be compared to Lewis Carroll's *Alice in Wonderland:* they can be fantasy entertainment at a child's level, or they can be catalysts of perception, moving the player toward a new or renewed awareness. They may be the first to establish the video game as a serious art form.

But perhaps the story of John O'Neill and his visual games belongs in the chapter on *Creation in Recreation.*

And God said, "Let there be a firmament
in the midst of the waters, and let it
separate the waters from the waters."
—The Book of Genesis

Chapter 2

Creation
in
Sound

The firmament separating the waters from the waters allowed for
the appearance of air, a primary medium for sound.

Sound begins when an object moves rapidly back and forth
(vibrates), causing similar motions in the air around it. The motions
in the air (waves of alternately compressed and attenuated air)
travel outward from the vibrating object and cause an eardrum to
vibrate. Sound is recognized when the vibrating eardrum transfers
its message to the brain.

Some waves of compressed and attenuated air are more regular,
or *periodic*, than others: the waves produced by a ringing bell, for instance, are more periodic than those produced by a thudding stick.
Usually, sounds that are organized in a coherent, aesthetically
pleasing way are called *music*. It might be said that birds and other
such creatures produce and hear music, but usually music is
thought to be a human creation which depends upon the aesthetic
reaction of a human listener.

91

Computers make sound, and music, by sending fluctuating levels of electrical voltage to a loudspeaker. The fluctuating voltages cause an alternating increase and decrease in the pull of an electromagnet inside the speaker, which in turn causes the cone of the speaker to vibrate, setting off corresponding vibrations in the air.

Such a loudspeaker is identical to the loudspeaker of a radio or a phonograph: all are activated by fluctuating levels of electrical voltage. The difference arises from the source of voltage fluctuations sent to the speaker. In the radio, voltage fluctuations come from amplified electromagnetic waves broadcast "over the air." In the phonograph, they come from bumps in the groove of a record, which cause a needle to vibrate; the vibrations of the needle are transformed into analogous "vibrations" or fluctuations of electrical voltage. In the computer music system, however, lists of numbers residing in a program, or generated by a program, define fluctuating voltages; the numbers are converted to fluctuating voltage levels by an additional system placed between the computer and the speaker.

1

Periodic vibrations of a musical instrument, and corresponding vibrations in the air, produce for the listening ear a single musical note. The perception of *duration*, of "how long the note lasts," is determined by how long the vibrations last. The perception of *volume*, of "loudness" or "softness" of a musical note, is determined by the intensity, the width or distance (back and forth) of the vibrations.

The perception of *pitch*, of "highness" or "lowness" of a musical note, is determined by the rapidity or frequency of vibrations. The pitch of Middle C, for instance, is produced when a musical instrument vibrates a little more than 261 times a second. The C below Middle C is produced when an instrument vibrates at half that frequency, about 131 times a second, while the C above Middle C is produced by a doubling of the frequency, or 523 times a second. The change in pitch from Low C to Middle C, or again from Middle C to High C, is described as an *octave*. One can hear a change in octave: the C notes all sound, in some not quite definable way, similar to each other.

Western European musical tradition from the Renaissance to the end of the nineteenth century was based upon a carefully defined structuring of pitches—eight pitches from one end of an octave to the other (do, re, mi, fa, so, la, ti, do)—allowing for some half steps (sharps and flats) in the sequence. In addition, traditional

Western music was based upon groups of predefined relationships between pitches, known as *keys*. A traditional piece of music would be written in a certain key, and harmonies in the piece would be based upon a sequence of pitches defined by that key, perhaps slipping in and out of related keys. The tradition was not particularly based upon an understanding of the modern science of acoustics (though mathematically precise relationships between particular pitches and the frequencies of vibrating strings had been noted as early as the time of Pythagoras). Rather, the tradition was based upon listening: it so happens that these interesting mathematical relationships produce pleasing sounds.

Most successful music, like successful art in general, combines the *original* with the *familiar*. The original delights and surprises, while the familiar provides orientation. Traditional music retained its familiarity not merely because it kept the traditional division of the octave. It also stayed within the harmonic structure of its predefined major and minor keys; it retained a larger structure of pitches known as the *melody* or *theme*; it was based upon relatively standard rhythms; and it used the familiar sounds of the standard orchestral instruments.

At the beginning of the twentieth century, however, certain composers in Paris and Vienna broke away from those habitual ways of defining music. Claude Debussy's tremendously successful *Prelude to the Afternoon of a Faun* was distinctive for its unusual and provocative "dreamlike" quality—caused in large part by delicate tones, a gentle but unorthodox shifting of keys, and a deliberate vagueness of theme. The listener—habituated to single-keyed, strongly thematic music—experienced a not unpleasant disorientation, perhaps similar to the disorientation of drifting on the edge of sleep. But while Debussy gently experimented with a fluctuating key, Arnold Schoenberg's music beginning in 1908 abandoned the use of dominating major and minor harmonic keys altogether, describing a revolutionary style of complete fluidity of key known as *atonality*. To the listening public, the change was a shock, and, in general, Schoenberg's music was not well received. When Schoenberg conducted a concert in Vienna in 1913 that included atonal works by two of his students, Alban Berg and Anton Webern, the police had to be summoned to control the audience. At about the same time, Igor Stravinsky was writing music in which, for the first time, rhythm could be a dominating force. When his *Rite of Spring* was performed in Paris in 1913, according to Stravinsky himself, "the first bars of the prelude...at once evoked derisive laughter. I was disgusted. These demonstrations, at first isolated, soon became general, provoking counter-demonstrations and very quickly developing into a terrific uproar."

The concert-going public may not at first have been receptive to these disturbing new forms of music, but the innovations of Debussy, Schoenberg, and Stravinsky broke forever the restraining bonds of musical tradition. Though many twentieth-century composers have looked back to eighteenth- or nineteenth-century tonality and compositional structure—to beg, borrow, and steal—no one since then has felt constrained by the old traditions.

The very meaning of music itself had begun to unravel. A piece of music no longer had to follow a rigid system of harmonies; it no longer had to possess a central melodic theme; its rhythm no longer had to be subservient to other elements. Additionally, the old idea that a musical composition consisted of a strict set of written rules to be carried out faithfully by the performer was questioned. Musial compositions were written that allowed for choice and improvisation by performers. Other new compositions contained significant random elements.*

Given such drastic changes in general assumptions about the definition of music, it should not be surprising that the meaning of musical instrument began to expand. Nineteenth-century composers occasionally used nontraditional sounds in their compositions. Mahler, for instance, included cowbells in one of his symphonies. But by 1913, Debussy anticipated the new experimentalism with sounds, particularly sounds associated with modern technology, when he stated: "The century of the aeroplane deserves its music." Virtually all musical instruments before Debussy's time were the products of an old Hand Technology, evolving slowly over generations, produced by craftsmen and their apprentices. But whether he had intended it or not, Debussy's statement was a call to apply the dramatic new Scientific Technologies to the production of musical instruments.

At first, the liberation in music encouraged musical productions that were particularly and self-consciously associated with modern technology. Erik Satie's 1917 ballet *Parade* included a typewriter and automobile horns in the orchestra. George Antheil's *Ballet Mécanique*, performed in Paris in 1926, included (amidst the clangor of eight pianos and eight xylophones) the tremors and tribulations of an airplane propeller and two doorbells. Arthur Honegger attempted to create the sound of a moving locomotive with his orchestral score for *Pacific 231*, performed in 1923. Luigi Russolo, calling for a "noise music" that could invoke the sounds of machines and factories, invented several mechanical noisemakers,

---

*One can find before this century occasional "inventions" of randomized music; William Hayes in 1751 satirically suggested composition by splattering ink on musical note paper, for example, and Mozart wrote a simple musical dice game. But Mozart's trivial game and Hayes' satirical comments are not really comparable to the quite serious attempts of modern composers to introduce randomness into music.

the *intonarumori*, which received some serious attention in Paris in the 1920s. As the century progressed, composers became less enamored of a "noise music" specifically associated with the new technologies, and instead became more interested in discovering new and interesting sounds from all kinds of sources. In 1938, John Cage experimented with a pitched percussion instrument he called the *prepared piano*, a piano with various objects of rubber, metal, wood, and so forth, affixed to the strings. Later, Olivier Messiaen wandered through fields (and had himself photographed doing so), writing down scores of birdsongs, which he then included in his *Chronochromic* (1960). But probably the emerging science of electronics, and an embryonic Information Technology, offered the most hope for a new kind of modern instrument, a true musical instrument of "the century of the aeroplane."

Music and sound are kinds of information (particular patterns), and the early stirrings of Information Technology in the nineteenth century were associated with sound information—the telegraph transmitted informative patterns of long and short clicks, the telephone transmitted informative vibrations of sound associated with

2. 1. Keyboard of Thaddeus Cahill's *telharmonium*
Photo: Historical Picture Service

speech. By the turn of the century, a few people began using regularly fluctuating electrical voltages to produce musical sounds. Thaddeus Cahill invented a *sounding stave* in 1897, a device that could influence the timbre of sounds by electrical means. In 1906, Cahill unveiled his *telharmonium*, a musical instrument that created sounds by interrupting an electromagnetic field with spinning, toothed wheels. Although the *telharmonium* was not particularly portable (weighing approximately two hundred tons), it was at least interesting enough to inspire composer Ferruccio Busoni to predict the coming of an electronic music capable of an "abstract sound, unhampered technique, and unlimited tonal material." The invention by Lee De Forest of an electronic *oscillator* in 1915, which could create regularly fluctuating levels of voltage (thus producing sounds at predefined pitches), was followed by a series of exotic electronic sound generating machines: Leon Theremin's *etherophone* or *theremin* (1923); Maurice Martenot's *ondes martenot* (1928); and Friedrich Trautwein's *trautonium* (1928). By 1929, Laurens Hammond had connected some electronic oscillating systems to a keyboard control and produced the first electronic organ—the Hammond organ.

2. 2. Leon Theremin and friend, playing *Music from the Ether* at the first public demonstration of the *theremin*
Metro Opera House, January 31, 1928. Photo: Historical Picture Service

Beyond perpetuating the family name, each of these inventors hoped to create a new kind of sound that might forge beyond the limited sounds of conventional instruments, and reach a level of universality. Perhaps the composer Edgar Varèse foresaw most clearly how electronic musical instruments would someday provide composers with universal sound-generating possibilities when, in 1917, he wrote, "I dream of instruments obedient to thought—and which, supported by a flowering of undreamed-of timbres—will lend themselves to any combination I choose to impose and will submit to the exigencies of my inner rhythm."

But these early electronic instruments—though they could call upon a wide range of pitches, and alter the duration and volume of any single pitch—were mostly able to produce only one *type* of sound, one *timbre*. In that sense, they were identical to traditional musical instruments: a violin may play a note at the same pitch, with the same duration and volume, as an oboe, but it still sounds like a violin, and is distinctly unlike an oboe. Why? The listener distinguishes the timbre of violins from oboes partly as a result of hearing different *spectra* of vibrations. Instruments have distinctive spectra because of subtle, "secondary" vibrations, or *harmonics*; the *fundamental vibration* may determine pitch, but *additional harmonics* determine a sound's characteristic spectrum. Since the early electronic instruments used single electronic oscillators to produce individual pitches, they were able to define only a fundamental vibration, without harmonics—in other words, without any way to vary the spectrum. But by 1954, the huge RCA Mark I analog synthesizer was plugged in. Like the electronic Hammond organ, the RCA Mark I made use of a keyboard control and several oscillators to define steady, periodic fluctuations of voltage for several pitches. Unlike the Hammond organ, the Mark I could also combine the voltage outputs of several oscillators at one time into one complex signal, to define a fundamental musical note plus distinctive harmonics; thus it was able to define distinctive types of sounds (timbres). By 1964, Robert Moog was selling commerical versions of his keyboard-controlled electronic synthesizer, the Moog Synthesizer.

For most of history, music has existed purely in time, existing only during the time of the performance, ceasing to exist after a performance. We consider that the visual arts endure in space, to some degree independent of time: an art museum or gallery can be considered a physical memory for visual arts. Music could claim no comparable memory until Thomas Edison and Emile Berliner invented the phonograph in 1878. The apparent advantages of memory are such, however, that today, a mere century later, the vast majority of music heard is produced from mechanical and magnetic memory files (records and tape recordings). But although, strictly speaking, musical memory has existed since 1878, no kind of memory was associated with a particular musical instrument until people used computers to generate sounds in the 1950s and 1960s.

Since the earliest computers were thought to be number machines, there was, at first, a conceptual problem. Someone had to recognize that numerical information could be transformed into the voltage fluctuations leading to sound. In addition to the conceptual problem, there was a more formidable technical problem. For the computer to be a music machine of any interest at all, it not only had to generate regularly fluctuating voltages, it had to be able to do that quickly, even semi-automatically (without impossibly complex tasks of programming) so that a programmer-composer could alter the fluctuations to define the many qualities of musical sound.

The necessary technical breakthrough was accomplished by Max Mathews of Bell Telephone Laboratories, who in 1957 first created the software known as Music IV. The Music IV program, and its offspring, Music V, included (1) the principle of *prepackaged digital oscillators* (containing prewritten lists of numerical wave definitions), and (2) *modifying units* that would easily alter (with simple arithmetic) whatever wave definition lists were within the oscillators.* Given such prepackaged oscillators and modifying units, composers and performers could write programs that relatively quickly defined pitch (modifying the frequency of the oscillation), loudness (modifying the amplitude, or intensity, of the oscillation), timbre (including more than one oscillation for a single tone), and so on. Computer music had begun.

The first computer music systems were large, required complex programming, and in general produced sounds that were similar to the electronic sounds generated on the analog synthesizers—the RCA Mark I, for instance, and the Moog. And like these early analog synthesizers, some computer music systems included keyboards, so that a composer could define sounds both by writing programs and by articulating definitions of sounds directly on the keyboard (as the pianist does). But of course the computer system possessed the added advantages of: (1) retaining a memory of any music played, so that a composer could listen to a piece, and easily return and revise that very piece; (2) a constantly expanding ability to define new sounds; and (3) an unusual precision. Today a great deal of computer music focuses on sound. A computer can theoretically define any sound; in practice, it can define a tremendous range of unusual or usual, beautiful or ugly, fascinating or boring sounds.

---

*How a computer makes music is described in more detail in Section 2 of this chapter.

At about the same time that Max Mathews was simplifying the process of computer-controlled sound production, other people were applying computers to music on an entirely different level. Music is sound existing in pattern. While Mathews worked on sound, others worked on pattern: musical composition.

The kinds of computer-controlled synthesizers built after Mathews' innovations made sounds that could be patterned by the numerical manipulations of programmers, as well as by the keyboard manipulations of performers. But this made little use of the computer's tremendous abilities to manipulate and rearrange and redefine its own information, and perhaps to make interesting decisions on its own about the direction of a composition, rather than remaining under the strict control of a human composer.*

Human composers combine a knowledge of the rules of composition (what has been done in the past) with some little understood creative production of new forms (what has not been done in the past). I like to consider this process to be the slightly miraculous combining of *goodness* (appropriateness) and *newness* (originality). Although the terms may seem simple, the event itself is anything but simple. A composer may spend half a lifetime formally and informally, consciously and unconsciously learning a set of rules for appropriateness within a given musical style, and then within a few hours or days produce a composition that in some remarkable way satisfies those rules yet simultaneously demonstrates a high level of originality. Newness or originality by itself is nothing: a madman can produce original combinations of sounds. Goodness or appropriateness by itself is nothing: any educated hack can produce perfectly imitative and sterile music by learning the standard rules of some style of composition. It is the dynamic combination of the two, by the human composer during an act of composition, that produces great music.

The problem in programming a computer to create musical compositions is similar. First, the rules of a particular style must be defined to the computer in a relevant way, that is, in clusters of mathematical-logical instruction. Second, there must be a system for introducing originality—for example, the introduction of dynamic conflict and interaction between two parts of a program, or the insertion of a randomizing factor.

---

*Having made compositional decisions, the computer might then automatically turn those compositions into musical sounds, using its own sound-generating abilities—but not necessarily. It is important to understand the separateness of these two tasks (generating individual sounds and patterning sounds into compositions). The important early work in computer composition produced numerical printouts on paper that were then laboriously transcribed into musical scores on paper, later to be played with conventional instruments.

Some of the rules of a particular musical style may be obvious and well defined. The rules of traditional counterpoint, for instance, are quite precise. One can easily look them up in a book and transform them into simple and unvarying instructions. Similarly, the rules of traditional harmony are precise. But what are the rules for creating a melody? We know that a melody is a sequence of differing pitches. We know that the sequence is usually thought to be, somehow, "pleasing." But what determines a *pleasing* sequence of pitches? Attempting to answer that question may be one way of establishing rules for melody, and ultimately it may be the most fruitful way: defining a psychology or physiology of musical aesthetics. But a much simpler way would be to analyze the melodic habits of existing human composers and simply imitate those.

Such was the procedure for the earliest computer compositions. In the early 1950s, Harry Olson and Herbert Belar built a machine that generated random numbers (without the assistance of a computer), and then applied those random numbers to what they had already learned about probable melodic sequences in Stephen Foster tunes. The result: some banal imitations of Stephen Foster. In the mid-1950s, M. Klein and D. Bolitho used a Datatron computer to analyze the simple melodies of one hundred popular tunes, arriving at tables of probabilities for pitch sequences (when pitch A occurs, the probability that the next pitch will be B is a certain number; the probability that the next pitch after B will be C is another number; and so on). Given those probabilities, Klein and Bolitho then proceeded to generate four thousand new pop tunes with the computer. They called their program *Push Button Bertha*. And at about the same time, Brooks, Hopkins, Neumann, and Wright used a computer to analyze thirty-seven hymn tunes and generate a probability table. Next they used the computer to generate random numbers representing pitches, and then the computer compared each number with the probability table to determine appropriateness. Appropriate numbers (pitches) were kept; inappropriate numbers were not. In addition, the computer was programmed to define all melodies only in C major and common meter, and to use standard note durations.

All this early work was derivative, however, and generally insubstantial: not until Lejaren Hiller and Leonard Isaacson began their work on the *Illiac Suite* in 1956, could it be said that anyone was seriously using a computer to attempt musical composition. As an undergraduate at Princeton University, Lejaren Hiller had studied classical composition (with Roger Sessions and Milton Babbitt) and chemistry. Receiving a Ph.D. from Princeton in chemistry, Hiller eventually became a professor of chemistry at the University of Illinois. Although successful as a chemist and a teacher of chemistry, Hiller continued his strong, albeit avocational, interest in music and musical composition.

Hiller learned about computers as a chemist, using them as tools in his research. At the University of Illinois, he and Frederick Wall, a well-known physical chemist, worked with a computer called the Illiac I, attempting to define the most probable dimensions of polymeric molecular structures in solution. The technique he used to arrive at these hypothetical dimensions was known as the Monte Carlo method—which involved simulating, in a numerically defined world, the combination of randomness and order involved in the structure of a molecule in the real world. The simulation began by having the computer spew out a complete "random universe," of random numbers. Next, the numerically defined elements of order in the molecule's structure were inserted, and the resulting combination produced an idealized (most probable) molecular dimension.

At some point it occurred to Hiller that he might substitute musical dimensions for molecular structure in such an experiment, and—with the assistance of another chemist on the project, Leonard Isaacson—he tried some contrapuntal exercises. From this and other small playful experiments grew a full-fledged musical composition in the form of a computer printout, transcribed into a musical score for a string quartet: the *Illiac Suite for String Quartet*. The 1956 performance of the first three movements of the *Illiac Suite* in Urbana, Illinois, generated tremendous publicity and much ink on paper. "Canny Computers: Machines Write Music, Play Checkers, Tackle New Tasks in Industry," proclaimed a September 1956 issue of the *Wall Street Journal*. "'Brain' Makes Like Bach for Scientists," announced the *Washington Post* in the same month. Later performances of the *Illiac Suite* continued to inspire curiosity, amazement, derision, and in general less interest in the music than in the concept of computer-assisted composition.

Having combined a randomizing system (a subprogram for a random number generator) in one part of a computer program, with the possibility of absolute definition and control in other parts of the program, Hiller recognized that he had a machine capable of moving from order to disorder virtually at will. His *Illiac Suite* was openly based on that principle, beginning with a chaotic generation of notes, and gradually imposing a more and more recognizable structure. And if there is one abiding principle or theory of music that Hiller maintains, it has to do with the dynamics of order and disorder. "When you talk about such things as Leonard Meyer's theories of musical effect," he stated in a recent interview with Coles Gagne and Tracy Caras, "you are really talking about order and disorder in the most broad and general sense: A person becomes more disturbed when the number of possibilities increases; disorder increases and you build tension, and then resolutions come when one arrives at more organized, static situations. This is what causes the ebb and flow of drama in a piece.''

The headlines and clamor and serious public recognition upon the first performance of the *Illiac Suite* were enough to convince various powers at the University of Illinois to retire him as a professor of chemistry, and make him a professor of music. Hiller subsequently established the second electronic music studio in the country at Illinois and continued with his new career. Since then he has written music with and without the assistance of computers in a wide range of styles and techniques—traditional and modern, computer-assisted and not, making use of computer-synthesized or traditional instrumental sounds as he wishes. He is called ''eclectic,'' and has been compared to John Cage (with whom he has collaborated) and Charles Ives. He continues to develop programmed systems for automating broad aspects of musical composition, and clearly derives much satisfaction from understanding the philosophical basis and the structural elegance of his compositional programs. But ultimately Hiller's approach is pragmatic: he listens. ''Can you hear what you programmed?'' he asked rhetorically in the Gagne and Caras interview. ''If yes, then perhaps it has some use; no, then you've gone off into a dead end.''

2

The basic task of any musical instrument is to produce *periodic vibrations*. When the violinist draws a bow across a stretched string, the string vibrates periodically, causing the whole violin to vibrate in a similar manner, causing waves of alternately compressed and attenuated air to move outwards, and causing the listener's ear to vibrate periodically. The flutist blows across the mouthpiece of a flute, producing periodic vibrations in a column of air inside the flute; the flute vibrates in turn, producing a motion of compressed and attenuated air, causing the listener's ear to vibrate periodically.

Musicians use a traditional musical instrument to produce periodic vibrations by causing the instrument itself (or air within the instrument) to vibrate. A computer, however, possesses no such physical components that could effectively be set into periodic vibration (try kicking one). Instead, it defines periodic vibrations by producing extended sequences of numbers; the numbers are converted by an external device into fluctuating voltages of electricity (you may think of these fluctuating voltages as waves, or, indeed, vibrations); the fluctuating voltages then cause a speaker to vibrate periodically.

The device that converts numbers into voltage levels for the computer music system is called a *converter*, or a *digital-to-analog converter. Digital* describes the discrete quality of individual numbers; *analog* describes the flowing, wavelike quality of regularly fluctuating voltages.

If we were to illustrate the process by which a traditional instrument makes music, it might look like the drawing in Figure 2.3. Here we see the vibrating instrument, the molecules of air being squeezed and drawn out, and the listener's ear, the inside of which is being set into periodic vibrations. It is painful to draw air, however, and tedious to draw things as if they were vibrating. It might be easier to represent such events with graphs. Graphs of periodic vibrations look more like the curves below.

2. 3. A vibrating flute causes the wavelike motion of alternately squeezed and drawn out air, which eventually causes an eardrum to vibrate.

Figure 2.4 depicts the actual vibration (the vertical axis shows distance to either side of a resting position) over time (the horizontal axis represents time) of a cello. Figure 2.5 shows a graph of the actual vibration of a flute. A graph of the vibrations of an eardrum during a cello concert, would look much like that in Figure 2.4, as

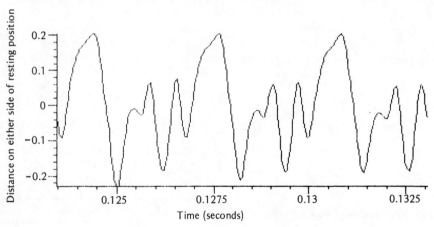

2. 4. Graph of the periodic vibrations of a cello. The vertical axis represents motion; the horizontal axis represents time.

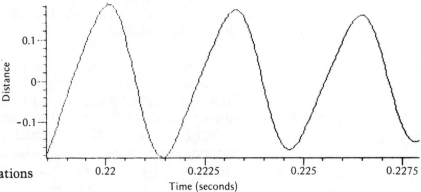

2. 5. Graph of the periodic vibrations of a flute

would a graph of the vibrations of a phonograph speaker, while the phonograph is playing a record of a cello. Similarly, the graph in Figure 2.5 would remain essentially the same whether it represented the periodic vibrations of flute, a loudspeaker producing sound from a flute recording, or an eardrum responding to either the flute or the recording of a flute.

Figure 2.6 presents an idealized periodic vibration. Although it does not happen to represent perfectly the typical periodic vibration of any musical instrument, it can be used to represent the idea of a periodic vibration. This particular curve, called a *sine curve*, is relatively easy to draw or define because it can be plotted by a simple mathematical formula. For the sake of simplicity, let us turn now to this third graph, the sine curve graph of an idealized periodic vibration.

How could a computer produce such a sound? The computer could simply calculate a table of numbers (call it a *wavetable*) that defines the height or depth of the wave at regular intervals. Those numbers could define the parameters, the "height" or "depth" (degree of electrical charge) of fluctuating voltages going to the loudspeaker. The result would not be a perfectly smooth wave of

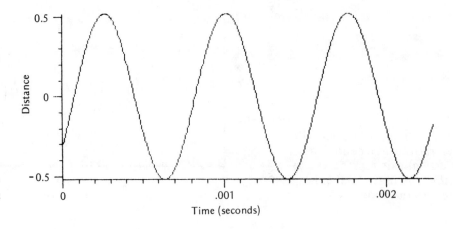

2. 6. An idealized periodic vibration: the sine curve

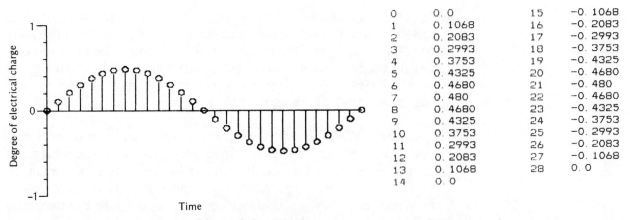

0	0. 0	15	−0. 1068
1	0. 1068	16	−0. 2083
2	0. 2083	17	−0. 2993
3	0. 2993	18	−0. 3753
4	0. 3753	19	−0. 4325
5	0. 4325	20	−0. 4680
6	0. 4680	21	−0. 480
7	0. 480	22	−0. 4680
8	0. 4680	23	−0. 4325
9	0. 4325	24	−0. 3753
10	0. 3753	25	−0. 2993
11	0. 2993	26	−0. 2083
12	0. 2083	27	−0. 1068
13	0. 1068	28	0. 0
14	0. 0		

2. 7. A computer uses a wavetable to define the sine curve in terms of discrete voltage levels.

fluctuating voltage, but rather a "stepped" wave, since the computer would have defined, with its numbers, a series of discrete voltage levels (as in Figure 2.7). But if enough numbers are used to describe that single wave, the final effect heard may seem identical to the effect of a truly smooth wave. (Alternatively, the rough edges of a digitally-defined wave could be smoothed out with filters.)

The single sine wave represents the cycle of a single periodic vibration. But sounds are produced when many vibrations occur within a second; Middle C, for example, is produced by 261 cycles of vibration per second. If the computer were to generate a single sine curve by calculating a wavetable of, say, 200 numbers, and then—if it attempted to generate 261 sine curves a second—this might require the calculation of 200 × 261 = 52,200 numbers a second. But such a task is a waste of time. It is much simpler for the computer to calculate the wavetable once, keep it in memory, and define voltages by reading through that same table again and again, from beginning to end, 261 times a second.

The values in a wavetable are sometimes called *samples*. The wavetable itself resides in a segment of software (sometimes also of hardware) called an *oscillator*.

When a computer defines periodically fluctuating voltages that are then sent to a loudspeaker, causing the loudspeaker to vibrate periodically, the computer is producing a musical sound. However, the musical sound I have been describing so far (defined by an eternally cycling sine curve) is useless. All musical instruments produce periodic vibrations, but *making* music means *manipulating* those periodic vibrations, producing different and distinguishable sounds, and patterns of different sounds.

The four major qualities that distinguish one musical sound from another are: *duration*, *loudness*, *pitch*, and *instrument definition* (or *timbre*).

Duration. Duration refers to the length of time an individual musical sound lasts. The duration of a single note on the violin lasts for about as long as the violinist draws the bow. The duration of a note on the flute lasts as long as the flutist blows. The duration of a single note from the computer music system lasts as long as fluctuating voltages are being sent to the speaker.

Loudness. When the violinist presses down harder and the flutist blows more intensely they produce stronger vibrations which are ultimately perceived by the listener as louder sounds. On a graph, increased volume means increased *amplitude.* The vertical axis of the graph, one may recall, describes motion (such as the back and forth motion of a violin string): increasing intensity of a vibration, thus, shows up on the graph as an increase in the height and depth of the curve. The word *amplitude* is used to describe that aspect of the curve: so, increasing intensity of the vibration results in an increased amplitude on the curve.

In a computer music system, altering the volume of a sound (that is, altering amplitude) means subjecting the values in the wavetable to simple multiplication or division. For example, if we wanted to double the amplitude of any wave, we would just multiply all the values by 2; if we wanted to halve the amplitude of a wave, we would divide all the wavetable values by 2 (see Figure 2.8). In this way stronger or weaker voltage fluctuations would be sent to the speaker, and louder or softer sounds would be produced.

0	0. 0
1	0. 2136
2	0. 4165
3	0. 5986
4	0. 7506
5	0. 8649
6	0. 9359
7	0. 960
8	0. 9359
9	0. 8649
10	0. 7506
11	0. 5986
12	0. 4165
13	0. 2136
14	0. 0
15	−0. 2136
16	−0. 4165
17	−0. 5986
18	−0. 7506
19	−0. 8649
20	−0. 9359
21	−0. 960
22	−0. 9359
23	−0. 8649
24	−0. 7506
25	−0. 5986
26	−0. 4165
27	−0. 2136
28	0. 0

2. 8. Multiplying a wavetable by 2 doubles the amplitude (thereby increasing loudness).

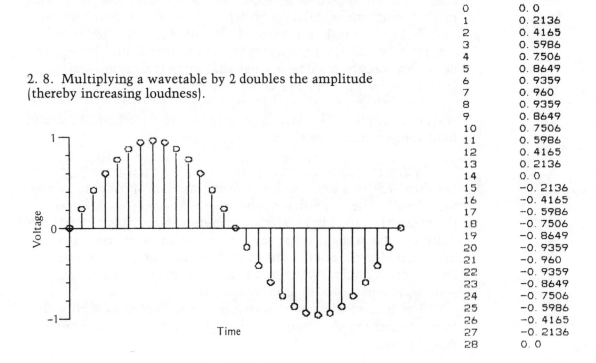

Pitch. When the violinist shortens the vibrating portion of a string by pressing down on the string with a finger, the result is faster (a higher *frequency* of) vibrations, and the listener hears a higher pitch. The violinist lengthens a string by taking away a finger: in this case, the string vibrates more slowly (at a lower frequency), and the listener hears a lower pitch. Pitch corresponds directly to frequency. Frequency is often described in terms of *cycles per second*.

How does a computer alter frequency in order to raise and lower the pitch of its musical notes? Let us refer again to the musical computer's act of reading numbers from its wavetable. Perhaps the wavetable contains 200 numbers, which describe a single wave cycle. Perhaps the computer is reading the wavetable 261 times a second, or, in other words, is sending out for conversion into voltage levels, 261 × 200 (or 52,200) values a second.

What if we want to double the frequency? Two possible methods are used by different computer music systems. One would be to double the speed of the reading; in other words, make the computer read through the full wavetable at twice the speed, thus sending out for conversion twice as many (104,400) values a second, thus defining twice as many cycles per second. The second way would be to keep the speed of the reading the same, but read out only every other value from the wavetable (see Figure 2.9). In that case, every cycle would be described by only 100 numbers instead of 200: your defined wave would be rougher. But because you are still sending out 52,200 values a second (your reading speed is unchanged), you are reading through the wavetable 52,200/100 = 522 times a second instead of 261 times a second.

Doubling the frequency raises the pitch by an octave. We will certainly want, however, to alter pitches by intervals smaller than an octave. How can we? According to the first method mentioned above, we would have to alter the wavetable reading speed by some non-whole number (for example, instead of multiplying the reading speed by 2, we would multiply it by 1.25). The second method

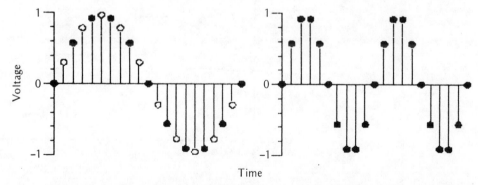

2. 9. A second method of doubling frequency: reading every other value in the wavetable

would have us choose numbers from the wavetable by approximation (for example, choosing only 160 numbers, in as evenly distributed a manner as possible, from the full progression of 200).

Instrument Definition (Timbre)

A violin and a flute may both play at an identical pitch and with an identical loudness, but we will still hear an unmistakable difference. Why? Each instrument has a distinct quality of sound, arising from (1) its *spectrum*: the distinctive combination of the fundamental frequency and the harmonics of an instrument's sound; and (2) the *amplitude envelope:* distinctive variations in loudness from beginning to end during any single note of an instrument.

Instrument Definition 1: Spectrum. A violin and a flute both playing a sustained note at the same pitch of Middle C are still producing different spectra. Most musical instruments produce not only fundamental vibrations—but secondary ones as well. These secondary vibrations, which occur with increased frequencies (in simple multiples of the fundamental frequency), are sometimes called *harmonics.* The flute is remarkable for producing a relatively "pure" tone, with few additional harmonics. A graph of the vibrations it produces would thus show a simple and regular curve, describing the smooth progression of essentially a single vibration over time. It would resemble the mathematically regular sine curve used in several of the earlier examples.

But all instruments in an orchestra, even the flute, produce both the fundamental vibration and some characteristic combination of secondary vibrations, the harmonic overtones. One way to represent such an event would be to plot both the fundamental and the secondary (harmonic overtone) vibrations on a single graph—superimposing two or more curves onto the same axes (Figure 2.10).

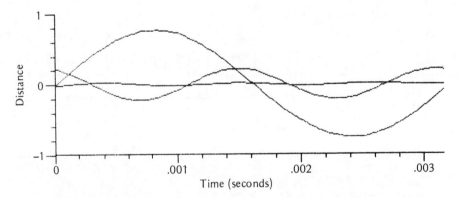

2. 10. Fundamental vibration and the harmonic overtone vibrations of a single musical instrument (a flute), superimposed on a single graph

Another way would be to *add* all the amplitudes of all the vibrations and plot the sum of the alterations in amplitude over time in a graph. In so doing, we produce graphs that display regular waves of *differing shapes*. For example, plotting the fundamental and harmonic overtones of a flute produces a *waveshape* somewhat like the one shown in Figure 2.11; a plot of the fundamental and the harmonics of a cello yields a waveshape like the one in Figure 2.12.

Since each instrument in an orchestra produces a distinctive spectrum, a graph of the waves produced by each instrument will have a distinctive shape. If a computer is to produce a sound resembling that of any particular instrument, it must thus be able to describe that instrument's particular waveshape. One way to do that would be to maintain numerical tables for different waveshapes in the computer's memory. But since the number of possible waveshapes approaches infinity, and since the number of waveshapes produced by existing musical instruments is large (furthermore, even one instrument will produce different waveshapes for different notes), storing prepackaged tables is not likely to be the most efficient system for defining waveshapes. A more efficient way is to maintain in the computer music system a group of oscillators that generate continual sine waves, and with those oscillators create new waveshapes by *adding* sine waves (similar to the process of adding fundamental and harmonic vibrations on the graph,

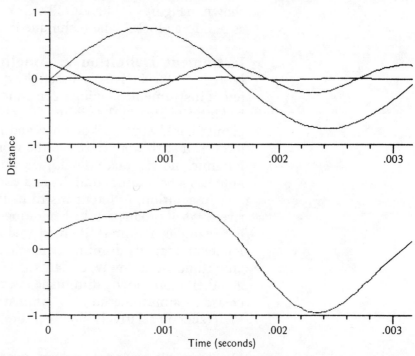

2. 11. Fusing (adding) fundamental and harmonic overtones of a flute into a single wave yields a distinctive waveshape.

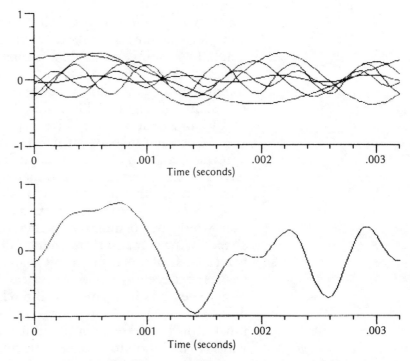

2. 12. Fusing the fundamental and harmonic overtones of a cello yields a distinctive waveshape.

shown in Figures 2.11 and 2.12). Groups of sine waves are thus used as building blocks. The technique is called *additive synthesis.* *

Instrument Definition 2: Amplitude Envelopes for Single Notes. So far, I have discussed the differing sound qualities of different instruments playing a continuous tone—as if the flute player had infinite breath, the violin player had an endless bow, or as if the pianist could strike a key once and hear a single sound continue forever. If such were the case, the world would be a much simpler, but much noisier place. Luckily, such is not the case. Each musical note has a beginning, middle, and end.

In addition, different instruments have different and distinctive ways of producing the beginnings, middles, and ends of notes. For example, a drum is likely to produce a sound that rapidly grows louder and rapidly diminishes to silence. A violin note increases in amplitude more slowly, remains at a constant amplitude for a time, and then more slowly diminishes. A note struck on a piano will increase in amplitude quickly (almost as suddenly as a drum), but then taper off relatively slowly (more like a violin). The occurrence

---

*Another popular method of synthesizing sounds, *FM synthesis*, will not be considered here. FM synthesis is much simpler, and therefore requires less expensive equipment, than additive synthesis; it is also less precise.

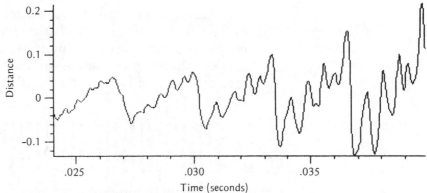

2. 13. Changing amplitudes in the regularly cycling wave-shape of an oboe: this shows the beginning segment of an amplitude envelope.

of harmonic overtones is certainly one reason we hear a difference in the sounds of different instruments, but even more important is the way different instruments produce their individual notes.*

If we graph the changing amplitudes of an individual note sounded by an instrument, we will arrive at something resembling Figures 2.13 and 2.14. Note that in these two depictions, the waves still have their characteristic shapes, but the amplitude at the peak of each wave changes in a distinctive pattern from beginning to middle to end.** Although it may not be as regular or symmetrical as the usual waveshapes in a single cycle of vibration, the *amplitude envelope* too is a kind of wave. Thus it is convenient to use another set of oscillators in the computer music system to define the shape of the amplitude envelope for an instrument's individual notes.

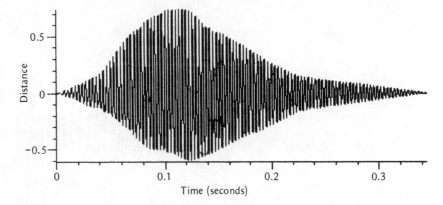

2. 14. Looking at a single note from a clarinet over time (about a third of a second), we see distinctive changes in amplitude from beginning to end (the full amplitude envelope).

*The spectrum (balance of harmonics) of a trumpet and violin are quite similar. Here the instrument's identity (at least for comparison purposes) is contained almost entirely in the variations in loudness over a single note (that is, the amplitude envelope).

**Put another way, waveshape describes amplitude variations occurring at a rate faster than the fundamental cycle frequency, while the amplitude envelope describes amplitude variations occurring in a larger frame of time, over several cycles.

At last, when we want our computer system to define, in terms of fluctuating voltages, the distinctive timbre in a particular musical instrument's particular note, we fuse the spectrum (the waveshape) defined by one set of oscillators, with the amplitude envelope defined by another set of oscillators; this process is graphed in Figure 2.15.

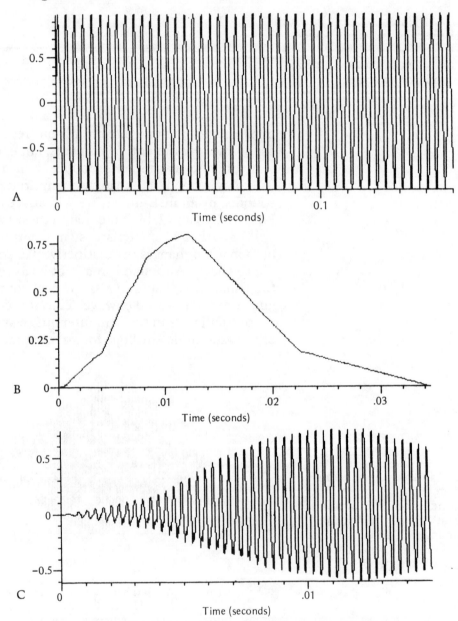

2. 15. Fusing a regularly occurring waveshape produced by one set of oscillators (A) with an amplitude envelope produced by another set of oscillators (B) defines the distinctive timbre of a particular instrument's particular note (C).

3

The Computer as Sound Creator and Manipulator. An orchestra of traditional instruments is capable of producing many types of sounds and manipulating those sounds in a wide variety of ways. A computer music system, on the other hand, is capable not only of imitating all the sounds of the orchestra, but of producing a vast range of new sounds, many never before heard, never before imagined. Additionally, a computer music system can manipulate sounds in ways never before considered: it can draw out single notes far beyond the ability of the flutist to blow or the violinist to bow; it can transform instruments; it can merge instruments; it can move instruments, so that the listener hears musical sounds traveling about through space in ways that even a musician with wings could not imitate. The fact is that computer music has opened up an entirely new dimension of listening possibility for which no standard vocabulary has yet evolved. What do you call a sound that seems halfway between string and human voice? Or a sound that in a single extended note transforms from string to reed to voice? How do you describe, with a word or two, a sound that resonates like a bell, with a metallic edge, but that strings on indefinitely like the smoothest cello?

Musical composition at Stanford University's Center for Computer Research in Music and Acoustics (CCRMA) is distinguished by the desire to achieve, through research in acoustics, psychoacoustics, and related engineering, high levels of control over individual sounds. This orientation has inspired many compositions of high musical quality, particularly at the level of individual musical sounds.

Mike McNabb's nine-minute *Dreamsong*, for example, composed in 1977–78 at Stanford University, succeeds as a surrealist montage of evocative sounds and transformations of sounds. It possesses that eerily fragmented quality of a dream, the sense of being carried from event to event with the flimsiest of logical connections. In a dream, one person may be transformed into another, or one thing or event may become another; *Dreamsong* moves, evolves through transformation. Naturally occurring sounds (voices) are processed (altered in numerous ways with digital techniques), and mixed with purely synthetic sounds to form a coherent continuum.

Dreamsong begins with the digitally recorded sounds of a murmuring crowd; it includes passages based on a recording of soprano Marilyn Barber; it ends with the digitally recorded fragment of

Dylan Thomas reading a poem.* The sound of the murmuring crowd, through *digital processing*, becomes smoother, is moved from speaker to speaker, begins to acquire pitch, becomes a melody that blends into a single extended soprano note. More synthetic, metallic-sounding tones appear, wavering then into a rolling concatenation of obscure sounds and strange music. Bell sounds appear in random pitches; gradually the overtones of the bells are transformed into the overtones of the soprano voice. Intimations of human voices, voice-instrument transformations lurk, appear and disappear throughout the composition: a ghostly, disembodied chorus, never fully articulate until the final, gradual emergence of the oracular voice of Dylan Thomas reading a poem fragment (as if, at last, we have awakened).

"I guess my main focus of attention in *Dreamsong* and in my later work," Mike McNabb explains, "is really integrating the use of recorded sounds, or sounds based on naturally-occurring sounds, with the whole world of synthetic timbres. With the computer it is possible to store in files a large number of 'instruments,' or timbres. The instruments can be purely synthetic sounds, or they can be based upon naturally occurring sounds; but the computer makes it possible for me to dip into this library of timbres and switch from timbre to timbre with an unbelievable fluidity. I find that to be a very compelling musical device, and, depending upon the context, it can be extremely expressive."

John Chowning, director of Stanford University's computer music laboratory (CCRMA), invented a technique for moving apparent sources of sounds, which he uses with aesthetic success in his 1972 composition, *Turenas* (tape, 10 minutes). Chowning's program for moving sound sources enables a composer to draw on the screen (using a graphics system) a moving path in three dimensions for any computer-defined sound; the composer can specify how fast the sound is moving along that path. The software calculates appropriate changes in reverberation (echoes from walls) as a sound source moves toward or away from the listener in the computer-de-

---

*One may think of digital recording as a simple reversal of the digital synthesis described in the previous section of this chapter: through a microphone, naturally occurring sounds are transformed into fluctuating voltage levels; the fluctuating levels of voltage are sampled at regular intervals (thousands of times a second) by an analog-to-digital converter, which describes such samples of fluctuating voltage as lists of numbers; the lists are placed in computer memory. Digital recording is superior to analog recording (such as normal tape recording) in that: (1) if the sampling is thorough enough (say, about 40,000 samples per second), the digital recording will provide higher accuracy, (2) the digital recording will retain its accuracy indefinitely (with no degradation of the signal due to simple physical problems—dust, oil, scratches, and so on); and (3) because all of the recorded samples can be manipulated mathematically, or *processed*, a composer is able to transform any or all of the qualities of the sounds.

fined space. It calculates whatever changes in volume for each of the loudspeakers would be appropriate as the sound moves.* And, after considering how fast the sound is supposed to be moving, it calculates an appropriate Doppler shift (in frequency). This Doppler shift occurs naturally whenever the distance between a source of sound and a listener changes; it is most noticeable when the change is rapid. Most people are familiar with the Doppler shift from the experience of standing near a railroad track and listening to a train whistle or bell as the train approaches and goes past: the whistle or bell not only becomes louder then softer, but it appears to rise, then fall in pitch. This happens because pitch is related to the frequency of sound vibrations; when the source of a sound is moving relative to the listener, that motion adds to (as the source approaches), and subtracts from (as the source recedes), the apparent frequency of the sound. Chowning's program, by coordinating variations in reverberation and changes in volume with changes in pitch calculated through a Doppler formula, can describe sounds that seem to whiz in precise paths through the air around the listener.

Turenas is a busy piece of music, intricate and broadly symmetrical—based upon the form of an arch, displaying a mirror symmetry in which the end broadly reverses the beginning. Sounds play and interplay, sweeping about the room of the listener. *Turenas* combines two distinct types of sound: low, dense, slowly emerging, slowly building and diminishing blocks or blankets or waves of sound; and a pitched percussion sound that appears throughout the piece, sometimes repetitious and syncopated, sometimes high-pitched and rolling impossibly fast, other times thudding like a drum, or whizzing about the room like a birdless birdsong, or transforming—becoming more and more resonant, becoming a bottle sound, a chime, a gong, with resonance increasing at every stroke as if, at last, the listener has entered a massive bell tower. "*Turenas* is the first piece of music where someone actually defines space as a compositional choice," Chowning comments. "I feel the piece is like sound sculpture, or the equivalent of dance in musical composition."

James A. Moorer's *Perfect Days* (tape, 6 minutes), composed at Stanford's computer music laboratory in 1976, uses a new musical instrument created by fusing the digital descriptions of a human voice and a flute, to "read" a poem. The result is both astounding and beautiful: a synthetic voice speaking comprehensible words, yet containing the breathy, silver sound of a flute reverberating in a large concert hall.

---

*Thus, it requires at least two separate sound channels and two speaker systems (stereophonic sound); obviously, quadraphonic sound, now commonly used with the Stanford system, would be even better.

Moorer began his musical poem with two digital recordings: one of jazz musician Tim Weisberg playing a flute, one of radio announcer Charles Shere reading the Richard Brautigan poem, *Perfect Days.* Moorer describes his compositional process: "I listened to the flute part, and I listened to the poem. Then I made a sort of map of them both, looking at the digital descriptions of the sounds, looking at exactly what times things happen. What time this syllable ended. What time this note on the flute ended. Here was the raw material, from which I composed the piece." First Moorer "whitened" the flute. That is, he simplified the flute's spectrum of sound for any single note. That process, by the way, ultimately introduced some random noise—an added hissing, breathy sound—which he chose to leave in. Next, he altered some of the voice recording, erasing some of the sound, leaving whatever seemed to be distinctive about word articulation—the making of vowels and consonants. Then he mixed small segments, or "snippets" from the two sources: "I decided what syllables I would apply to what flute phrases, and ran the appropriate programs. In some instances, the flute phrases were either longer or shorter than the spoken passages, so I would either slow down or speed up the passage. Generally, I slowed down speech segments to match flute phrases. So finally I had produced a set of short, cross-synthesized passages, about fifty or sixty little snippets."

At this point, Moorer had three basic colors on his composer's palette. He still had all the digital information about the original voice. He still had the original flute. And he had those "snippets" consisting of cross sections of the two. The final act of composition was arranging those elements in time, deciding which came where and after what, and what loudness was to occur in what speaker. He added some programmed instruction to produce concert hall reverberations, and there it was: a series of programmed instructions to fuse, to alter and combine the two earlier digital recordings, producing finally a "voiceflute."

The Computer as Performance Instrument. Most Stanford computer music concerts are taped, rather than live, performances. Stanford composers produce careful, complete works that allow for no interpretation by performers: they are finished when the composer is finished, and exist in fixed form. A concert might consist of a bare stage, a tape recorder plus speakers, and a composer who turns on the recorder at the beginning and then turns it off at the end.

Bill Buxton, director of an experimental music studio at the University of Toronto, has worked for many years on developing computer compositional systems that are easily accessible for musicians and composers who have no knowledge of computer science or programming. Additionally, Buxton has been concerned with using the computer in live performances.

A Buxton performance begins with laborious compositional work in the Toronto studio. Here, a "mothership" computer is attached to smaller computers. Buxton works with the keyboard and screen of the small computer, but much of the complex computing involved in composition—the interpretation of instructions, the experimentation and reexperimentation with sounds and sequences of sounds—is taken over by the large, mothership computer. For performances, however, the smaller computer is unplugged, placed in the back of a car (along with sound-generating equipment and interactive performance hardware), and driven to the concert hall, wherever that might be. At the concert hall, Buxton sets up his equipment. The computer and synthesizer go backstage, and the performance hardware goes on stage, placed on a table. Often, Buxton works with dancers and professionally designed stage sets, so the table and the performance equipment are likely to be integrated into some larger stage event.

The table is about two feet deep, over waist high—Buxton will be standing behind it—and about as wide as a small piano keyboard. The performance equipment includes a screen and a typewriter keyboard. Buxton will be able to key in, on the typewriter keyboard, some basic instructions to the computer. The screen will display information about the process of the music both to Buxton and the audience. Additionally, a small piano keyboard is placed on the table: several parts of the composition may be modifiable by the pitch, speed, and duration of notes Buxton can produce with the piano keyboard.

So far, Buxton's system is not much different from many other computer performance instruments. Many commercially available synthesizers include a piano keyboard input. Reaching across the keyboard, however, Buxton will also be able to influence his composition by drawing on a standard graphics tablet: a plastic and metal tablet, fourteen by fourteen inches, on which he "draws" with a circuit-completing stylus. Buxton's graphics tablet has been modified, though, so that instead of sending drawn pictures to the screen, it sends increase-decrease signals, for any of several different aspects of a composition, to the sound generating system.

Buxton might begin by drawing on the tablet with a stylus in his right hand, with the results appearing in the sound. With his left hand, he may manipulate one or two treadmills. These are small devices supporting plastic loops; the loops can be pushed or pulled, and the direction and speed at which this happens is read by a simple optical scanner reacting to dark bars printed on the plastic (a process similar to that of optical bar readers in supermarket checkout stands). With a foot, or with his right hand, Buxton might also input signals with a device having a pressure sensitive membrane. This membrane can respond to simple toward-and-away, or right-and-left motion with a hand, as the graphics tablet does, but it is also sensitive to degree of pressure. Thus, it may be ideal for putting percussive or rhythmic information into the composition. None of these performance tools, by the way, is "hardwired" into the computer; all are under software control. This means that the way they influence any particular composition depends entirely upon the specifications of the composition, not the nature of the machine.

Buxton can pull the loudness up or down, alter the tempo, the richness, the resonance; he can start or stop aspects of the composition. The computer itself is capable of defining up to sixteen instruments at once. And any of the performance tools can be used to modify one of the instruments, or several. Also, the tools can be used to modify different instruments in different ways—for instance, to decrease the volume of one group of instruments while increasing the volume of another. If the musical performance is integrated with a dance performance, which itself may contain improvised sections, Buxton is able to watch the dancers and gesture to his musical system in ways that are more immediately appropriate than simply turning a dial: "I like to think that we are in some ways returning to the idea of the conductor—who with a single sweep of the hand or baton can cue in one group of players and cue out another. Ultimately, though, my actions produce transformations of the original piece. In that sense, I am more of a performer, or perhaps a jazz musician who improvises on the spot. I take this structure, my original composition, and stretch, twist, turn it. I can put it in different juxtapositions with itself, so that you have five or six or seven versions of the same thing happening at once, in different combinations."

The tremendous flexibility of control with such a system is leading, Buxton believes, to an unusually dynamic concert hall situation. Speakers can be placed anywhere in the hall, and the conductor-performer has the ability to move the music, or segments of the music, out to any of those locations with a single gesture. The result may be something akin to sculpture in sound. "Sounds can be placed in space, so that spatial location itself becomes another element of the composition, a new basis for musical organization." Further, the fact that computer music now can be played live, and modified and improvised live, means that the musician is no longer limited to solo performances. Buxton himself has played in concerts with other musicians who have brought their own systems.

Buxton believes that the development of live performance tools has begun, in the last two or three years, to give computer music some greater legitimacy. "I think there's an incredible new vitality in the concerts of today, and it has to do with the improvement of instruments, and getting away from tape recorded concerts. You can get far more complex structures and far more beautiful sounds by doing tape pieces—and I don't want to deny the significance of the large-system studios who are doing that. But I believe the live component, within the dynamics of the concert hall, is really what will push this music past its adolescence, into some kind of maturity."

The Computer as Composer. We might ask: Why write a musical composition in the form of a computer program, using some peculiar programming notation? Why not write, as composers have for centuries, a musical composition in the form of a "program" for performers, using standard musical notation? One answer is that a computer composition can directly make use of the computer's sound-generation capabilities. Another is that a computer can be programmed to generate much grander, more complex, more intricate compositions than an individual composer can through traditional means (marking notes on lined paper).

For example . . . on July 4, 1976, as a commissioned work for the American bicentennial celebration, Lejaren Hiller's *Midnight Carnival* cascaded around the streets of downtown St. Louis to an audience of twenty to thirty thousand people. *Midnight Carnival*, a computer-generated composition of both computer-synthesized sounds and *musique concrète* (mixed or processed, prerecorded natural sounds), included forty-six separate channels of sound on tape, emanated from numerous loudspeakers over several city blocks, and lasted hours.

Another example: in 1967, John Cage was invited to work with Lejaren Hiller on the computer composition of a piece of music for seven harpsichords and prerecorded, mixed, computer-generated sounds, called *HPSCHD* (pronounced "H–P–S–C–H–D" or "Harpsichord," whichever is most congenial). Though he had never before composed with a computer, and has not since, Cage accepted the challenge: "It's almost a principle in my behavior that if certain doors are opened, then I go through. And so I tried to think of something that would be, well, like when you go to a restaurant you want to order something that you can't cook yourself, and so I wanted to think of something to do with the computer that wouldn't be done without it, or that would be difficult."

Since 1950, Cage had been using the Taoist oracle, the *I Ching*, as a formal way to remove his music from his own control. The *I Ching* serves, in his words, as a "discipline, to free my work from my likes and dislikes, from my memory and taste. And to free me." One of the first things Cage and Hiller did together, in 1967, was to preserve the *I Ching* selection principle in the form of a subprogram for the computer. The *I Ching* consists of a large number of prophetic statements; the participant tosses sticks, or coins, in groups of six; the results are used to select from statements within the *I Ching*. Cage and Hiller's subprogram, then, imitated the process of tossing six coins, arriving at a number from 1 to 64. The number would then be used to make choices from different sorts of musical material.

The first musical material to which they applied the digital *I Ching* was simply another computer program for generating sounds similar to the plunks of a harpsichord. Using the *I Ching* subprogram to define a twenty-minute sequence of such notes, Cage and Hiller then tape recorded the results fifty-one times, producing fifty-one different versions of a computer making sounds similar to those of a harpsichord.

The second musical material was a written score to be played on a real harpsichord. Cage and Hiller decided to modify it seven times, for seven different harpsichords. They began with a score for harpsichord attributed to Mozart, known as the *Musical Dice Game*. Mozart's original score allows for randomizing certain sequences by tossing dice: Hiller and Cage simply substituted their *I Ching* selection for the dice tossing. Though tossing dice, as in the original *Musical Dice Game*, may be considered a procedure for randomization, Cage is certain that the *I Ching* is not simply a fancier technique for randomization. ''The idea of randomness,'' he says, ''is in the mind of some scientist; and it is the equal distribution of the elements of whatever universe you're dealing with. But the *I Ching* doesn't deal with equal distribution. The *I Ching* is curious; it appears as you work with it to be temperamental. It seems to become fond of certain numbers, and stay with them, and then leave them, much as the experience in nature of finding certain plants growing in a group and then not growing. In other words, nature is not random, nor is the *I Ching*. Randomness has nothing to do with nature. It has to do with man's desire to predict the future, and therefore to control the future. The *I Ching* if anything is a renunciation of that desire. You accept what happens. I think there are as many composers attempting to increase control, now, as there are, like myself, deciding to renounce control. This is one of the things that's encouraged me to do it: the race as a whole would lose nothing by my not controlling things, since other people are controlling them. Through my activities, the species would learn what happens when we do that.''

In any case, Cage and Hiller used their *I Ching* subprogram to select a score for the first harpsichord. Using similar schemes, they next produced other scores for the other six harpsichords. The second score began with sequences selected by the *I Ching* from the *Musical Dice Game*, but then the *I Ching* was used to insert pieces from other works by Mozart. Later scores began in the same way, but then the *I Ching* inserted selections from works by other composers—moving stylistically through history. The seventh score was simply an instruction to the harpsichordist to do something of his or her own choosing as if there were an audience listening, or as if the performer were practicing at home.

With seven scores for seven harpsichords and fifty-one computer-generated tapes, *HPSCHD* was complete except for the instructions for performance. The instructions allowed for the playing of anywhere from one to fifty-one of the tapes, either in sequence, all at once, or in any combination. At the same time, according to the instructions, from one to seven harpsichordists could play either one of the scores at a time, or all seven at a time, or any combination. A sample performance, for instance, might include a stage with fifty-one tape recorders scattered in the midst of seven harpsichords. Someone would decide when to turn on a tape recorder, and a harpsichordist (or two or three) would wander about the stage, sitting down to play through a score when the moment seemed appropriate, perhaps taking a break to smoke a cigar, then moving to another harpsichord to carry out another score.

HPSCHD was, in fact, performed in a large, circular building at the University of Illinois in 1969. Included with the performance were seven harpsichords, multiple speakers and amplifiers playing the continuous tape recordings of a computer's imitations of a harpsichord, and a light show generated by several movies running at once and eight thousand slides that Cage and Hiller had prepared. Cage describes the performance: "As you approached this enormous, round building from the outside, the entire building was flashing with lights made by the images. It was just extraordinary! The concert itself was marvelous because you went through the historical progression from chamber music into orchestral music—that kind of density—and then you went beyond that to something we're not familiar with. There has never been, since then, a production of *HPSCHD* to equal that."

Laurie Spiegel is a professional composer who has used computers extensively in her work for several years. Spiegel received her formal musical training at the Juilliard School of Music in New York, and in the late 1960s she began composing electronic music on an *analog synthesizer.* One might think of the analog synthesizer as an electronic music generator without a computer. It is likely to have a keyboard at one end, speakers at the other, and in the middle, electronic oscillators and other devices to transform keyboard work into vibrations in the speakers. Like an organ, it is capable of producing a wide spectrum of sounds.* Spiegel found it particularly congenial as a composition tool because she could experiment with and listen to many sounds as she was composing, rather than having to wait for other musicians to play what she had written on paper. "Instead of being dependent on someone else to turn my work into sound, I could hear the work as I composed it, decide which ideas to pursue and which to throw out, and have them done exactly the way I wanted, without an instrumentalist as a middleman to alter them. I found I could learn much faster about form and pacing and musicality than I would have, working on paper without getting to hear my ideas."

2. 16. Laurie Spiegel composing at the keyboard
Photo by Carlo Carnevali

In preferring not to begin with notations on paper, Spiegel had one distinct disadvantage, though. Writing on paper has a permanence. It is a form of memory. Like all earlier musical instruments, the analog synthesizer responds immediately to a musician's desires, but without memory: the music flows through without leaving a trace. In 1973, Spiegel contacted composer Emanuel Ghent and computer music pioneer Max Mathews, who were able to give her access to a large computer music system. Although it took her a year to compose her first work on the digital

---

*An analog synthesizer has many knobs and other input devices that can be *patched*, at the whim of the user, to define parameters of sound (pitch, amplitude, timbre). The small, rock-group-oriented, highly commercial synthesizers popular about a decade ago were relatively organ-like, in that they all pretty much limited the generation of pitch patterns to a keyboard control. But larger, modular systems are much more flexible. According to Spiegel, "The analog synthesizer continues to be musically expressive and wonderful in ways that digital systems are only beginning to approximate now."

system *(Appalachian Grove I*, available from 1750 Arch Records in Berkeley), she found computers to be such productive tools that she has used them ever since.

Aside from memory, digital synthesizers give a composer greatly expanded abilities to automate parts of the composition process: prewritten sections can be incorporated, and pieces can be programmed to evolve on their own. "Instead of specifying each individual note, as you do in old-fashioned composing, you can set up a system in which the machine creates and evolves the music, making decisions and taking care of specific sounds according to the instructions you give it." Additionally, a composer can choose to create music through various interactions with the computer: "I usually work with a lot of input devices going into the machine, to alter the music it's generating while it's generating it."

One of Spiegel's first interactive pieces began with the computer playing a prewritten simple melody over and over, gradually incorporating into it some music she was simultaneously playing on the keyboard, then gradually evolving back into the original melody. She later transcribed the full piece to paper, and published it as a piano score (in *Heresies*, #10). Other works of hers that make use of computer interaction (or, as she prefers to describe it, "real time interaction with computer algorithms") can be heard on her record, *The Expanding Universe* (Philo Records #9003).

The League of Automatic Music Composers—John Bischoff, Don Day, Jim Horton, and Tim Perkis—produces spontaneous performances through the dynamic conflict and cooperation of four automatic composition programs running through four interconnected small computers.

Each member of the league writes his own composition programs, but the programs contain interactive elements: each is designed to fuse with some signals from the others, ideally producing an unpredictable musical whole. Jim Horton's program, for example, might generate a series of musical pitches that move up and down the scale in a randomized fashion. Don Day's program may be designed to "listen" to the signal from Horton's computer, waiting for a pause. When it finds one, it may take the last note played, and generate from that an ascending or descending scale. Tim Perkis' program might mimic, in a different pitch or tone, something from either program, while John Bischoff's program might continuously search for the occurrence of two parts of a three-part harmony. Upon finding that, it generates the third part. Each member of the league is capable of altering elements of his individual program during a performance, and John Bischoff controls a mixer board, influencing the volume of any part of the combined signal.

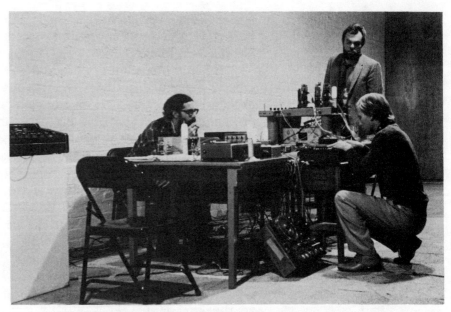

2. 17. Three-quarters of The League of Automatic Music Composers.
Photo courtesy The League of Automatic Music Composers

Perhaps surprisingly, the resulting music conveys a feeling of unity. As Bischoff says, "What we noticed from the very beginning was that when the computers were connected it sounded very different from pieces just being played simultaneously. If you imagine four pieces of music together at the same time, then coincidental things will happen. But by actually connecting the computers together, and having them interchange and share and interact on information, there seems to be an added dimension. It's hard to describe, but there seems to be a mindlike quality attached to the thing. All of a sudden, the music seems not only to unify, but it seems to direct itself. It becomes independent, almost, even from us."

A performance. The composers sit at four sides of a table loaded with complex electronic equipment, laboring quietly away with keyboard or switch controls as the music emanates from a bank of large speakers in a dramatic, sometimes appealing, sometimes appalling fashion. Here a series of notes breaks away, dashing madly through scales and variations of scales like a cat on a keyboard. There heavy, sonorous tones struggle, move, interact. Then quiet. Suddenly a new sequence beats over and over and over the same progression of notes. Then the pattern repeats in another key. A note dives. Higher notes like clarinets engage in battle. Lower notes appear and disappear in fast, sometimes warbling tones. The piece seems not to have any beginning, middle, or end. Rather it is a continual unfolding of sound. Sometimes a musician sits back and puts hands in pockets. Other times, he bends studiously over the keyboard, or stares at a monitor. Sounds like a cricket lost inside an amplifier. Then, a rapid, toned percussive sound, like drum sticks paradiddling on the string of a base violin. Ascending whistles. Then a sequence that sounds like a church organ. Then a slightly atonal pairing of two or three notes drives through a sequence that reverts to the percussion in low tones. Finally the music seems to take off, faster and faster and faster repetitions of a troubled offkey tone culminating in a violent, buzzing roar. Fade.

David Behrman prefers to create music that includes a computer music system as an interactive compositional element, along with live performers playing traditional instruments. Behrman's *On the Other Ocean* (recorded by Lovely Music) is performed by two musicians playing flute and bassoon according to a loosely defined score, and two synthesizers—one analog, the other digital. Whenever either musician hits one of six particular pitches in this piece, pitch-sensitive triggers activate an electronic generation of the same pitch on both synthesizers. The computer synthesizer produces a perfectly steady pitch, while the analog synthesizer produces a slightly drifting pitch. The slow, meditative notes on the flute and bassoon—combined with electronic music generated from two sources, one slowly wavering, slowly converging with and diverging from the pitch of the other—create at last an ornate, appealing, finely-textured blanket of music.

Setting: Stage is empty except for a compact collection of impressive-looking electronic gear and a chair in the center. Panoramic projections by artist Jacqueline Humbert appear on three or four large screens arranged around the back and sides of the stage.

Enter (stage right): Composer David Rosenboom. Rosenboom quietly sits in the chair, flicks on some switches. A computer screen begins to glow. Other switches are turned on and a low, single-pitched humming sound, a drone, begins flowing out of the speakers. Rosenboom makes some adjustments, and the drone is brought to a single, low volume. The audience becomes quiet. An assistant begins pasting the ends of long electrical wires to several places in the performer's scalp. Once Rosenboom is wired up, he quietly calibrates the computer's sensitivity to his brainwaves. The assistant leaves the stage. Rosenboom finishes his calibrations. He turns on a last switch, and sits back in the chair, ready. The meditative drone ceases. Tonight, the music will be from a biofeedback composition entitled, *On Being Invisible.* The composer will conduct.

The music begins.

We hear first seemingly random sounds: percussive yet gentle and toned sounds, plucks, mild squeaks, bloops, blops. One imagines an orchestra of plunking and percussive instruments tuning up, or a backyard full of miscellaneous objects, with rain falling slowly at first in random splots and splashes on bottles, tin cans, oil drums, a wooden table, an old toy drum. The piece progresses. Sounds resonate—sometimes, as refined as sounds from a fine musical instrument; sometimes jagged and buzzing, rain on scrap metal. Sometimes there seem to be solos, then an orchestra. Now a single sound, wooden, percussive, beats rapidly in a regular measure. Now it changes pitch and tone and evolves gradually into a slower rhythm of ascending and descending notes. Now it becomes louder, with the same rising and falling pitch. A new quality of sound appears, a soft almost indistinguishable whistle, and now a low, low humming like a church organ, lurking in the background, now warbling. A distinctive theme appears: a repetition of three syncopated notes, bop-de-bump, bop-de-bump, repeating with variations in pitch. The syncopation turns into a whirl of sounds for a moment, then reverts to its old pattern, bop-de-bump, bop-de-bump. Now like a child striking on a broken drum. Now like a mocking voice: *Don't do that, don't do that.* The music recedes, the rain has passed, only a few raindrops striking a few resonating pieces of metal in the backyard. One last drop strikes a clean sound like a bell. End of Part I of *On Being Invisible.*

Rosenboom studied musical composition at the University of Illinois in the mid-1960s, at that time one of the key centers of elec-

2. 18. David Rosenboom with electrodes attached to monitor brain signals during a performance of *On Being Invisible*
International Festival on Music and the Future in Mexico City, 1978
Computer signal analysis and sound-generating equipment are shown to the left.

tronic music experimentation and research in the world. Lejaren Hiller was continuing his pioneering work at Illinois, begun in the 1950s, on programming computers to create automatic compositions based upon theories of musical aesthetics.

After leaving Illinois, Rosenboom went to New York, where he set up shop as a free-lance composer and established a small company specializing in custom electronic design for artists and galleries. Interested in general issues of musical perception, he began to study neurophysiology with guidance from Dr. E. E. Coons. "One day Coons called me up and said, 'I've just been to the laboratory of a friend of mine who has been able to attach electrodes to a person's brain and allow aspects of the brain's signal to control a tone. You've got to come and see this.'" The friend turned out to be Les Fehmi of the State University of New York at Stony Brook. Indeed, Fehmi had one of the early biofeedback systems that responded to what we now call Alpha waves, one of the many distinguishable kinds of electrical activity in the brain. The Alpha waves happened to be fairly large signals, not hard to observe after simple electrical amplification, and very closely related to visual activity. Rosenboom tried the biofeedback system, and discovered he could alter the production of a sound simply by altering the quality of his attention.

In the early 1970s, Rosenboom was offered a faculty position at York University in Toronto. York was starting a new music department and offered Rosenboom support for what he had become interested in: relationships among modes of neural information processing in the brain, states of consciousness, and aesthetic experience. He set up a laboratory to develop techniques of measurement and analysis of brain signals that could give information about how these signals change during aesthetic experiences—with a primary concentration on music. "We had set up a very elaborate feedback loop consisting of the person, the ability to do sophisticated analysis of brain signals, and the ability to generate complex relationships in sounds." Immediately the department began experiments, some of which led Rosenboom back into his earlier interest in integrating computers and musical composition. His composition, *On Being Invisible*, is one product of that interest.

When *On Being Invisible* opens, the computer simply begins making sounds—these early sounds can be composed beforehand and inserted into the program, or they can be randomly generated. A second part of the program contains a model of perception, which predicts what kinds of changes in sound are likely to be perceived by the average listener as "important structural landmarks." In essence, then, the computer generates music and analyzes the music according to its own programmed model of musical language.

When it finds a sound that was predicted to be an important structural landmark, it activates a third part of the program which analyzes the brain signals of the performer sitting in the chair, and looks for a particular type of short-lived brain signal known as an *evoked response*. Evoked responses are transient brain waves associated with mental events such as shifts of attention, sudden alertness, the salience of a stimulus to the person. *On Being Invisible* is programmed to search for one particular *peak* of an evoked response wave, known as *P300*.

The computer examines evoked responses, and tries to find out whether or not its prediction (that the musical event is indeed an important structural landmark) is confirmed by the brain signals of the listening performer. If it is confirmed, and the computer finds that peak P300 is growing or increasing, then it moves to increase the probability that the kind of musical changes associated with this mental reaction will continue to occur. In other words, the computer tries to continue stimulating the occurrence of peak P300. It does this on all levels of musical production. It looks at changes in tonal quality, changes in pitch and loudness, and changes in patterns of notes. When the P300 peaks diminish in size or frequency, the performer may be either bored with the music or deliberately diverting attention. Whatever the case, the computer responds by introducing more randomization into its production of sounds, looking again for the steady occurrence of a P300 waveform. "What you have is a piece of music that converges and diverges in structure and general quality following your own sequences of attention and boredom, or altered interest," Rosenboom explains. "You find that you can relate to the piece in a number of ways. You can be passive, and simply be another element of the circuit, in which case it's just a process piece in which the convergences of the sound into a coherent musical piece are the result of nonvolitional shifts of attention. Or you can try to direct your attention, and try to make it go where you want it to."

4

Every tone on the traditional musical scale vibrates precisely twice as fast as the tone an octave below it: thus the curiously circular movement one hears in singing across a full octave—do, re, me, fa, so, la, ti, do. Although we recognize a movement upwards in pitch, we also recognize some kind of a circular "starting over," caused by a precise doubling of the original frequency. Music is based upon intuitively understood physical principles of sound, the physics of regularly vibrating objects. Music is structured in periodicity and the resonance of tones, and in the harmonic relationships between tones. On a thematic level (the broad interrelationships of individual notes over time), music is an intermingling of order and chaos—the periodic creation of resonance, and the resolution of tonal patterns.

It has always been possible for a visual artist to create an image that in some way resembles the spirit or feeling of a musical work. At least since the beginnings of cinema, though, some artists have wanted to create a visual equivalent of music. But until the computer was invented, it has been markedly difficult to do so.*

John Whitney is an inventor, artist, and an internationally recognized pioneer in the field of technologically assisted art. He was one of the first artists to begin using computers. He was one of IBM's first artists-in-residence. He is recognized as the originator of several special-effects techniques used in motion pictures and television. Whitney's work led to the stargate-corridor sequence in *2001: A Space Odyssey*, the time-warp sequence in *Star Wars*, and the streaked titles of *Superman*. Most significantly, though, since the 1940s Whitney has experimented with ways for creating a visual complement to music. According to Whitney, "It has been only in the last ten or fifteen years, with the development of computer graphics, that we can construct a visual art of graphic periodicity. Music is a periodic phenomenon. The entire history of music has been associated with very elementary periodic relationships of sound structures using the octave, the fifth, and the fourth, and the common intervals of the music of all cultures. With current computer graphics devices, we can foresee a visual domain that has equal potential."

Whitney works at his own studio in Pacific Palisades, California. There he maintains some specialized equipment for the composition of music, as well as a computer graphics system with a screen positioned directly in front of a camera. He defines, with computer programs, resonant geometric images on the screen. Once the computer has drawn an image—which may take a second, several sec-

---

*A visual music could mean motion, precision, and the play of periodic transformations from order to disorder to order. Two years after Vasily Kandinsky began painting entirely abstract canvases (1910), Léopold Survage, son of a Russian piano maker, began his studies—ultimately a series of two hundred abstract water colors—for an abstract visual art that would be put in motion through techniques of animation on film. Although his studies were never filmed, Survage is considered the first in a long tradition of abstract animators. "It is the mode of succession of their elements in time," Survage wrote in 1914, "which establishes the analogy to music, sound rhythm, and colored rhythm, whose realization I am advocating by means of cinematography." In 1921, Walter Ruttmann's brief *Lichtspiel Opus I* [*Lightplay Opus I*], the world's first abstract animated film, was shown in Frankfort. Abstract animators following the lead of Survage and Ruttmann—Viking Eggeling, Hans Richter, Oskar Fischinger, Mary Ellen Butte, and others—often continued to see their work in terms of music. For a thorough history of abstract and experimental animation, including today's abstract animations done with the assistance of computers, see Russett and Starr, *Experimental Animation*.

onds, or longer—the camera automatically photographs the computer's screen display, then the computer program draws the next image in a gradually changing sequence. The computer, of course, generates images more slowly than in cinematic "real time," patiently producing image after image in a long sequence. But once the camera has captured a full sequence, the developed film can be played back at normal movie or television speed, twenty-four or thirty frames a second.

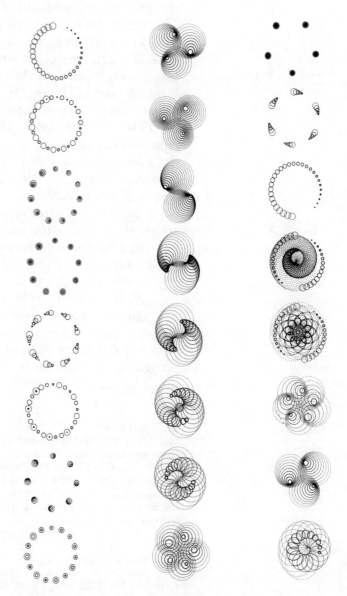

2. 19. Sequence of patterns based upon the Digital Harmonic computer programs
Courtesy John Whitney

Whitney's productions are meant to succeed as animations. The stills are very simple. Only rarely (as in Color Plate 8B), do his stills suggest the impact of full animation. "I am not concerned whatsoever with the 'looks' of a frame or a single pattern. I am concerned with the moving event, with the dynamics of imagery. I may work with a dynamic array of points, or simple geometric objects, drawing out over time patterns that often seem disordered, but which at significant fractional points fall into very orderly harmonic patterns." In motion and with music, Whitney's work comes dramatically alive. His animations indeed seem to articulate some fine visual equivalent to music, moving into and out of geometric form, surprising and delighting. If you have ever closed your eyes at a concert and experienced that synaesthesia of quickly changing abstract visual patterns seeming to dance in time and form with the music, then you have already begun to understand Whitney's work . . . but certainly the work of John Whitney belongs in the previous chapter on *Creation in Light*.

So out of the ground the Lord God formed every beast of the field and every bird of the air, and brought them to the man to see what he would call them; and whatever the man called every living creature, that was its name.

—The Book of Genesis

Chapter 3

Creation in Symbol

Naming begat language. Language begat thought. Even when the beasts and birds no longer passed directly before his eyes, Adam now could represent them with his tongue and in his mind. Too, he could represent them to others: he could communicate. And when he learned to carve symbols on wood or scratch them on paper (symbolizing the sounds from his tongue in phonetic writing, or the sights before his eyes in pictographic writing), Adam could communicate across time and space.

1

In his great satire of English politics and society, *Gulliver's Travels* (1726), Jonathan Swift described an automatic writing machine:

133

We crossed a walk to the other part of the academy, where, as I have already said, the projectors in speculative learning resided.

The first professor I saw was in a very large room, with forty pupils about him. After salutation, observing me to look earnestly upon a frame, which took up the greatest part of both the length and breadth of the room, he said, "Perhaps I might wonder to see him employed in a project for improving speculative knowledge, by practical mechanical operations. But the world would soon be sensible of its usefulness; and he flattered himself, that a more noble exalted thought never sprang in any other man's head. Every one knew how laborious the usual method is of attaining to arts and sciences; whereas, by his contrivance, the most ignorant person at a reasonable charge, and with little bodily labour, might write books in philosophy, poetry, politics, laws, mathematics, and theology, without the least assistance from genius or study." He then led me to the frame, about the sides whereof all his pupils stood in ranks. It was twenty feet square, placed in the middle of the room. The superficies was composed of several bits of wood, about the bigness of a die, but some larger than others. They were all linked together by slender wires. These bits of wood were covered on every square, with paper pasted on them; and on these papers were written all the words of their language, in their several moods, tenses, and declensions, but without any order. The professor then desired me "to observe; for he was going to set his engine at work." The pupils at his command took each of them hold of an iron handle, whereof there were forty fixed round the edges of the frame, and giving them a sudden turn, the whole disposition of the words was entirely changed. He then commanded six-and-thirty of the lads to read the several lines softly, as they appeared upon the frame; and where they found three or four words together that might make part of a sentence they dictated to the four remaining boys, who were scribes. This work was repeated three or four times, and at every turn the engine was so contrived, that the words shifted into new places, as the square bits of wood moved upside down.

Six hours a-day the young students were employed in this labour; and the professor showed me several volumes in large folio, already collected, of broken sentences, which he intended to piece together, and out of those rich materials, to give the world a complete body of all arts and sciences; which, however, might still be improved, and much expedited, if the public would raise a fund for making and employing five hundred such frames in Lagado, and oblige the managers to contribute in common their several collections.

Gulliver is shown the Grand Writing Machine during a visit to Laputa, an island floating in the air whose walleyed inhabitants ab-

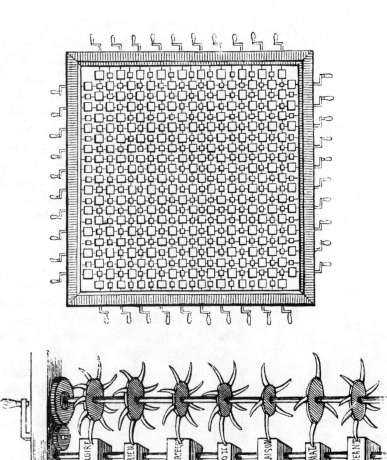

3. 1. Grandville *The Lagado Writing Machine*
French edition of *Gulliver's Travels* (1838). From Print Collection, Art, Prints and Photographs Division. The New York Public Library: Astor, Lenox and Tilden Foundations

sorb themselves in intellectual speculation. As a distinguished visitor to the island, Gulliver is given a tour of its primary academic institution, the Academy of Lagado, where he observes a number of strange souls engaged in speculative projects: a person who has spent eight years trying to extract sunbeams from cucumbers; an old, bearded man who wants "to reduce human excrement to its original food, by separating the several parts"; another who is trying to turn ice into gunpowder; a blind man and his blind apprentices, who mix colors for painters. Other speculators hope to produce colored silk by feeding spiders colored flies; to breed sheep without wool; to produce pillows by softening marble. In the school of languages, three professors speculate about a scheme to improve language by eliminating all words. And, of course, Gulliver is shown the Grand Writing Machine.

The Grand Writing Machine is described in more detail than any other project in the academy. Perhaps Swift considers it the most appropriate idea for ridicule. Where did the idea come from? In 1678, it seems, one John Peter published a pamphlet entitled "Artificial Versifying, a New Way to Make Latin Verses," which was briefly mentioned and ridiculed in an early eighteenth-century periodical, *The Spectator* (Number 220), in 1711. Most likely, Swift had the *Spectator* piece in mind as he developed his portrait of the Grand Writing Machine. However, the island of Laputa bears a telling resemblance to the mythical South Seas island described by Sir Francis Bacon in his allegorical introduction to scientific method, *The New Atlantis* (1627): on that island, English savants at an institute known as Salomon's House spend their energies in experimentation and observation. Bacon may not have originated the idea of learning based upon science, but his book gave it currency and force, and clearly Swift's satire is an attack against the idea of scientific method in general. Swift mocks the whole notion that the lot of mankind can be improved through invention based upon pure research—which he portrays as mindless speculation.

Sunbeams out of a cucumber? Gunpowder out of ice? The ideas are patently absurd, and we laugh or sneer right along with Swift . . . for a moment. Nevertheless, sunbeams out of a cucumber is finally no more absurd than sun-energy from a lump of coal. Gunpowder out of ice is no more ridiculous than bombs from pitchblende.

Swift's satirical presentation of the Grand Writing Machine resembles our own modern fear that machines will dehumanize us by supplanting those mysterious qualities we consider most human: intelligence and creativity. The Professor of Lagado tells Gulliver that the machine would enable "the most ignorant person" to write books in philosophy, poetry, and so on, "without the least assistance from genius or study." A disturbing thought indeed. In any case, the Professor of Lagado was mistaken, and Swift missed the point. The Grand Writing Machine was nothing more than a clumsy device for producing random combinations of words. It was never designed to replace human intelligence and creativity. Words written on pieces of paper were arranged at random on the blocks. The forty pupils randomly turned the cranks that turned the blocks. But note that, in the end, the only combinations of words chosen were those that made sense, that aroused interest: "where they found three or four words together that might make part of a sentence, they dictated to the four remaining boys who were scribes." In other words, the machine produced interesting combinations of words, but the final output depended entirely upon human choice and intelligence: of the professor, in choosing the words and deciding where to put them on the blocks; of the thirty-six lads, in the choices they made and called out; and also of the four scribes, in their decisions about what to write down, given what they heard. The Lagado writing machine ultimately depended upon human intelligence and creativity as much as a typewriter does.

Why have a writing machine at all, if humans still control the quality of its results? Certainly, one thing that the machine can do well is to produce new, unthought of, unusual combinations of words. It can stimulate creativity by breaking up staid, stable patterns of language and thought and meaning, applying the forces of randomness to the habits of tongue and brain.

The early twentieth-century Dadaists would have loved such an absurd machine. The Dadaists, by elevating the spontaneous, the obscene, the absurd to the highest levels of art were pursuing a number of goals: to dog the cats of tradition in art and literature, to validate despair, to identify themselves to each other, to have a good time. But above all: to curse meaning. Meaning was rationality, bourgeois communication. Meaning was the limited kind of thinking and belief that led to traditionalism, nationalism, and the Great War. The Dadaists cursed meaning, and in its place they erected an art and literature of nonmeaning.

Dadaist Tristan Tzara wrote a poem which stated that the way to write a Dada poem was to cut up any newspaper article into its constituent words, put the words in a bag, shake the bag, and take out the words one by one. Copy the words down as you pull them out, and you'll have a Dada poem: ''The poem will resemble you and you will find yourself to be an infinitely original writer with a charming sensitivity even though you will not be understood by the vulgar.'' Tzara was not the only person in this century to suggest, with some degree of irony, randomizing schemes to produce ''literature.'' In 1938, William Cook published, under the title *Plotto*, lists of characters, plots, scenes, conflicts, resolutions, and invited his readers to construct stories and novels from them. Beat generation author William Burroughs and friends tried such an approach, the results of which where published in Paris under the misleadingly comprehensible title, *Minutes to Go* (1960).

When computer programmers and a few poets first produced machine poems based upon much the same principle as that of Tristan Tzara—of words shaken gently in a paper bag, that is, of randomness—they did not see themselves as the odious speculators in Swift's Academy of Lagado, nor as poets in the Dada tradition. Mostly, they were light-hearted experimenters, trying to discover the work-manipulation possibilities of a new machine.

Louis Milic, an English professor at Cleveland State University, may have created the first computer poetry. In 1963, Milic programmed a computer to generate absurd English sentences. First he would describe, in the program, the frame for a simple sentence—subject, verb, object. Then he would provide lists of words that could be inserted randomly into that general frame.* The results were nonsensical sentences, but Milic soon noticed that the sentences reminded some people of modern poetry. "Apparently," he states, "when people don't understand something they say it's poetry. Of course, this is more likely to be true for the twentieth-century reader than, say, the eighteenth-century reader, who demanded as much coherence in poetry as in prose." At the same time, it occurred to Milic that the creation of poetry through word randomization was interestingly similar to a technique Dylan Thomas occasionally used. Thomas kept a notebook of words. Whenever a interesting or odd word arose in conversation, the poet would write it down in his notebook. When he wrote poetry, he would sometimes refer to the notebook to see if there were any combinations of words that looked interesting, often regardless of whether they made particular sense.

Thus provoked, Milic began using a computer to manipulate poetry. First, he took a poem written by Dylan Thomas, called *In the Beginning*. Milic randomly scrambled all the verbs, adjectives, and nouns, and asked his students to sort out the original from the recombinant versions. Frequently they were unable to. Next, he began creating original poems based upon prewritten sentence frames, with randomized words taken from lists of semantically similar words. The results were not, of course, great poetry. But they were interesting, and useful in the classroom. "In the preface to my poetry booklet, *Erato*, I say that writing poetry with a computer is like eating spaghetti with implements a yard long: it can be done, but it's very difficult. The human mind so easily and remarkably programs the language, whereas the computer does it with such great difficulty. People who work with computers, as I do, usually are more aware of their limitations than their capacities. . . . Perhaps the most useful thing I acquired from all that was a renewed admiration for human poets and poetry." The following is one of Milic's computer-generated poems:

---

*How could a computer, such a precise and nonrandom machine, produce random sequences of words? One simple way would be for the programmer to list within the program sequentially numbered words. Next the programmer could put into another part of the program a table of random numbers (such tables are published and can be found in a library). Finally, the computer could be instructed to proceed through the random numbers list, using each random number selected to refer to some word in the sequentially numbered word list. There are also ways of programming a computer to *generate* random (or approximately random) numbers, rather than simply referring to a predefined list of such numbers.

Old Woman

Above the eager folds of the stream,
Above the windy pleats of the beach,
I loved upon a noble step,
I, an old woman in the space of the flower.

Above the eager faces of the surf,
Above the early flounces of the shore,
This is my message to the world:
Set your lively figure, my comrade,
Sing to me in the chaos of the gloom.

A number of programmers, poets, and would-be poets followed Milic's example, and in the end, some bad poems were produced through programming by bad poets, and a few good or interesting poems were produced by a few good or interesting poets. The quality of the poetry depended almost entirely upon the quality of the program; the computer itself provided only two additional virtues. First, it could combine and recombine sequences of words mindlessly, thus producing poetry devoid of the normal habits, hesitations, and censorships a human can be expected to introduce. Second, it could combine and recombine sequences of words effortlessly, for months or years at a time.

Richard Bailey, editor of a volume of computer poetry and author of several articles on the subject, has reported on one of the most significant uses of that second virtue. According to Bailey, several years ago a certain Robert Gaskins programmed the computer in a large institution to produce endless *haiku* (a tightly-structured, traditional Japanese poetry form) on the screen of a particular monitor, when it was not otherwise in use. The haiku appeared at the bottom of the blank screen, rose slowly to the top, and disappeared forever, as new haiku appeared at the bottom. Hundreds of thousands of haiku were produced in that fashion—decorative, occasionally intriguing pop zen wallpaper—without wasting a single sheet of paper.

Marie Borroff, poet and professor of English at Yale University, was one of the more serious poets to experiment, albeit briefly, with computer poetry. She learned computer programming, and wrote several poetry programs to run on an IBM computer more than a decade ago. "I had seen some computer poetry, and so I decided to do some myself. I discovered that there is a range of extremes, depending on how much you specify and how much you leave to chance. I think the alternatives are either to structure it highly, or to allow a random number generator to do something for you, and what I did in particular was to acquire vocabularies by random means and then invent frames into which the computer inserted words from my vocabularies, also randomly." Typically, her programs began with verbal frames containing a number of empty slots. The frames consisted of traditional poetic devices or patterns—invocations, exhortations, and the like—and the slots were to be filled with words randomly chosen by the computer from appropriate vocabulary lists, each of which might contain fifty words.

One poetry program she wrote provided nineteen different vocabulary lists. Each list contained words meant to serve a particular function, to fill a particular slot—concrete or abstract nouns, descriptive or lexical adjectives, intransitive verbs, for instance—but given that limitation, for each list Borroff selected twenty-five words by poking her finger at random into the pages of an anthology of classical English poetry, and an additional twenty-five from the pages of an anthology of avant garde poetry from the 1960s. Then she instructed the computer to choose words from each of the lists to fill corresponding slots. Some of the computer's choices were random, while others were only semirandom—having been determined by previous word choices. The results were, as Borroff describes it, "an absolutely zany but sometimes quite effective kind of verse." *Five Poems from the Chinese* is one of her more successful computer poems.

Five Poems from the Chinese

Gracious is money
And avuncular are the buttonholes of its bed;
But it is among the berries, and there only,
That the graciousness of money may guard us
And the buttonholes of its bed may be judged.

Furtive is mahogany
And delirious are the shadows of its pants;
But it is among the pastures, and there only,
That the furtiveness of mahogany may uplift us
And the shadows of its pants may be dissolved.

Base is darkness
And passionate are the lungs of its shape;
But it is among the fields, and there only,
That the baseness of darkness may know us
And the lungs of its shape may be wronged

Stiff is music
And deep are the steeples of its caress;
But it is among the trees, and there only,
That the stiffness of music may create us
And the steeples of its caress may be judged.

Transparent is flesh
And ancient are the shadows of its spittle;
But it is among the trains, and there only,
That the transparency of flesh may breed us
And the shadows of its spittle may be quenched.

In the early 1950s, E. Mendoza, a professor of physics at Manchester University in England, had an amusing conversation with a colleague about the quality of undergraduate physics essays. The colleague half-seriously asserted that students never really learned physics, they just learned a vocabulary of appropriate-sounding words, which they hung together in random order on examination essays. Tired teachers then scanned the papers looking only for those words, and graded the papers on that basis.

Mendoza decided to test his colleague's theory. He wrote a program that would randomly select phrases from four lists (combined with one minor deterministic element), and place them in a sequence generally reminiscent of an English sentence. He deliberately kept his grammatical structure simple, used unimaginative verbs, and tried to place the weight of the sentences on the nouns, "making the sentences all very dead," Mendoza wrote, "to imitate the style of physics textbooks."* Mendoza's program began generating endless physics essays much like the following:

> The absolute the entropy of the universe which determines microscopic disorder implies the increase of disorder while quantity of heat statistically increases in a reversible process. Statistically the entropy of the universe determines irreversibility. Disorder causes $dS > dQ/T$ but the entropy of the universe which causes a decrease of free energy for the universe is conserved while energy is conserved.

Continuing the experiment, Mendoza surrepetitiously inserted one such essay into a batch of first-year examination papers and awaited the results. "Unfortunately it was marked by a very conscientious man who eventually stormed into the Director's office shouting 'Who the hell is this man—why did we ever admit him?' So perhaps my colleague's hypothesis was wrong and students are a little better than we think."

Mendoza's charming joke demonstrated not much except that: some people really do read physics examinations at Manchester University; and, without some strong and intelligent structure, computer-generated prose cannot be taken very seriously. Structure can be created in a number of ways and at different levels. Much of the computer prose written after Mendoza's experiment has depended upon the creation of plot structure through simulations,

---

*This and further quotes are from Mendoza's article in *Cybernetic Serendipity*.

or models, of human behavior, combined with subprograms that generate grammatical English sentences to describe the simulated event.

In 1973, for instance, Professor Sheldon Klein of the computer sciences and linguistics departments of the University of Wisconsin together with a group of his students, developed a complex program (actually, an entire programming language) to simulate verbal and nonverbal human behavior in social groups; as the program generated abstract simulations of social behavior, it represented that behavior internally with a "semantic code" (a symbolic representation abstract enough that it can be translated into the various surface structures of English). A subprogram then translated this abstract semantic information into English text.

The program's first test case was a set of rules modeling the kinds of social behavior typically described in murder mystery detective stories. The result: a set of 2100 word detective stories generated on a UNIVAC 1108 computer in less than nineteen seconds each. The next test case, in 1974, was the automatic generation of hundreds of Russian folk tales (in about two and a half seconds each). Generating folk tales seemed an attractive task largely because a folklorist, Vladimir Propp, had already carried out some mathematically precise structural analyses of Russian folk tales. The following are two sample tales from that experiment:

The Popoviches live in a certain kingdom.
The father is Baldak.
The oldest son is Nicholas.
The younger son is Marco.
The youngest son is Emelya.
The oldest daughter is Dunia.
The younger daughter is Maria.
Boris also lives in the same land.
Boris is of miraculous birth.
A bear walks into the certain kingdom.
The bear asks Vasilisa where is the heart.
Vasilisa says that the heart is in the hut.
The bear cuts out Baldak's heart.
Baldak is replaced with the bear's son.
Baldak calls for help from Boris.
Boris decides to search for the heart.
Boris leaves on a search.

Boris meets a stove along the way.
The stove proposes that Boris eat the meal which it has
   prepared.
Boris does not respond.
The stove asks again.
Boris refuses.

The stove asks for a third time.
Boris responds by partaking of the meal.
A magic sword, a magic bird and a magic hen are given to
  Boris.
Boris travels to the location of the heart in the other king-
  dom.
Boris travels by the magic bird.
The heart appears from the magic hen.
Boris starts back home.
The bear tempts Boris by changing into an alluring object.
Boris escapes by avoiding the temptation.
Boris returns home.

*   *   *

The Popoviches live in a distant province.
The father is Nicholas.
The mother is Maria.
Katrina is the only child.
Erema also lives in the same land.
Baldak is Erema's child.
A dragon flies into the distant province.
The dragon disguises himself as an old lady.
The dragon uses a magic pin on Nicholas.
Nicholas falls asleep.
The dragon threatens to eat Baldak.
Erema calls for Nicholas.
Erema announces that the dragon threatened to eat Baldak.
Nicholas decides to search for the dragon.
Nicholas leaves on a search.

Nicholas meets a witch along the way.
The witch is fighting with Emelya over a magic carpet.
The witch asks Nicholas to divide the magic carpet.
Nicholas tricks the disputants into leaving the magic carpet
  unprotected.
The magic carpet is seized by Nicholas.
Nicholas travels to the location of the dragon in an other
  kingdom.
Nicholas travels by the magic carpet.
Nicholas finds the dragon.
They engage in a competition.
Nicholas wins with the help of cleverness.
Nicholas starts back home.
Nicholas returns home.

In 1980, Klein and his students began work on a new version of
their simulation program, designed for small computers, called
"| | | | |" (Bar Bar for short), and capable of generating from a single
semantic code not only a verbal description, but visual and musical

output on videotape as well. The first simulation generated from this program (with the assistance of an Apple and a Terak) was an opera, *Revolt in Flatland*, based on Edwin Abbott's *Flatland*, a nineteenth-century fantasy about life in a two-dimensional world. According to a recent *New York Times* article, Professor Klein recognizes that *Revolt in Flatland* falls short of *Don Giovanni*. "I'm not keen on showing it because, to be perfectly frank," he is quoted, "the music is superb but the action is quite dull. . . . Most of what's happening in the current version is that little squares and triangles and polygons are moving slowly from one house to another. The action only happens occasionally, when they meet."

Klein and his group are currently working on programs to search a plot for interesting dramatic values and edit out boring scenes, and to generate analogical variants and surrealistic versions of the opera. Ultimately, though, their work is concerned with more than literary production. Klein himself is interested in cognitive anthropology, and one of his major motivations is to test the structuralist theories of Claude Lévi-Strauss.

In 1976 at Yale University, Jim Meehan described a program similar to Klein's, that generated stories by simulating characters and their behavior in a fictional world. Meehan's program, called *Tale-Spin*, was designed to test certain models of human behavior. Because his model was simplistic, a gross reduction of the complexities of real human behavior, Meehan decided to give the characters whimsical animal names, thus giving his generated stories the charming, unpretentious quality of Aesopian animal fables.

The *Tale-Spin* world consisted of three separate but interacting elements: (1) the characters themselves (their personalities and the states of their interests in certain goals—acquiring food, drink, rest, or sex, otherwise known as "fooling around"); (2) the interpersonal environment (how the characters felt about and dealt with each other); and (3) the physical environment (rivers, trees, roads, and so on). Such elements of the modeled world were described in the program as lists of rules. (For example: If you wish to acquire some object, first you ask, "Do I own it?" If you don't own it, you ask, "Is it free for the taking?" If someone else owns it, you ask, "Is the owner a person I can bargain with?" If not, you ask, "Is my conscience such that I would steal it?")

The action of *Tale-Spin* begins when someone defines to the computer the main character and his or her primary goal, and the other characters participating in the story. Characters in *Tale-Spin* have certain inherent goals, such as self preservation, and other characters may acquire goals in response to events in the story—but it is the assigned goal of the main character that drives the action. The story thus becomes an adventure in problem solving. What makes such generated stories unpredictable, of course, is the complexity of the rules activated whenever a main character pursues a goal.* The following *Tale-Spin* story illustrates very well, I think, how a character's goals create action, and how action is resolved once the goals are satisfied.

Lulu, Peggy, and Maggie

Once upon a time Lulu Bear lived in a cave. There was a nest in a maple tree. Peggy Bird lived in the nest. Lulu knew that Peggy was in her nest. One day Lulu was famished. Lulu wanted to get some honey. Lulu wanted to find out where there was some honey. Lulu liked Peggy. Lulu wanted Peggy to tell Lulu where there was some honey. Lulu was honest with Peggy. Lulu wasn't competitive with Peggy. Lulu thought that Peggy liked her. Lulu thought that Peggy was honest with her. Lulu wanted to ask Peggy whether Peggy would tell Lulu where there was some honey. Lulu wanted to get near Peggy. Lulu walked from her cave down a pass through a valley across a meadow to the ground by the maple tree. Lulu asked Peggy whether Peggy would tell Lulu where there was some honey. Peggy liked Lulu. Peggy trusted Lulu completely. Peggy didn't have much influence over Lulu. Peggy was indebted to Lulu. Lulu trusted Peggy completely. Peggy was very generous. Peggy was honest with Lulu. There was a beehive in a redwood tree. Maggie Bee lived in the beehive. There was some honey in Maggie's beehive. Peggy told Lulu that the honey was in Maggie's beehive. Peggy told Lulu that Maggie had the honey. Peggy told Lulu that Maggie was in her beehive. Lulu was usually honest. Lulu wanted Maggie to give Lulu the honey. Lulu was inclined to lie to Maggie. Lulu disliked Maggie. Lulu didn't have much influence over Maggie. Lulu decided that Maggie wouldn't give Lulu the honey. Lulu wanted Maggie to get near the ground by the redwood tree. Lulu wanted to get near Maggie. Lulu walked from the ground by the maple tree across the meadow through a valley to the ground by the redwood tree. Lulu grabbed Maggie with her paw. Lulu let go of Maggie. Maggie fell to the gound by the redwood tree. Lulu wanted to get near the honey. Lulu took the honey. Lulu ate the honey. The honey was gone. Lulu was not hungry. Maggie thought that Lulu was not hungry. The End.

---

*As with the Klein programs, all the action is first carried out symbolically, and then described in the form of English sentences by a language-generator residing in another part of the program.

Often, *Tale-Spin* has generated absurd stories because of unexpected conflicts in rules, or the incompleteness of certain parts of the model. *Tale-Spin* produced one story, for example, about a certain Henry Ant who fell into a river while trying to get a drink of water. The portion of the program that generated this event described it as "gravity pushed Henry Ant into the river." However, one of the rules of the model was that whenever someone pushed someone, both characters moved. Suddenly, because forces and characters had not been clearly distinguished within the program, it described a situation in which both "gravity" and Henry Ant were in the river. Gravity had suddenly become, in terms of the internal logic of the program, a character. When characters fell into the river, the program rules stated that their inherent drive for self-preservation automatically superseded all other goals. The program then went through lists of possible means of self-preservation in the river: if the character has legs it can swim; if the character has wings it can fly; if the character has friends it can call for help. Since gravity had none of these, the computer reported this sad message: "Gravity drowned."

Meehan, certainly, was not especially interested in generating entertaining stories. He meant to test and refine models of human behavior. On the other hand, many of the stories turned out to be charming, and Meehan believes that it is possible, given complex enough models of human behavior and environments, for a computer to generate stories of some interest. However: "I don't think *Tale-Spin* is a threat to Shakespeare, or even *The National Enquirer*," he says, "and I don't expect computer-generated stories to be very interesting, as literature, for a long time. The problem may be that the world is very complex, and very difficult to model."

In the nightmare totalitarian society envisioned by George Orwell in *1984*, all books are conceived by committees and composed by machines. Books are designed as packaged products having two purposes only: to promote "proper" political thinking with propaganda and to stupefy the masses with pulp. A central character of *1984* works as a mechanic on one of the novel-writing machines. She doesn't like to read, though. "Books were just a commodity that had to be produced, like jam or bootlaces."

No one so far expects computers to replace authors. Computer-generated writing is of far more interest to the computer scientist looking for new solutions to old programming puzzles, and to the psychologist looking for provocative models of human creation and cogitation, than to the literary artist. Even the more sophisticated plot-generating programs rely on simplistic, mechanistic models of human behavior and experience which are then allowed to run a serendipitous course.

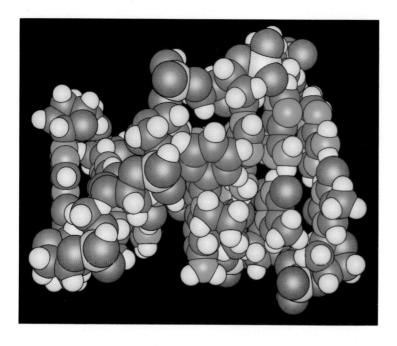

Plate 1A (left). Nelson Max, *Computer-generated model of a segment of a DNA molecule.*
Photograph taken by Nelson Max at Lawrence Livermore National Laboratory, University of California. Permission to reproduce granted by the University of California. This photograph was taken by a contractor of the U.S. government under contract W-7405-ENG-48. Accordingly, the U.S. government retains a nonexclusive, royalty-free license to publish or reproduce the published form of this contribution, or to allow others to do so, for U.S. government purposes.

Plate 1B (lower left). *Computer-aided design of a jet.*
Courtesy Evans and Sutherland.

Plate 1C (lower right). *Calma's Multicolor Raster Display (MRD) used to design an integrated circuit.*
Courtesy Calma Company.

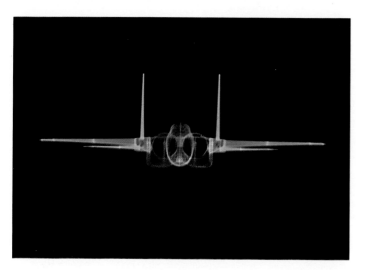

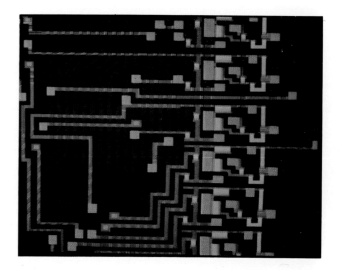

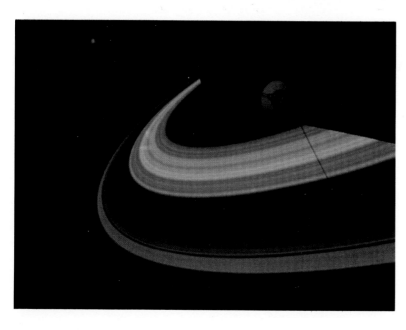

Plate 1D (left). James Blinn, *Saturn Flyby Simulation.*
Courtesy Jet Propulsion Laboratories.

Plate 2A. *Table Top Scene Simulation.*
Courtesy Information International, Inc.

Plates 2B and 2C. Loren Carpenter, *Mountain Scene
Simulations.*
By permission of Loren Carpenter.

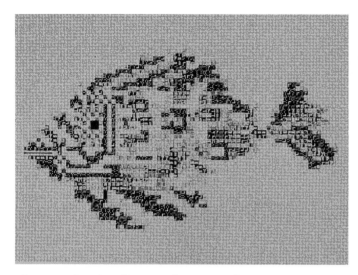

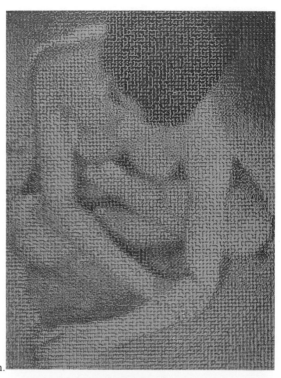

Plate 3A (above). Lillian F. Schwartz, *Fish*. 1972.
© Lilyan Productions, Inc.
Image by Lillian F. Schwartz; program by Ken Knowlton.

Plate 3B (right). Lillian F. Schwartz, *Nude*. 1972.
© Lilyan Productions, Inc.
Image by Lillian F. Schwartz; program by Ken Knowlton.

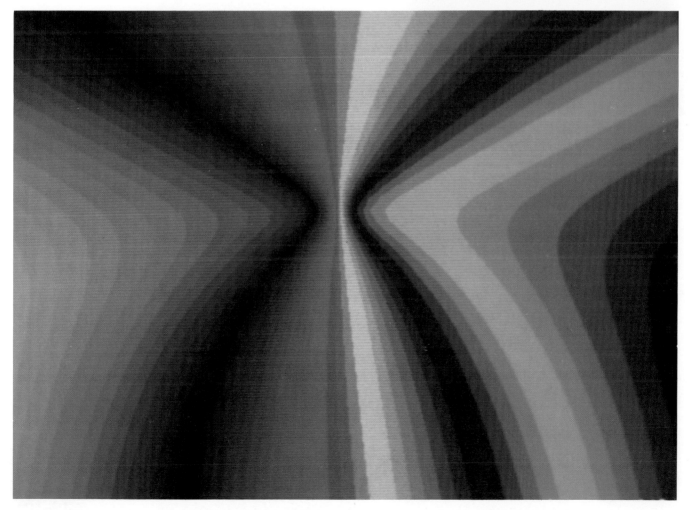

Plate 3C. Lillian F. Schwartz, from the animation *Metathesis*. 1979. © Lilyan Productions, Inc. Image by Lillian F. Schwartz; program by John Chambers.

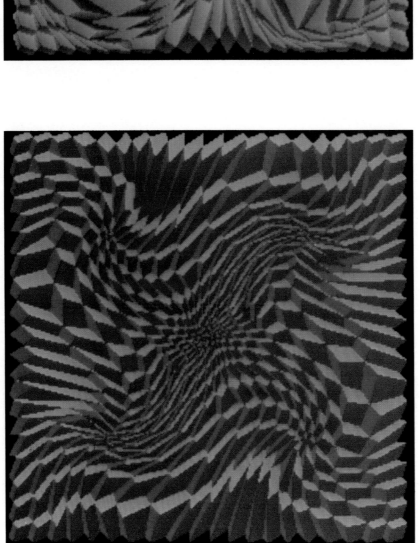

Plates 4A and 4B. Ruth Leavitt, from the animation *From Blue to Yellow*. 1978.
© 1978 by Ruth Leavitt. By permission of Ruth Leavitt.

Plate 5A (above). David Em, *Transjovian Pipeline*. 1979.
Artist: David Em.
© 1979 by David Em.

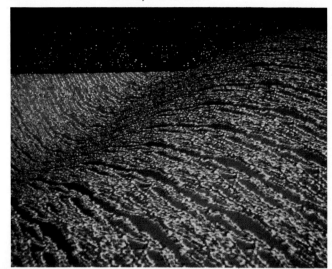

Plate 5B (below). David Em, *Wave*. 1979.
Artist: David Em. © 1979 by David Em.

Plate 5C. David Em, *Escher*. 1979. Artist: David Em. © 1979 by David Em.

Plate 6A. Darcy Gerbarg, *Image created at NYIT Computer Graphics Laboratory.*
By permission of Darcy Gerbarg.

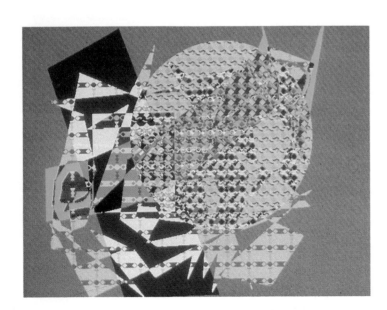

Plate 6B. Darcy Gerbarg, *Image created on a Ramtek Color Display.*
By Permission of Darcy Gerbarg.

Plate 6C. Darcy Gerbarg, *Image created at Aurora Imaging Systems.*
By permission of Darcy Gerbarg.

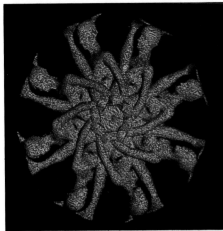

Plate 7A. Duane Palyka, *Pinwheel 1.*
This image was generated by
NYIT's Computer Graphics Lab.
Artist: Duane Palyka.

Plate 7B. Duane Palyka, *Picasso 2.*
This image was generated by NYIT's Computer Graphics Lab. Artist: Duane Palyka.

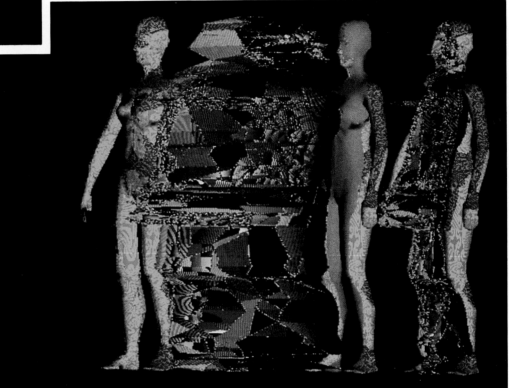

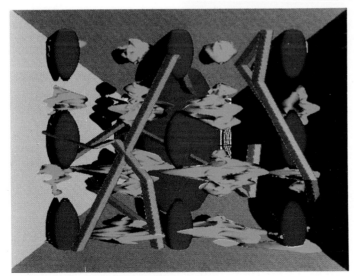

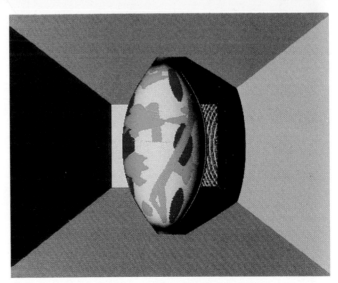

Plate 7C. Duane Palyka, *Space-Carrots.*
This image was generated by NYIT's Computer Graphics Lab.
Artist: Duane Palyka.

Plate 7D. Duane Palyka, *Space-Carrots on Soid.*
This image was generated by NYIT's Computer Graphics Lab.
Artist: Duane Palyka.

Plate 8A. Harold Cohen, *Colored Drawing.* 1982. 20 × 30 inches. Photographer: Becky Cohen.

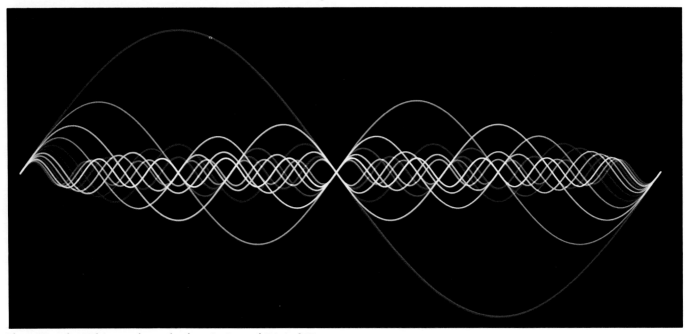

Plate 8B. John Whitney, from the frontispiece of *Digital Harmony.* 1980. By permission of John Whitney.

Ezra Pound once remarked that literature is "language charged with meaning." The problem with computer literature generators is that their greatest precision of meaning resides in the original program: as the program runs, its precision of meaning runs down, much like a toy unwinding, scattering into higher levels of entropy and lower levels of meaning. To expect serious literature, "language charged with meaning," after scattering a program through systems of serendipity and randomness appears to be like trying to create a choice cut of steak by passing a cow through a grinder: the result approximates meataphor more than metaphor. On the other hand, there is certainly a demand for hamburger, and one potential use of a future writing machine (containing programs more sophisticated than those we have now) would be to generate very quickly vast stacks of literary hamburger, thus lowering the prices of supermarket paperbacks and sexy bestsellers. Instead of having to labor over a manuscript for one or two months, a supermarket author could ask his or her agent simply to press a button and let the computer produce it in an hour.

For the sake of enterprising author-programmers, I should mention that the proper structure for such a program already exists and has been well defined.* In January of 1980, Simon and Schuster hired an advertising agency to determine the most attractive formula for books in their projected series of mass-market paperback romances, known as the Silhouette Romances. The agency decided to poll romance readers in Dallas, San Diego, and Oklahoma City to find out exactly what kind of book format, plot, and characterization would sell the most. Said a member of the agency: "We use this method all the time in the packaged-goods area—with deodorants, with toothpaste. . . . There was no reason it couldn't apply to books as well." The results of that survey were then passed on in a three-page tip sheet to potential authors of the Silhouette series, and can be summarized as follows. The story should be between 50,000 and 56,000 words long. There should be no violence, no pain, and no "slangy, obscene or profane" language. The hero and heroine may not appear in bed together unless they are married. The heroine is an innocent with few troubles beyond those of love. She is a virgin between the ages of nineteen and twenty-seven who neither drinks nor smokes. She is "not beautiful in the high fashion sense," and her makeup and dress are "modest." The hero is between eight and twelve years older than she is. He is definitely "virile," but "not necessarily handsome." In the story he is never married to anyone except the heroine, but he can be a widower. He is allowed to be divorced only if his former wife initiated the divorce. If there

_____

*See Kakutani.

is another woman, she must be "mean, oversophisticated and well groomed." The story is, of course, a love story. It ought to take place in an exotic setting that can "transport the reader" (presumably out of Dallas, San Diego, or Oklahoma City), and it is good to provide a map of the setting to appear on the inside cover of the book. In the end, of course, all the tribulations of love should be resolved and the hero and heroine should get together. Once they are safely married, a tasteful and discreet love scene in bed is acceptable.

2

According to Captain Grace Hopper of the U.S. Navy (the only woman ever honored with the Data Processing Management Association's Computer Science Man of the Year award), the idea of computers being disrupted by bugs originated at Harvard University in 1945. The eight foot high, fifty-five foot long, glass-and-steel encased computer known as the Harvard Mark I was not working. Technicians and repair people descended on the machine, located the troubled circuitry, and a specialist with tweezers pried loose a big moth. This was the first bug in a computer. Most later "bugs" existed not in the hardware or circuitry, however, but in the software. *Word processing* began as a sort of electronic tweezer used to extricate bugs from programs.

Programs have to be perfect. When programs were entered into computers in the form of continuous punched paper tape, a single bug in the program might require revising the entire tape. Thus, computer users were strongly motivated to design a system for the editing of programs. Such a system typically included something known as the *symbolic editor*, and a piece of office equipment, the Friden Flexowriter.

The Friden Flexowriter was a fancy typewriter of sorts, used for creating punched paper tape program inputs. The programmer typed programming instructions on the Flexowriter keyboard, and the Flexowriter punched the code onto paper tape. By itself, however, the Flexowriter system had one serious weakness: if the programmer typed an error, or if a bug in the program was later discovered, the entire program would have to be retyped. Thus, the invention of a symbolic editor.

The symbolic editor was a piece of software that connected the Flexowriter to the computer, and took advantage of the computer while a program was being written. With the symbolic editor, the programmer typing on the Friden Flexowriter keyboard would see all the programming instructions on the computer screen (one line at a time, at first) before they were punched on paper tape in binary code. Additionally, whatever was on the computer screen could be erased or altered by simple commands on the Flexowriter keyboard. This meant that errors in typing or bugs within programs could be extricated without anyone having to retype the entire program. The symbolic editor automatically adjusted correct programming text around the altered text. At last, when the programmer was satisfied with whatever text appeared on the screen, he or she could instruct the Flexowriter to punch the program into binary code on paper tape.

As time passed, editing systems were tinkered with and improved. People added a capacity to type out programs in regular numbers and letters on regular paper in regular print, instead of binary codes on strips of paper tape. Once this happened, a few enterprising scientists, programmers, and hangers-on recognized that the symbolic editor provided an amusing way to write personal letters and Christmas greetings when the boss wasn't looking, and for several years such clandestine activity continued until it was no longer clandestine. At some point (precisely when is unclear, but it was associated with computers becoming smaller, less expensive, and more accessible), using the symbolic editor to produce letters and documents became an appropriate activity in itself. Thus originated computerized *text editing*, eventually known as *word processing.*

What is a *word processor*, or *word-processing system*? A word processor or word-processing system consists of (1) a computer (plus its usual peripheral elements, the screen, the keyboard, the program disk device), (2) a special program, and (3) a printer. The person using such a thing types at the keyboard, and instantly sees whatever he or she has typed on the screen as text. It looks much like a typewritten page of text except that it glows. That's attractive and entertaining. What is useful is that the program inside the computer allows a user to modify—alter, edit, delete—whatever text is on the screen, and whatever text may be stored in memory. With disks or other storage devices, one can stash endless text in memory, one page or a million.

With the possible exceptions of Jack Kerouac and the Beowulf Poet, writers find that their first drafts are imperfect. Perhaps the drafts contain spelling errors, or grammatical errors. More likely, they just don't work in places. A scene is flat. A character is unconvincing. A description needs to be expanded. A paragraph needs to be deleted. A sentence needs to be inverted, converted, or introverted. Common sense demands this, modesty demands that, immodesty demands a third thing, an editor demands a fourth and fifth. It is common for writers to revise their work three or four, five or ten times. And in the days of quill pens, such revision was done by scratching out, scrabbling and scribbling in, and in the end physically rewriting page after page, time and again. In the days of typewriters, an author went over the first draft of a manuscript with a pencil, crossing out, making notes in the margins. Next came the cut-and-paste stage: the author moved sentences and paragraphs around physically by cutting them out and pasting them elsewhere. A section might be expanded by physically cutting it open, typing additional material on another piece of paper, and pasting the entire mess together. As soon as the mess became unbearable: back to the typing stage again. Type the whole piece over, and look at it again. Probably the resulting second typed draft would again need to be revised, and cut and pasted.

A word processor allows the writer to revise electronically. Comes a misspelling or typographical error, the writer simply calls up the appropriate section on the screen, and with a few simple strokes on the keyboard, corrects the error: the entire remaining text is adjusted automatically. There are no erasure marks, no gaps, no signs anywhere of any correction or alteration. Comes a useless paragraph, the writer simply calls it up on the screen and deletes it: the gap closes up as if it had never existed. Comes a sentence that needs to be altered, the writer simply alters it. Again, the rest of the text is adjusted automatically. Comes a paragraph that should be elsewhere, or a word used throughout the text that should be changed in every instance, the program most likely will take care of that as well. If the writer is a terrible speller, he or she might add a spelling dictionary to check automatically the spelling of most words. If a writer wants italics, or special mathematical characters, he or she might buy the software and hardware for that. If at any time the writer wishes to see what the full *oeuvre* looks like on paper: press a few special keys, specify margins and spacing of lines, specify if the pages are to be numbered, specify if right margins are to be as perfectly aligned as the left margins, and so on. Then press the final command, and the printer begins spewing out the hard copy, the printed version—which can look like our standard idea of a computer printout (letters composed of lots of dots), or it can look precisely like any typewritten version, except there will never be signs of erasure. Don't like that printed version? Go back and work on the memory of it, as it appears on the screen, page by page, make your alterations, then print out *that* copy. Like the first version better? Go back to that extra disk you've stored in the desk drawer.

The primary function of word processors is seen to exist in the editing stage of writing. But in fact, word processors make a written text so fluid that they influence the compositional side of writing as well. With a typewriter, any false starts, weak ideas, errors are there, on the paper. They are *in the way*—disturbing, intimidating.

3. 2. Writing memoirs with a word processor
Photo: United Press International

You feel that constant urge to erase them, or type over them. Or you try to ignore them, as you bravely go on your way, composing. That must be why many writers have never been able to compose directly at a typewriter. Instead, they write a draft or two with pen on paper first, then transfer that to a typewriter. With a word-processing system, however, many writers find they can compose directly at a keyboard. False start? Weak phrase? Never mind. It can be instantly altered, or saved and easily altered later. Have a good idea or a nice sentence or chapter that might be useful later but not now? Never mind. Write it out on the screen, save it in memory, and call it up later when you want it. What we have, in other words, is something drastically different from an expensive typewriter: an entirely new medium.

Excellent word-processing systems based on small computers (plus software, plus printer) can be purchased for the price of two or three expensive typewriters. With such a system, contents of an entire book manuscript can be encoded into magnetic patterns on a single disk (or a handful thereof, depending on the capacity of the disks). The disk or disks can be stored indefinitely; alternatively, their contents can be run back into the word-processing system and modified in any way the author chooses; or, their contents can be sent, with the help of a special inexpensive device called a *modem*, over a telephone to another computer. Computers have long been used in typesetting, and thus it is merely and clearly a matter of time before authors, publishers, editors, and printers will use a single computer system, or a series of coordinated systems, to produce books far more efficiently. Publishers are beginning to establish such systems. Even now, certain periodicals are published "electronically." The subscriber (for instance, a library) receives a computer terminal and printer instead of a paper journal. People who have access to the terminal can call up the current table of contents on the screen. If they see an article of interest, they merely instruct the terminal to print out that particular article.

3

Scott Kim is an unusual kind of calligrapher, often supplementing his pen with a computer. Kim's specialty is *inversions:* the representation of words in visually telling, usually symmetrical or reversible, ways.

Kim's *Infinitely Spiralling Infinity* began with the word *infinity* written in such a way that, in a straight line, the word was identical to its inverted (upside-down and reversed) form. Next, he defined that calligraphic form to a computer. Had he possessed almost infinite time, Kim might have defined the image by describing numerically (with coordinates on a numbered grid) each point of all

3. 3. *Invertible Infinities*
By permission of Scott Kim

the edges of all the letters, at last instructing the computer to make enclosed spaces black. To save time, though, he merely defined important points on the edges, instructed the computer to connect them with mathematically defined curves, and then instructed it to fill in the enclosed spaces. All of this produced a straight-line, continuous, invertible, *infinity*. Finally, Kim added a set of instructions (written by John Warnock of Xerox PARC) that transformed all the points on a straight line into a gradually shrinking spiral; and he arrived at the remarkable calligraphic infinite spiral shown below.

3. 4. *Infinitely Spiralling Infinity*
By permission of Scott Kim

Aaron Marcus practices an art at once minimal and conceptual. Minimal: few pretty pictures. Conceptual: Marcus is preoccupied with meaning more than form. He is the first person in history to speak to himself—using two adjacent pay telephones in the United Nations building—on a long-distance circuit that circled the Earth.

A Zero-Circle Around the Earth 24 October 73   Aaron Marcus

3.5. Documentation photograph by Mr. C of *A Zero-Circle Around the Earth* 24 October, 1973

A good deal of Marcus' work with computers explores an intersection between image and language. Sometimes he appears to be an aesthetic theoretician. At other times, he becomes a *concrete poet*, creating objects of meaning in language by using the computer to mold the visual form of words, the concrete shape of the poem itself. Visual art has often been considered somehow parallel to written language, capable of conveying its own symbolic messages. In a time when most people were illiterate, artists like Michelangelo transformed religious stories into visual representations on cathedral walls and ceilings. Among the first to begin the reverse, transforming words into meaningul visual form, was the nineteenth-century French poet, Guillaume Apollinaire, whose *Calligrammes* became a model for later poets and printmakers. "Most poets," Marcus says, "are happy to see their work printed in a book, and the form of it is not too important. The concrete poet says, 'Wait! I take these utterances of my mind that came out of my mouth and set them down. Suddenly I notice these markings are arbitrary. Why are my words black and not green? If I say *the* and write *t-h-e*—I may notice that the *t* is shaped in a peculiar way. What does that mean? What does it mean that the capital letter at the beginning of my utterance is supposed to invoke a visual beginning to this composition? Why are my words all running in lines? Well, the words stream out of my mouth, but that may or may not relate to the emotional or conceptual content of what I'm saying. The experience in my head is not in a line, but I've had to push it out of my mouth in a line. Why do I have to do that on paper?' With a computer I don't. The computer begins to make colorful, dynamic, visual poetry easy. I can twist the knobs, or change the program, and suddenly I have

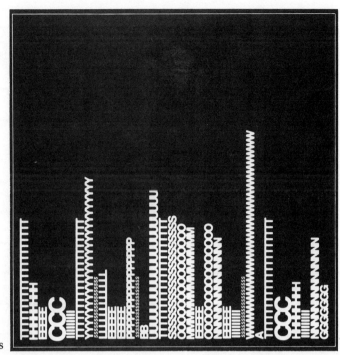

3. 6. Aaron Marcus *The City Sleeps,*
but Someone is Watching 1972
Photoprint, 15 × 19 inches
Reproduced by permission of Aaron Marcus

control over the visual symbolism of my writing. Suddenly I have
something halfway between verbal discourse and painting.''

At least two previous reproductions of Aaron Marcus' concrete
poem *The City Sleeps, But Someone Is Watching* were mistakenly
placed resting on one side instead of upright: illustrating the poem's
peculiar combination of meanings symbolic and visual. Tilted on
its side, the language content is quite clear, but the significance of
the image becomes less clear. Aligned as it was originally intended,
the language content is slightly less obvious, but the image of a city
skyline becomes a good deal more apparent.

Some of Marcus' work may remind one of the paintings of Paul
Klee: dreamlike images of vaguely pictographic content in apparent
suspension on canvas or paper. Other work seems static, and provocatively, or irritatingly, abstract and hieroglyphic. ''I have always
had in mind a kind of colorful, dancing spatial environment of symbols. I'd like to make out of symbols an architecture. Aside from
keeping the rain off and heat in, architecture gives us symbolic
tableaux, symbolic structures distributed in space. The computer's
architecture of information makes us freer than ever before to create
forms, to move around, twist and turn, to create markings and symbolic monuments, to produce something as animated as a ferris
wheel at a carnival, or as static as a cemetery.''

But excuse me! Aaron Marcus and Scott Kim certainly belong
in the chapter on *Creation in Light*.

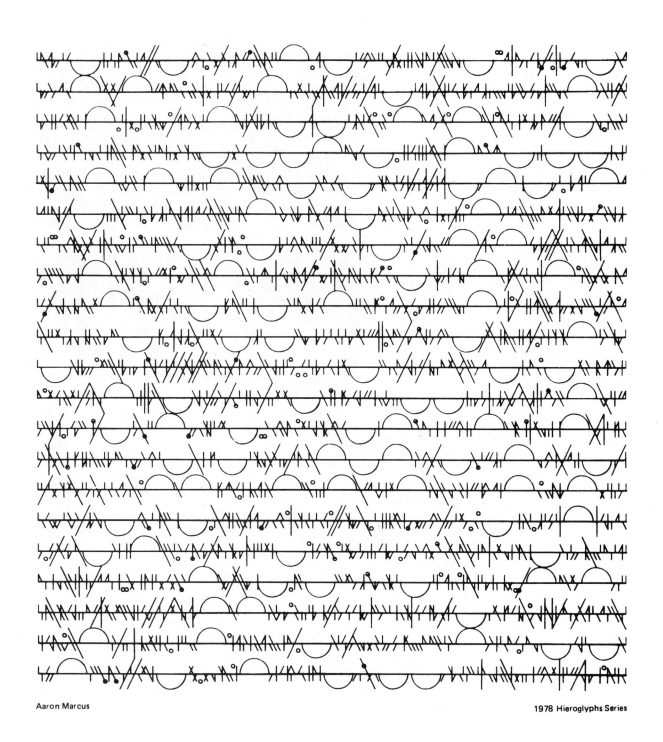

3. 7. Aaron Marcus *From the 'Hieroglyph Series'* 1978
Reproduced by permission of Aaron Marcus

And on the seventh day God finished his work which he had done, and he rested on the seventh day from all his work which he had done.

—The Book of Genesis.

Chapter 4

Creation
in
Recreation

1

Life is the immediate sequence of events and actions in the material universe. Art is a mirror or lens acting upon that immediate sequence to produce an image or model or enduring impression. Art, as mirror, can reflect life with realistic accuracy. As lens, it can *refract* life in surprising, interpretative, nonrealistic ways. Often in his work, artist M. C. Escher practices a mirroring, a realism so highly precise as to make us on the one hand almost forget the mirror. On the other hand, with a single violation of the laws of realism, he hits us over the head with that mirror. His lithograph *Drawing Hands*, for instance, presents the portrait of a pair of hands drawn so accurately as to look "really real," as though they actually exist in life, interacting with the elements and tools of art—pencil,

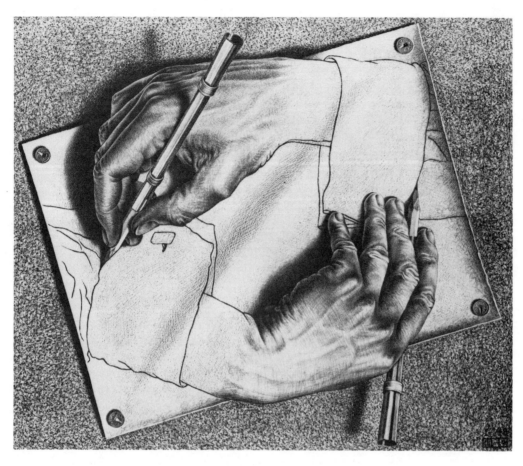

4. 1. M. C. Escher *Drawing Hands* 1948
Lithograph $11\frac{1}{8} \times 13\frac{1}{8}$ inches
© Beeldrecht, Amsterdam/ VAGA, New York 1982
Collection Haags Gemeentemuseum

paper tacked to a surface. The hands seem to leap from the drawing, three dimensions emerging from two. A closer look shows that the "drawing" itself appears to exist in a three-dimensional world, emerging from the two-dimensional surface of the actual lithograph. The result inspires admiration, surprise, pleasure—and it does so by teasing the distinction between art and life, at last reminding us boldly of the paradox of all finished works of art: they at once exist and stand apart from existence.

Games are a form of art. Call them participatory art. Like all other art forms, games invite the observer to step aside from daily life and enter a fantasy world where life is experienced vicariously.

Life is continually compared to games in daily speech, in

numerous game metaphors.* "The game of life" is a cliche we hear more often than necessary. When we compare life to a game, we say we are giving ourselves perspective, which more accurately means that we are altering our perspective, trying to step back and see our lives from a cosmic point of view. We are attempting to distance ourselves, to say: "Life should not be taken too seriously." And it may be that this concept of *seriousness* can tell us as much as anything about games. Games are smaller than life. They are not as serious as life; that is, games arouse less intense psychological involvement than life does.

Though smaller than life, games are also *models* of life. First, a game always has a goal. So does life, both in its long-term aspect (the goal of survival: to endure), and in short-term aspects (the day-to-day goals of survival: going to work, cooking dinner, eating dinner). Second, in pursuit of goals both the player in a game and the participant in life encounter resistance or opposition in two forms: directed or willed opposition, and nondirected or random opposition. Directed opposition in a game usually consists of other players; in life, it consists of other people with other goals. Nondirected opposition in a game usually consists of some explicit randomizing factor such as a roll of the dice or turn of the cards; in life, it consists of all random experience.** Of course, just as visual art

---

*All his life Simon dreamed of running for the office of President of the United States. At last, he had his time at bat. Although most Monday Morning Quarterbacks considered him a dark horse candidate, some smart teamwork combined with an ace up the sleeve and a hole in one enabled him to clear the first hurdle in style. The die was cast, and so far he was batting a thousand. At the nominating convention, however, just when it seemed that he was nearing the home stretch, Simon was forced into a stalemate. A coalition of opponents (though mere pawns in the party) forced his hand and played a wild card by suggesting that his New Deal deals were way out in left field. Such dirty dealing from the bottom of the deck ultimately turned the convention into, as the expression goes, a whole 'nother ball game. What a sticky wicket! What a raw deal! Suddenly he found himself behind the eight ball. Although he was quite teed off, Simon managed to remain poker-faced as he sat on the sidelines for the rest of the convention. Though he knew what had happened wasn't exactly cricket, he played the game as it was expected of him, down to the last turn of the cards—until in the end, sadly, he lost all his marbles and was sent to the bench. Poor Simon: outrun in the race for the Presidency, a loser in the game of life.

**Standard, cubical dice (consisting of six equal, square faces) were used in India and Persia as early as 3000 B.C. Before the manufacture of cubical dice, people threw *astralgali* (a small bone found under the heel bone of a sheep or dog; instead of having six equal faces, the astralgalus has four faces, two of which are rounded.) Extensive caches of astralgali have been found in prehistorical campsites dated as early as 40,000 B.C., while Egyptian paintings from about 3500 B.C. show various deities tossing astralgali alongside mortals, and keeping score on counting boards. Astralgali, and then symmetrical manufactured dice, were often used as tools of divination. Toss them in the air and unseen forces of suprareality make the cast, while the priest interprets. Part of the attraction of randomized games, particularly gambling, has to do with a latent or unconscious sense of participation in unseen worlds of divine will or fate.

can be realistic or abstract, so games can be realistic or abstract models of life-action. The game of *Monopoly* is a realistic model of life-action in a capitalistic world. The game of chess is a semi-realistic model of the life-action of war in a feudal world. The game of darts might be considered a highly abstract model of the life-action of hunting.

We sometimes model the real world to understand it better. But in the case of games, we model the real world first to be enticed or stimulated by it, and second to back away from it—in other words, to have the luxury of tasting its pleasures without suffering its pains. Games grab our attention because, as models, they trigger the same biological responses and drives that life triggers; but ultimately, they lead us gently into a protected setting. In real-life real estate speculation, for instance, one can go broke, be humiliated, face actual poverty and deprivation, and perhaps in the end, jump out a window. In the game of *Monopoly*, however, one can have the luxury of experiencing (imaginatively) acquisition and power without having to face the real-world risk of bankruptcy. Because games stimulate biological impulses, we call them *entertaining*. Because they are nonserious, and avoid for us the stresses of real loss or failure, of deep involvement, we call them *relaxing*. In many ways their function resembles the function of dreams, and since games have existed in every culture known to history, we might conclude that they are psychologically as essential as dreams. We enjoy them, as we enjoy other forms of art, for ultimately obscure reasons, perhaps for the same reasons we enjoy dreams. They are at once an escape and a confrontation, an inner stage for psychic rehearsal.

2

In 1949, in a talk before the National Institute of Radio Engineers, Claude E. Shannon of Bell Laboratories proposed applying large computers and considerable computing time to the problem of teaching a computer to play chess. In a *Scientific American* article of 1950, he gave the following justification: "This problem, of course, is of no importance in itself, but it was undertaken with a serious purpose in mind. The investigation of the chess-playing problem is intended to develop techniques that can be used for more practical applications."*

---

*A century earlier Charles Babbage, inventor of the Difference Engine and the Analytical Engine, noted that the rules and procedures of certain games of skill, such as chess and "tit-tat-to," could be mathematically codified, and thus could be played by machine. He briefly, perhaps facetiously, entertained building such a machine in the form of a humanoid automaton and charging people for a machine

A serious purpose? More practical applications? What did Shannon have in mind? It is important to remember that in 1950 computers had existed for less than a decade. In comparison to the computers we have today, they were very expensive, very big, and very crude. The scientists who ran them thought they possessed wonderful, high-powered machines capable of doing prodigious mathematical feats. Shannon, however, thought that computers one day could be used in "tasks of a semi-rote, semi-thinking character" and he gave the following list of practical possible uses: "designing electric filters and relay circuits, helping to regulate airplane traffic at busy airports, and routing long-distance telephone calls most efficiently over a limited number of trunks." Shannon believed that one good way to research "semi-rote, semi-thinking" computer applications would be to work on computer chess.

Why chess? In the first place, the rules and goal of chess are precisely defined. As a problem, chess is difficult enough to be productive but not so difficult as to be intolerable. And it seemed potentially a good measure of machine intelligence because it could always be opposed by and compared to a human player. Most important, however, chess would be the first problem presented to a computer for which there was no approachable correct answer.

Of course, theoretically there is a correct solution to the chess problem. The correct solution is the perfect game, the game in which one has played with infallible accuracy the best responses to each move by an opponent. To do that a person has only to figure out in all cases the perfectly best response to any move and to all possible sequences of moves. To find the perfect game, in other words, one has to consider all possible games. How many games is that? If we estimate that there are about thirty possible choices of play per move, and that the average game consists of about forty exchanges (moves and responses), we begin to see that there are a lot of possible games. If you can make thirty possible plays and your opponent can respond in about thirty possible ways to each of your thirty possible plays, that gives nine hundred possible games in the first exchange. Each one of those nine hundred possible games can be modified nine hundred possible ways by the end of the second exchange, giving 810,000 possible games. By the end of the third exchange, there are some 729 million possible games. What you have, in other words, is a geometric progression, not a simple upward ex-

game of "tit-tat-to"—thinking that he might thereby develop enough income to complete his Analytical Engine. Babbage's ideas of a similar machine for playing chess were a little simplistic, however: "Allowing one hundred moves on each side for the longest game in chess, I found that the combinations involved in the Analytical Engine enormously surpassed any required, even by the game of chess."

pansion of numbers but a self-multiplying explosion, the same kind of event that makes mathematicians shudder when they consider population growth. By the end of the fortieth hypothetical exchange, according to people who like to figure out such things, there would be somewhere around a million-times-itself-twenty-times possible games: enough games that even an extremely fast computer would have to survive well beyond the life of the universe in order to test them all. And what if it made a mistake in its original evaluations and had to do everything all over again? In other words, there may be a correct answer to the chess problem, but it is impossible to find.

Shannon's proposed solution was to look at the way people play chess and imitate that. People are seldom so foolish as to examine all thirty possible plays per move, and they usually recognize the impossibility of anticipating moves very far ahead in the game. Instead, they quickly zoom in on two or three or four promising moves and anticipate as far ahead as they can tolerate—two or three exchanges ahead, or, if they're expert players, a few moves beyond that.

By 1958, two scientists working at IBM, Alex Bernstein and Michael Roberts, had designed a chess program for the monstrous IBM 704 that was good enough to beat a human novice chess player.

4. 2. The IBM 704 without its chess board
Photo courtesy IBM archives

The computer took about eight minutes to ponder a move, accompanying its cogitations with a dramatic flashing of lights, at last printing out a diagram of the board showing its decision. At the end of the game, it printed out the score, and the ambiguous statement: "THANK YOU FOR AN INTERESTING GAME." Bernstein and Roberts acknowledged their debt to Shannon, and indeed their chess-playing program was based upon Shannon's original idea.

Like any human player, the program began with a basic knowledge of the game's rules and values. That is, in memory the computer stored information about the layout of the board, the capacities for motion of the various pieces, and the various freedoms and restrictions—what could and couldn't be done with the pieces. It also kept information about values—values of the various pieces (according to chess experts), and of certain positions on the board and certain moves (keeping the king well protected, for instance, is of high value).

Given that basic evaluative ability, combined with enough memory to consider various moves and the consequent alterations of the board, the computer again followed the human model. Instead of seriously considering the approximately thirty possible choices of play, it examined all squares of the board and quickly considered only seven "good" possible plays (by asking ranked questions having to do with strategy and position, such as "Is the king in check?" and "Is a piece threatened?"). Next, and again as a human player would, it never anticipated all possible consequences of those seven hypothetical plays, but rather proceeded for two exchanges (four moves—play, response, play, response) to examine possible consequences. For each of the seven hypothetical "good" plays, it considered seven "good" possible responses, and for each of those it considered seven responses, and for each of those seven again, producing at last a consideration of 7 times 7 times 7 times 7 or only 2,401 combinations of moves and responses. The computer would examine each combination of moves, and attach a numerical value to each move. Having considered all 2,401 hypothetical events, the computer would select as its actual first move the one of seven first plays that produced the highest total score, both for its own hypothetical sequence of plays and its opponent's (thus anticipating that its opponent would be playing a good game).

It quickly became obvious to these early developers of computer chess that there are some ways in which a computer will almost certainly be superior to a human opponent in chess. For one thing, the computer will never have lapses of attention, and it will never, through fatigue or laziness, overlook a possible direction of play. Thus, a computer is not likely to make the sort of foolish play that even chess masters occasionally make. Additionally, in any situation where sheer ability to consider alternatives becomes important, the computer clearly has the advantage—in a linear fashion, it can calculate alternatives very, very quickly. On the other hand, the human brings to the game a high level of flexibility—a quick ability to learn from past mistakes and to size up an opponent, playing to the opponent's particular prejudices and weaknesses. As Bernstein and Roberts noted when describing their IBM 704 chess-playing program, anyone who could put together a sacrifice trap (the deliberate loss of a piece for significant position advantage) could beat it. Ultimately, as Shannon himself pointed out, the frustrated human player can always reprogram the machine so that it loses.

One of the limitations in computer chess at that time was simply the sophistication of the values placed on various moves. How much is this position worth? How much is that attack worth? To improve such evaluations, chess experts were enlisted to lend advice. Another limiting factor in computer chess was time. Obviously, the computer must take only an amount of time that a human opponent finds tolerable. Bernstein and Roberts thought eight minutes was tolerable. In timed tournament chess, three minutes is the limit. But computers became smaller and faster, and a computer in 1968 taking the same time that the IBM 704 did in 1958 would actually be playing a much more thoroughly considered game. Also, since in real chess the opening plays tend to be standardized, programmers realized that they could save time by storing in memory one or two hundred classic opening games. Thus, the computer didn't really need to waste time "thinking" until the fifth or sixth or seventh turn.

At computing centers across the country, in Europe, and especially in the Soviet Union, groups of programmers and computer scientists began working away on their versions of chess-playing systems. Informal competitions began. By 1974, thirteen computer chess programs from eight different countries competed in the first World Computer Chess Championship, at the Birger Jarl Hotel in Stockholm. The great American hope was a program known as *Chess 4.0*, originally developed by three students from Northwestern University—Lawrence Atkins, David Slate, and Keith Gorlen. Since most of the programs were written for very large computers, only two computers actually made it to the hotel; the rest communicated their moves by telephone. The winning program was the Soviet Union's *Kaissa* (named after the mythical goddess of chess), running on a large British-made computer based in Moscow. *Kaissa* played a series of superb games, and moreover astonished everyone by making many of its plays after a few seconds' deliberation—a feat it accomplished by continuing to

4. 3. Cartoon by Claude Shannon
From ''A Chess-Playing Machine''
Copyright © 1950 by
Scientific American, Inc.

INEVITABLE ADVANTAGE of man over the machine is illustrated in this drawing. At top human player loses to machine. In center nettled human player revises machine's instructions. At bottom human player wins.

analyze possible plays during an opponent's turn. *Chess 4.0* from Northwestern University placed a highly respectable second. Although it played to a draw with *Kaissa*, it had already lost to another program.

By 1976, however, *Chess 4.0* was making a comeback. It had grown a little, and thus was now called *Chess 4.5*; and its inventors and promoters, Lawrence Atkin and David Slate, ran it on one of the most powerful computers in existence, Control Data's Cyber 176. In the summer of that year, Atkin and Slate entered Chess 4.5 in a human tournament, the Paul Masson Class B Championship, and it won. Class B, by the way, is one category above C, the class of an average serious tournament player. Emboldened by that victory, in March of 1977 they entered the program in a tournament for human Class A, or expert level players. It won that too. At last, Slate and Atkins decided their program (by then known as *Chess 4.6)* was ready for the long-awaited rematch with *Kaissa*. They took it to the 1977 World Computer Chess Championship in Toronto. It beat *Kaissa* once to take the championship; then it turned around to whup it a second time in forty-four plays in an exhibition game. *Kaissa* limped home in disgrace.*

Meanwhile, the Fredkin Foundation had established a grant of $100,000 for the first programmer to design a chess program that could not be beaten by human opponents. In a 1982 tournament in Pittsburgh, Pennsylvania, the designers of a number of chess-playing programs, including Northwestern University's great *Nuchess*, hoped to win that purse. But the computers were soundly defeated (two wins, two draws, and eight losses) by local chess players from the Pittsburgh area. The human chess players simply studied the machines' styles and deliberately played against those styles. One of the human players even went so far as to repeat the precise plays another player had already used to defeat the same machine. The computer had no understanding of this tactic, and played precisely the same responses, losing once again.

Needless to say, beating the Russians (in the 1977 World Chess Championship) was a serious thing to do. Trying to win the $100,000 Fredkin Foundation grant in 1982 was also serious. By the end of the 1970s, however, computer chess no longer had to be serious. Small, inexpensive computers were suddenly on the market, and anyone could play chess against a computer for very little money. People could play chess for chess' sake!

By 1980, one could buy a program *(Sargon II)* costing a mere thirty dollars that would run on the little Apple II computer and that

---

*Dreading the rumored prospect of internal exile.

seemed fully capable of beating very good human opponents. *Sargon II* played within the limits of tournament time. It kept in memory standard "book" openings. It showed whatever moves it was considering. It entertained you with pleasing graphics on the screen, while you were being beaten. *Sargon II*, playing at its highest level of difficulty, seemed reasonably matched against a human player with a United States Chess Federation ranking of about 1700 (distinctly above the novice level). By 1981 *Sargon 2.5*—an entire chess-playing unit including computer and program—was being marketed for less than four hundred dollars. *Sargon 2.5* contained the same decision-making program as the earlier version, but it existed in a complete unit small enough to rest in the palm of one's hand. In addition: it had seven levels of skill; it gave advice to its human opponent; and it could work out strategies during its opponent's playing time, thus frequently giving quick responses to an opposing move.

Computer chess, as Shannon promoted it, was supposed to be a model for human decision making. However, in many areas of human decision making chess is not really a very good model at all. For one thing, other than the opening choice of sides, there is virtually no element of chance or randomness in a chess game. For another, everything about the game is clear and open. There are no hidden or obscure elements.

Given those two limitations, some computer scientists have asserted that poker is a more interesting game to study as a model of many real-life situations requiring human decision.* Poker does have unknown elements—the cards still lying face down in the deck, the cards suspended in an opponent's hand—not to mention the interesting and unpredictable human element known as *bluffing*. The outcome of a poker game depends only partly on the actual cards one is dealt; decisions made by the players are just as important. Thus, players try to bluff their opponents into making the wrong decisions. At the same time, players must determine when their opponents are bluffing high or bluffing low, and whether there are any consistent patterns of bluffing. So it becomes necessary, in computer poker, to design a program that not only deals with uncertainty (by figuring out probabilities of an unplayed card turning up or being in an opponent's hand, and calculating mathematically correct strategies of betting), but that also tries to create uncertainty (by attempting to outbluff its human opponent).

Decision making in chess can be divided into two elements. First, one must evaluate a single board situation, calculating the

---

*See Findler.

values of immediate moves and their immediate consequences; second, one must project into the future, considering the values of long-term strategies and consequences. Hans Berliner, a computer scientist and chess expert (one of the top twelve chess players in the United States for a decade and a half), worked on computer chess programs for a long time, and then decided that it would be more interesting to find a game that focused on immediate evaluations. "What I wanted," he wrote in an article in *Scientific American*, "was a domain where it is possible to compare two situations and make a judgment about which one is the better without having to worry about the exhaustive analysis that chess positions require." Berliner at last decided that the game of backgammon suited his purposes, and proceeded to develop a computer backgammon game that he named *BKG 9.8*. By 1979, he thought his game was good enough to challenge Luigi Villa, then the world champion at backgammon, in a $5,000 tournament at the Winter Sports Palace in Monte Carlo, Monaco.

BKG 9.8 was run on a PDP–10 computer at Carnegie-Mellon University, and its decisions were sent to Monaco by satellite, where a fancy robot, named Gammonoid, carried the decisions out on the board. At one point, Gammonoid was introduced on stage with an orchestral accompaniment from the theme of *Star Wars*; nonetheless, the audience seemed unimpressed.

When the actual tournament began, the audience was small and at first unenthusiastic. Apparently, Luigi Villa was strongly favored. But as the tournament proceeded and *BKG 9.8*, with some surprising and clever moves and serious strategies, won the first three games, more and more observers entered the room. According to Berliner: "The television room was now full of spectators, who groaned and cheered as the game swung back and forth between the combatants. It was like the semifinals and finals of the world championship, when the room was packed with aficionados who argued about which moves were best and which side was in the better position." When at last *BKG 9.8* won the championship, with a tournament score of 7 to 1, the audience went wild. The dethroned Luigi Villa was devastated, and Hans Berliner felt moved to console him: "I told him that I was sorry it had happened and that we both knew he was really the better player." But that day, in July of 1979, marked the first time in history that a machine had taken the world championship in any game away from a human player.

3

For a few hundred dollars one can now buy a small computer that will play a superb game of chess, or poker, or backgammon. The programs may cost anywhere from five to fifty dollars, and will come on either a tape cassette or a small, magnetic disk. Many of the programs offer the option of playing at several levels of skill. Not interested in chess, poker, or backgammon? How about checkers, *Monopoly*, *Clue*, or Go? How about bowling, golf, football, hockey, or baseball? By now, just about every traditional game and sport has been modeled by a computer program. However, one can also play a large number of nontraditional games on a small computer—specifically designed to take advantage of one or another of the unique qualities of the computer.

Skill and Coordination Games. These games require intense concentration and a quick trigger finger. On the screen you have fast action, dramatic motion and event, and typically an imaginary setting of space exploration and high technology. Although such games are usually thought of as fodder for young boys, for many years they were played—often in secret—by computer professionals on large, institutional systems.*

The first game of this sort, known as *Spacewar*, was created in 1961 by an irrepressible group of students and young programmers in the electrical engineering department at the Massachusetts Institute of Technology.** Before that time, computers at MIT were of the million dollar variety, identical with or similar to the IBM 704 Alex Bernstein played chess on in 1958. The IBM 704 had a room of its own, and specialized caretakers, or operators who ran it. Mere programmers were not allowed in the room. Then, in 1961, came Digital Equipment's PDP-1. It was carted into MIT in a few large boxes, and plunked in a corner of a room.

Many things about the PDP-1 were new and exciting. It connected directly to a typewriter, so you could type a character in and see it appear right on the screen. Also, it had a TV screen that allowed you to display points and make a picture or a graph. Most significantly, though, the PDP-1 only cost a little over a hundred thousand dollars. This meant that more people could touch it, and use it, and not have to justify their use so severely as before.

---

*One enterprising programmer developed a game that looked, on the screen, like a standard piece of accounting software; thus he could play it while "at work." In another instance, a large group of computer professionals colluded to play games on their institutional system during off hours; they passed among themselves printed rules, a narrative background to the game, and other pertinent details; those who were involved refuse to talk about it even now (years after the fact), even in the most general terms.

**Once again the issue of seriousness and games arises. Computer chess developed because Claude Shannon managed to convince the scientific community that in certain circumstances chess was somehow more than a game: it could be a serious type of problem for study by computer scientists. *Spacewar*, however, was never thought to be particularly serious. Instead, the computer itself became less serious—that is, less expensive.

4. 4. The PDP-1. By permission of Digital Equipment Corporation

One of the people who watched as the PDP-1 was carted into MIT was Stephen Russell, a programmer. He gives the following account: "I saw this thing come in, and admired it, and thought it was kind of neat. Among my friends the machine was the subject of some conversation. We thought it was a neat, new piece of technology, and we wondered what we could do with it. I personally got a rather bad itch to do something with it, just to find out what it was like to use. Also, there was a serious frustration because it had this wonderful screen display and at the time it wasn't used very much. We had a number of bull sessions on the subject of what would be a good demonstration program for the computer, which would, among other things, make good use of the video display."

In one of those sessions, Russell and his friends and roommates observed that displaying the physics of a rocket ship in space would be easy enough—much simpler than the physics of an airplane, for instance. Also, at the time Russell had just finished reading the Lensman science fiction series, four books written by E. E. Smith in the 1930s that contained dashing, fast-paced, high-action space adventure. Something of that spirit, with lots of action, seemed an interesting thing to try: "We had several more bull sessions on the subject, and eventually started talking about how this program ought to look. Basically, two space ships could be moved around on the screen, the player might control their motion, and they could fire torpedoes at each other. Everybody else thought it was a good idea, and they kept telling me, 'Gee, you really ought to write that.' I kept inventing excuses: I didn't want to think about all the ugly numerical analysis, and so on. But finally I sat down and started writing." Russell wrote a program for a two-player game. Each player had control of a spaceship that looked like a little triangle of light on the screen and could be rotated right or rotated left. A player could fire the spaceship to make it accelerate, or fire a torpedo. The torpedo went in a straight line, and could be used defensively (to blow up other torpedoes), or as an offensive weapon (to blow up an opponent's spaceship).

4. 5. *Spacewar:* Ready!
Screen photo by J.M. Graetz

The ships were given a limited supply of fuel (that is, limited time and ability to move across the screen), and when a player fired the rockets to accelerate, a little flame flickered out the end of the triangle. Torpedoes looked like slivers of light, but when one hit its target the computer made an appropriate "explosion" by displaying a random burst of dots on the screen.

4. 6. *Spacewar:* A direct hit!
Screen photo by J.M. Graetz

To make the game easier to play, Russell and his friends built two control boxes. Each box had a "fire" button for the torpedoes, a directional lever for the ship, and a second lever for acceleration, or—when pushed all the way out—for something they one day hoped to add, tentatively called *hyperspace*.

4. 7. The control box
Drawing by J.M. Graetz

Russell continues the story. "Well, that sat around for a while, and then a fellow by the name of Peter Samson wrote a program he called *Expensive Planetarium*, which had dots moving slowly across the screen, which represented stars. We decided to add it to the *Spacewar* game I had already written, so that now it had a star background and looked a little more realistic." Samson's *Expensive Planetarium*, by the way, was a careful representation—both in location and intensity—of the stars as they appear in the night sky in this hemisphere.

By this time, a few people had become reasonably adept at playing the game, and it began to seem too simple, too . . . straightforward. The gang decided to put some curves in. "My friend Dan Edwards did some head-scratching and figured out that it was possible to do gravity on the ships in real time; that is, to calculate the effect of gravity on the ships without actually slowing down the display, without causing a flicker and so on. So he took the program and added gravity—from a hypothetical sun in the center of the screen—and that gave it orbits." This apparently made the game more interesting and more of a challenge. Now the spaceships no longer moved in straight lines. They were pulled into orbits around the central sun, and players had to learn how to compensate for gravity. At that time, the computer did not have enough room in memory to make the spaceships' torpedoes respond to gravity as well, so *they* continued to fire in straight lines. Any apparent paradox was solved by calling the torpedoes *photon bombs*—unaffected by gravity.

Among other things, the addition of gravity led to a classic opening move in the game. In the beginning of the game, the two rockets start out at opposite corners of the screen. With the addition of gravity, players quickly learned that the best, or at least most dramatic, opening gambit was to move their rockets into very close orbits around the central sun, providing an extra kick of acceleration. This classic opener was called *the CBS opening*, because the rockets appear to form a CBS "eye" on the screen.

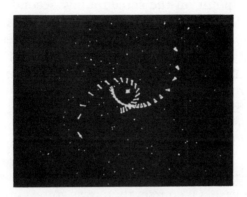

4. 8. The CBS opening
Screen photo by J.M. Graetz

That was the definitive version—all except for *hyperspace*, on which one of Russell's roommates and collaborators, J. M. Graetz, had been tinkering for some time, and which he at last added to the program in 1962. Hyperspace was what Graetz calls "the ultimate panic button." According to Graetz, "The idea was that when everything else failed you could jump into the fourth dimension and disappear."*

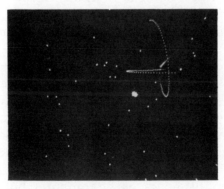

4. 9. A ship disappears into hyperspace
Screen photo by J.M. Graetz

---

*Some of my information about *Spacewar* comes from Graetz's excellent article in *Creative Computing*, August, 1981.

To make hyperspace more interesting, Graetz included a fancy screen pattern that represented the disappearance of a ship into hyperspace. To make hyperspace seem a reasonable element, instead of intrusive magic, Graetz included the concept of *MK I unreliability:* the rockets used Mark One Hyperfield Generators that hadn't been sufficiently tested—after they were used three times, they would conk out. Thus, with the complete game, a player in trouble could simply hit the hyperspace control and the threatened ship would disappear from the screen, only to reenter at some unpredictable point on the screen a few seconds later—but such an escape could only be used three times per game.

Soon there were a number of copies of the *Spacewar* program, and they quickly spread to all the other PDP–1 installations across the country (about fifty). Other programmers began writing *Spacewar* versions for other computers. Even though many people were having fun with the game by the end of 1962, generally it was still necessary to conceal at least some of the fun. As Russell puts it, "I had to get permission to use the computer, and I must say I didn't emphasize that I was writing a game. Instead, I said I was learning to use this new machine and educating myself, and that was certainly the case. Of course, there was some complication with people who just wanted to play. Later on, most installations felt it necessary to make it very clear that playing *Spacewar*, unless it was some sort of special demonstration, was absolutely the lowest priority of things the computer would do."

Time passed. Other features were added and variations began to appear. In the variation known as *Minnesota Spacewar*, the rockets themselves were invisible, but whenever you accelerated, the flame appeared on the screen. Scoring on the screen was added. And a ship could be partly damaged by a torpedo and crippled, instead of always being obliterated. In the variation known as *Two-and-a-Half-D Spacewar*, each player had a separate screen, and instead of seeing the ships as if from a distance, the players had the view that a pilot, inside a ship, might have. Part of the task was to find the enemy ship.

By 1972, the First Intergalactic Spacewar Olympics was held on a PDP–10 at the Artificial Intelligence Center of Stanford University. Now there were five ships on the screen at a time, and the scores (number of kills) for each ship appeared in appropriate places on the screen. To complicate the screen, orbiting mines had been added. Needless to say, the Intergalactic Spacewar Olympics was held during off-hours for the computer, but by this time, the terrible truth was obvious. No longer did enthusiasts feel compelled to presume or pretend that *Spacewar* was a "demonstration program" or a way of "learning how to use the machine." It was a game! People played it for the frivolous purpose of having fun. At the same time, computers and computer circuitry were becoming inexpensive enough that the first coin-operated *Spacewar* games began appearing in bars and pizza parlors.

Now it is possible to buy software based on the original *Spacewar* game and play it at home on a personal computer. Or one can play a large number of imitations, variations, or mutations of it, including the highly successful *Space Invaders.*

Space Invaders made its mark as a video arcade game in Japan. A video game is not precisely a computer game, because computers are, by definition, universal and programmable machines. Video arcade games are, instead, complete, dedicated units made up of computer components, containing fixed programs locked away inside the machine. They are not programmable. The dedicated nature of such games, though, means that whatever circuitry is used can be concentrated more fully on producing exciting sound effects and animation. Taito Corporation of Japan began manufacturing and distributing the yen-in-a-slot arcade units in 1968. By 1980, some 300,000 *Space Invader* video arcade games were in use in Japan, and an additional 60,000 in the United States.

The game is fast, demanding skill and reflex, rather than thought and strategy. Put your quarter in the slot, and on the screen appear the weird images of fifty-five alien invaders in orderly rows in the sky, descending to the horizon of Earth, firing laser beams as they descend. On Earth (at the bottom of the screen) you are aiming and firing defense lasers, one at a time, from three laser bases. Above the many orderly rows of attacking aliens, a single saucer flies about, also threatening the peace and survival of Earth-bound defenders.

Players at the controls of the machine are dancing about, firing lasers, trying to pick off the descending aliens one by one—picking up various scores for various kinds of aliens. The lone saucer, when hit, is worth scores ranging from fifty to three hundred points, depending on when in your sequence of shots it is hit. Meanwhile, maddening electronic music pulses in your ears. If you are good enough, for one quarter you can defend the Earth and monopolize the machine forever. Be forewarned, though: after shooting down all the descending attacking aliens, a whole new horde of fifty-five aliens appears, this time closer and firing more lasers. Your skills, your reflexes must be faster, and the hypnotic, repetitive music beats faster, just to remind you. Each wave of attacking aliens begins a little closer, until the tenth wave, when the aliens begin an attack formation at their original position again. The game ends either when all three Earth laser bases have been destroyed, or when an alien manages to evade the lasers and land.

When they first put out the game, the people of Taito Corporation allowed only four digits for scoring, presuming that no one would ever surpass a score of 9,999. What fools these manufacturers be! Soon after the game appeared, players were commonly reaching scores in the 5,000 range, and records began climbing well above the four-digit capacity. By 1980, an official score of 95,000 was recorded in the United States.

The only people who seem to understand the immense, addictive fascination of this and similar video games are adolescents, mostly boys—and they're not talking. The video game known as *Pac-Man* may be an exception. Girls like to play it too, perhaps because a player scores points without firing guns. In any case, rumor has it that *Space Invaders* provoked a minor monetary crisis in Japan, because so many yen were temporarily suspended in so many coin boxes. In addition, Japanese newspapers were provoked into massive editorializing over the decline in studiousness and the rise in delinquency associated with the game.

While video game arcades have recently been closing down in Japan, however, in America the rise of *Space Invaders* was just the beginning. Currently, 32 billion quarters a year are clicking into the coin boxes of American video games. And while children spend their allowances playing *Space Invaders*, *Pac-Man*, *Donkey Kong*, *E.T.*, and the like, parents are becoming alarmed. "Watch a teenager dumping quarters into a machine," pronounces one parent, "see the zombified look in that child's eyes. Is this what we want for our future generations?" A number of American cities and towns have banned video arcades altogether, while many more have severely restricted their locations and hours. On the other hand, some people think the game is beneficial to children, teaching concentration, coordination, a practical sense of Newtonian physics, and at the same time keeping them away from the television set.*

Computer Simulation Games. At the beginning of this chapter, I suggested that all games are models—either realistic or abstract—of events in real life. *Simulations* are *deliberately realistic* models of events in real life. Computer simulations are based on mathematical representations of real-life processes. In the form of games, they require thought more than action, but the earliest computer simulations were not intended to be games at all.

---

*Some U.S. Army recruiters have been hanging around video arcades, asserting that kids who love the games are good candidates for the military. Further, at the urgings of some Army officers, Atari has revised one of its arcade games, called *Battle Zone*, so that the control panel bears a marked resemblance to a particular infantry personnel carrier. This new version might become an inexpensive way of helping train soldiers.

In the 1930s, some people at MIT began thinking about systems called *servomechanisms.** Servomechanisms are systems, real or theoretical, that are self-modifying or self-directing. Perhaps a good example would be a heating system controlled with a thermostat.

The thermostat consists of two elements. First, it has a device sensitive to *feedback*. The feedback in this case happens to be the temperature of the air around the thermostat, and the device in the thermostat sensitive to temperature is an internal thermometer. Second, it has a device for activating the system namely an internal switch that turns on the heater when the temperature is too low, and turns off the heater when the temperature is too high.

A person may walk into a cold room in which the temperature is 50 degrees, and immediately walk over to the thermostat and set the little dial to 70. At this point the thermostat has been instructed to respond in the following way to feedback: whenever the temperature is below 70 degrees, the switch should be turned on, causing the heater to generate heat. Whenever the temperature is above 70 degrees, the switch should be turned off, allowing the room to cool down.

It should be apparent why the term *feedback* is used in this context: it is the nature of the servomechanism to establish conditions (in this case the temperature of the room), and continually "feed" information back to itself about those conditions. When feedback indicates that room temperature is moving toward the ideal temperature (below 70 but getting warmer, or above 70 but getting cooler), we call it *negative feedback*, because the difference between the real temperature and the ideal temperature is decreasing. Most, perhaps all, man-made servomechanisms are designed to move a system toward an ideal point; that is, to produce events that cause negative feedback, to reduce continually the difference between the real and the ideal state.** *Positive feedback* in the system means that the difference between the real and the ideal temperatures is increasing. In other words, climatic events outside the room (heat or cold) are more powerful than the heating system. When the temperature is actually at 70 degrees, we might say that the system has reached a state of balance, or *equilibrium*. Steady equilibrium seems to be the goal of the servomechanism. In the case of the heating system, we expect that the temperature of the room

---

*Engineering uses of servomechanisms were described as early as the nineteenth century; one of the earliest was to stabilize the motorized steering of large ships.

**If our hypothetical system also had a cooling device that was activated whenever the temperature became warmer than the ideal, it would be a better example of a servomechanism: it would *actively* tend to produce negative feedback whether the room were too hot or too cold.

will hover around 70 degrees, and we would be disturbed indeed if it kept fluctuating between, say, 50 degrees and 90 degrees.

That may be an interesting way to think about heating systems. It was also an interesting way to think about weapons. For instance, one could design a missile or torpedo to guide itself, as a servomechanism. One could give it some information about the direction of a target, include a feedback system, and then fire it. If it begins moving off course to the left, the feedback system activates a steering device which causes it to bear toward the right. It bears to the right until it reaches the correct course, or equilibrium, and the right-bearing system is turned off.

In the 1950s, Professor Jay Forrester at MIT began to examine events occurring in nature and in society as if they were servomechanisms. An apple grows until it stops growing, that is, until it reaches some kind of equilibrium. Cities grow in size, and then stop growing, or reach an equilibrium. In the case of cities, general growth past an ideal size (positive feedback) might be caused by lack of opportunity in the countryside and the promise of jobs in the city, whereas reduction in population toward the ideal size (negative feedback) might be caused by rising unemployment and crime. At first glance, it might appear slightly foolish to look at natural and social events, apples and cities, as if they were servomechanisms. It is, after all, only a metaphor, or a model. But for Jay Forrester there were at least two things about the metaphor that seemed useful. First, the metaphor seemed fitting and appropriate. Of course, neither an apple nor a city is as simple as a thermostatically-controlled heating system. They are complex systems. But it seemed to Forrester that if you examined them as if they were *interlocking and dynamic networks* of several different servomechanisms, you had an interesting and useful model indeed. The second useful thing about looking at natural and social events in terms of the metaphor was that servomechanisms are easy to describe with simple mathematical logic, and thus can be written as part of a computer program.

By the late 1950s, Forrester was trying to predict the results of corporate planning and policy with computer models. By the late 1960s, he had applied his simulation techniques to study the processes of growth and decay in cities. In June of 1970, Forrester was invited to a meeting of an organization known as The Club of Rome, in Bern, Switzerland. The Club of Rome is a private club of seventy-five individuals from several different countries, who share the common interest of considering large-scale world problems. They suggested that Forrester create a model of the world for the formal prediction and consideration of future world events. Forrester did, and the results of his computer simulation of the world are described in his book, *World Dynamics*.

Forrester's model of the world was a dynamic, mathematical description of five interrelated parts having to do with: population growth, capital investment, natural resources, agricultural investment, and pollution. The five parts of the system might be seen as five highly complicated and interactive feedback loops. In the example of a feedback loop system I gave earlier—the thermostat—the process of feedback was relatively simple. The thermostatically controlled heating system monitored and responded to the heat it produced. In a dynamic system, however, the nature of the feedback becomes a good deal more complex. In Forrester's world model, each of the five feedback loops fed back information both to itself and to the other four systems. As the population element of the model increased, for example, it increased pollution, but pollution reached a point where it began to decrease population (causing diseases, disrupting food production, and so on). As population increased, so did investment in agriculture, which produced more food, which encouraged more population, until there was no more land for agriculture, and starvation began to reduce population growth. As capital investment increased, pollution was stimulated until eventually population growth was discouraged.

Part of his model was based on a concept Forrester called *limits to growth*. Briefly, *limits to growth* suggests the following. No matter how sophisticated our agricultural methods are presumed to be, a limited amount of land can be used for agriculture. Thus there is a limit to how much food can be produced. No matter how much pollution the ecosystem can tolerate initially, there is a limiting point at which the pollution can no longer be dissolved or washed away, and it becomes poison. In Forrester's model, reaching a limit to growth was quite like reaching 70 degrees on the hypothetical thermostat. Once the temperature of the room has gone past that limit, positive feedback begins indicating that the heater should be turned off.

Forrester tried several scenarios for the future of the world by varying the weights of the model's five different components. What would happen, for instance, if governments decided to concentrate on controlling pollution? He was able to try this scenario out on his model and examine the results. What would happen if governments tried to eradicate world hunger by massive investments in agriculture? He tried that one out. The computer gave the results of these different scenarios by printing out a series of line graphs, showing over time the progression of various parts of the world system simulation. The time portion of the graph ran from the year 1900 to the year 2100, thus providing both backward and forward results. Looking backward on the model was a way of checking accuracy, since one could compare model results with historical reality. Looking forward was the purpose.

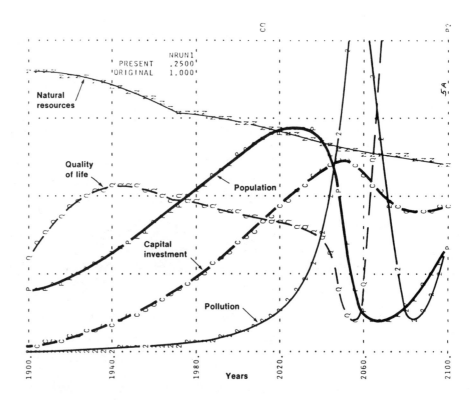

4. 10. Gradually reduced use of natural resources combined with continuing rise in population leads to a pollution crisis.
Graph reproduced by permission of MIT Press.

Why build a model, when one can see, hear, and experience directly what is going on in the world? Forrester never claimed that his model was infallible, or even very good. But he noted that it had the one advantage of being a conscious and deliberate attempt to look at the world realistically. In a mathematical simulation we know exactly what the elements are and we can examine and criticize them rationally. By contrast, the mental models of the world from which people often act can be laden with unexamined assumptions, prejudices, and beliefs. For all the potential faults of computer modeling, at the very least it can be seen for precisely what it is, and it can be criticized on rational grounds. Further, Forrester believed that his model often uncovered behavior in dynamic systems that was in direct opposition to unexamined "common sense" models of the world. For example, one run of the model shows a pollution crisis, a point at which the limits of the Earth's capacity to absorb and dissipate pollution has been reached—as a result population declines from various diseases, declining food production, and so on. Common sense might suggest that before such a crisis people would at last recognize its approach and begin to place massive limitations on industrial pollution. But Forrester's model suggested, contrary to common sense, that at that point in time the higher levels of population would be absolutely dependent upon a certain level of industrialization. To control pollution would require controlling industrialization. People might be facing an almost impossible choice—disaster by deindustrialization, or disaster by pollution—and be unwilling or unprepared to act.

What overall conclusions did Forrester's world simulation suggest? First, we are entering a transition phase in which growth as an answer to world problems is no longer possible. Second, when growth passes the limits to growth, the resulting feedback tends to move the system toward equilibrium. Third, in Forrester's world simulation, equilibrium often was approached by very rough fluctuations, analogous to the heat in a room fluctuating between 50 and 90 degrees. On the graph, such fluctuations would show up as a sudden collapse in a line representing population, or quality of life, or amount of natural resource, and so on. The term Forrester used to describe such a sudden fluctuation was *crisis*. And fourth, it may be possible to reach that inevitable equilibrium without massive fluctuation, without crisis or catastrophe, by consciously limiting the forces of growth (population and industrialization) through consistent and intelligent planning on a large scale, instead of waiting for natural catastrophe to apply the limits. "It is certain," he wrote, "that resource shortage, pollution, crowding, food failure, or some other equally powerful force will limit population and industrialization if persuasion and psychological factors do not."

Today, you can choose from a large number of simulation games written for the personal computer, all of which follow Forrester's original big-computer simulation in style and programming technique. Perhaps the main difference is that Forrester's world simulation produced its results in the form of line graphs printed on paper, whereas current small computer simulations usually rely on the computer screen, often producing entertaining graphics, as well as verbal and numerical results. Also, in game simulations the player becomes an imaginary participant in the simulated event or process.

Computer Bismarck (available in slightly different versions for the Apple and the TRS-80 personal computers from Strategic Simulations) simulates an historical event of World War II: the emergence into the Atlantic of the German battleship Bismarck. The game begins at high noon on May 22, 1941. There are two sides, the Germans and the British, that can be played by one or two players. If there is only one player, the computer itself plays for the Germans. The British objective is to sink the Bismarck while protecting their merchant convoys that run back and forth from the United States. The Germans are trying to disrupt those convoys and also sink British warships.

At the beginning of the game and at appropriate times during play, the computer displays a map showing the locations of one's own planes and ships, and the locations of any enemy forces "spotted" during the last turn. Each turn in the game represents four hours of time in real life, and at the start, players search for the enemy by instructing the computer to move each of their various planes and ships into new areas. Extraneous factors—such as the weather—are likely to influence the efficiency of this initial search. Once the searching commands have been punched in by both players, the computer calculates the new positions and informs players of any sighting of the enemy. Once the enemy has been sighted, the combat phase begins. In this phase, bombs, torpedoes, and whatnot are fired at the enemy, and the computer calculates the number of hits and total damages. A ship must be hit a certain number of times before it sinks. Until then, it limps along in damaged condition, with reduced speed and firepower—less of a threat in future combat with the enemy. Once a combat volley has been exchanged, the game returns to the search phase. The computer also keeps track of the amount of ammunition, and the potential for reinforcement. Gaining a lead of thirty points, or reaching eight o'clock in the morning of May 27, 1941, will end the game, but clearly the best way to end the game is to sink the Bismarck.

Three Mile Island (published by Muse Software for the Apple home computer) is based on the accident that took place in March of 1979 at the Three Mile Island nuclear power plant in Middletown, Pennsylvania. The player, as operator of the simulated power plant, begins the game by firing up a turbine that generates electricity. The player monitors the plant's operation by calling to the screen any of three different charts and four different animated diagrams, and makes appropriate decisions. The operator must run the power plant on a routine basis and produce a profit: that is the object of the game. But of course, this is the simulation of a power plant that had an accident. Thus, as time passes, various things are sure to go wrong, randomly—valves fail, gauges become inaccurate. Beyond making a profit, then, the operator must maintain a schedule of routine maintenance and also respond correctly and quickly to emergencies.

George Blank's *Santa Paravia and Fiumaccio* is a classic small computer simulation (available from Instant Software in slightly different versions for the Apple, Atari, PET, TI 99/4, and the

TRS–80 home computers). The game, based on historical research, makes the player ruler of a fourteenth-century Italian city-state.

As ruler, your job is to run the city-state in style, avoid disaster, and increase your own power and prestige. First, you must deal with a restless population of serfs. They are hungry. They want more food, and ask for grain from the grain reserves. If you don't take care of them, they may begin fleeing to other provinces, but if you use too much of your grain surplus now, out of season, you risk catastrophe should a drought occur. In addition, rats are continually decreasing the size of your unused grain surplus. Aside from placating the serfs, you probably ought to maintain at least a small army. For one thing, your ambitious and unscrupulous neighbor, Baron Peppone, is likely to invade at any time. For another, with an army you might be able to increase your landholdings and wealth. Alas, it takes money to make money—to raise an army you need gold. Selling grain from surplus can bring you gold; alternatively you may choose to tax the merchants and nobles, or increase customs duties. Just be careful you don't alienate anyone who has the power to strike back! If you wish to increase your prestige, you might use gold to build a new cathedral or palace. You may keep track of your lands, your possessions, and your defenses, simply by asking the cartographer to show you the latest ''mappa'' (on the screen). Your final goal is to gather enough power and prestige to be recognized as an undisputed Royal Highness.

The *Energy Czar* game, by Atari, simulates the energy situation of the United States. The player has been appointed by the president of the United States to be an Energy Czar with full legal powers to raise or lower energy prices, raise or lower taxes, increase or decrease environmental controls, promote or restrict energy development, and ration or leave unrationed energy sources. Each of these five policies is implemented differently with eight different kinds of energy sources: coal, oil, natural gas, nuclear, hydroelectric, solar, wind, and biomass (which includes synthetic fuels and methane taken from decaying organic material). The game begins with the energy situation of 1980, and the player can call up five different graphs on the screen, which show prices, taxes, deaths, supply, and usage—for each of the eight energy sources.

On the prices graph, the player sees, in units of a billion dollars per quad (quadrillion British Thermal Units), the current prices of each of the eight energy sources. The player now has the choice of legislating a freeze on the current price of each, or allowing it to fluctuate with the market. On the taxes graph, the player is shown current tax levels and is allowed to levy taxes (a billion dollars at a stroke), on each of the energy sources (up to eight billion total).

However, the player ought to remember that he or she will be able to use only one-tenth of the total taxes collected. The rest goes to waste and other federal projects. Also, higher taxes mean higher prices—meaning lower popularity for the Energy Czar.

On the deaths graph, the player examines how many deaths have occurred during the last period, as a result of industrial accidents and pollution, for each of the eight energy sources. The player then can choose to tighten or loosen environmental controls. Tightening them decreases the number of deaths, but it also means higher prices. Attempting to eliminate deaths would probably lead to economic catastrophe.

The supply graph shows in quads (quadrillion British Thermal Units) the amount of energy produced during the last period, and gives the Czar the ability to influence supply during the next period by choosing to promote or restrict any of the eight sources. The usage graph shows, in quads, energy consumption over the last five years. The Czar can ration supplies for any of the eight sources (an action that is bound to be unpopular, but in certain circumstances, perhaps necessary), or the Czar can allow energy use to float freely in response to market demands.

Policies are implemented every five years, beginning with the year 1980. After each turn (of implementing a five-year plan), the computer shows the results. Three types of results appear on the screen—economic growth, deaths (from pollution and industrial accident), and inflation. After the numerical listing of each of the three results, the screen shows a figure representing the percentage of people in the American population who are favorably disposed to the Energy Czar, for each of the three. At the bottom of the screen, the average public opinion is shown. If any of the three percentages is under twenty percent, or if the average of these three percentages is under thirty percent, the Czar is ignominiously kicked out of office and the game is over. If the overall opinion of the Czar is seventy-five percent favorable, he or she becomes a National Hero and may retire to the country and write an autobiography. If the Czar is neither such a failure nor such a success, he or she may quit voluntarily or choose to go on for another five-year term.

At the beginning of the game, the player must choose a bias. On the screen, the possible biases are listed as pro fossil, pro nuclear, and pro solar. Part of the reason for this initial choice of bias has to do with the results of the pregame research into the real energy situation: the researchers found that information and statistics available varied according to the biases of the authors. Thus, for instance, background material written by a pro-fossil author (in favor of coal and oil, the fossil fuels), might show nuclear energy as being more expensive to develop and more potentially dangerous, than would background material written by a pro-nuclear author. The game represents this fact by entering this initial choice of bias into the equation determining results.

Elements other than bias and policy influence the equation in this game, however. For instance, the simulation reflects the reality that coal and oil are abundant in 1980, but are nonrenewable and therefore likely to be scarce in a few decades. It also reflects the reality that adequate energy from renewable sources, such as solar power, wind power, and biomass, will be difficult to establish by 1985, but once renewable sources of energy are established, their output is going to be constant. Thus, the player who chooses a pro-fossil bias has a better chance of becoming a National Hero within the first twenty years of the simulation, while the pro-solar player has a more favorable chance of becoming a National Hero after about forty years. And to make the game even more realistic, the player can choose energy policies which, though they will result in utter disaster within fifteen years, are likely to make him or her a National Hero at the end of five years. That gives nine or ten years for the retired National Hero's autobiography to achieve best-sellerdom before the book burnings.

Exploration and Role-Playing Fantasy Games. Computers are based on binary circuits, and the first generation of computers could be controlled only by instructions written as a coded series of binary commands—on or off, 1 or 0. Such a fundamental level of program is called a *machine language* program, and programming a computer in such a manner was indeed an arduous undertaking. The first improvement over this state of affairs occurred when programmers and computer scientists began writing secondary programs that had no function other than to translate easier-to-remember (because they more resembled English) groups of letters and numbers into that abstruse machine language. Such groups of letters and numbers became, in fact, a second language, known as a *programming language*. Programming languages were as precise and demanded the same rigorous lack of ambiguity as machine language. They were simply easier to use.

A number of programming languages have been developed, and since each provides some distinctive translation between the user and the machine, each seems differently suited for different tasks. But since the primary purpose of a programming language is to make the computer more accessible to people, in some ways the ideal programming language may be *natural language*—everyday speech. Some computer scientists hope one day to develop a translating program that will allow a completely computer-naive person to make full use of some computer system simply by turning on the power and typing in an instruction phrased in his or her own native, natural language. Perhaps a request like: "Please let me know what I should do to find out about albino zebras in zoos." Of course, the kinds of programs necessary to translate between an extremely unpredictable, complex, and often imprecise natural language input and an absolutely precise machine language would have to be sophisticated indeed. Such a program has yet to be designed.*

Given an internal vocabulary (a list of words to compare with words typed on the keyboard), and a series of instructions about how to respond to different words and different structures of words, however, a computer could react usefully to a very limited group of *seemingly* natural language instructions. One possible use of such a program might be to send some apparently meaningful words or sentences out to a typewriter or screen, and thus make it appear that the user is conversing with the program.

Joseph Weizenbaum of MIT developed the first such conversational program in 1966. He named the program *Eliza*, in honor of Eliza Doolittle of Pygmalion, the Cockney girl whose social rank rose as she learned to speak proppah English. Weizenbaum's *Eliza* consisted of a language-analyzing portion and a script. The language analyzer reacted to someone's natural language input typed on a computer keyboard, by selecting key words and apparent themes. The script portion contained a series of rules allowing the computer to improvise sentences that were based on themes it determined in the language analyzer. *Eliza might* have appeared to converse on a variety of subjects, but Weizenbaum gave *Eliza* a script for mimicking a Rogerian psychotherapist. He thought this would be especially easy to carry out, since Rogerian therapists are trained to be nondirective—that is, their responses are typically neutral and often simply reflect the patient's own words. The following is an example of an exchange between a person and the *Eliza* program:

Men are all alike.
IN WHAT WAY
They're always bugging us about something or other.
CAN YOU THINK OF A SPECIFIC EXAMPLE
Well, my boyfriend made me come here.
YOUR BOYFRIEND MADE YOU COME HERE
He says I'm depressed much of the time.
I AM SORRY TO HEAR YOU ARE DEPRESSED

---

*A genuine natural language translating program must be prepared to deal with some astounding levels of complexity and ambiguity—large vocabularies, complex and variable rules of syntax, idiom, slang, context, connotation, levels of diction, and so on.

It's true. I am unhappy.
DO YOU THINK COMING HERE WILL HELP YOU
NOT TO BE UNHAPPY*

Eliza indeed possessed nothing resembling an understanding of the contents of the "conversation." The program simply cued in on key words or phrases and molded responses according to some preestablished formulas. Thus Weizenbaum became legitimately concerned when, as the program became widely known and surprisingly popular, a number of people presumed that *Eliza* demonstrated a potential of computers to automate psychotherapy.** Weizenbaum was alarmed not only by the naivete of these reactions, but also by the emotional readiness with which people adopted such beliefs. He was indeed disturbed by what he saw as an eagerness to attribute human qualities to a machine, and to presume that such a significant human interchange as psychotherapy could somehow be reduced to cold mechanics. What happened, of course, was that *Eliza* was one of the first programs that computer-naive people could use and appreciate and interact with. As Weizenbaum himself noted, "Most other programs could not vividly demonstrate the information-processing power of a computer to visitors who did not already have some specialized knowledge, say, of some branch of mathematics. . . . Its power as a demonstration vehicle was further enhanced by the fact that the visitor could actually participate in its operation." Its immense popularity was predictable—and so was the naivete of responses to it.

The inclusion of a similar conversational program is one obvious way to make computer games accessible to noncomputer people, and the first person to intuit this was computer scientist Will Crowther, who sat down before a PDP-10 one day, during off-hours at his place of employment, and wrote the original *Adventure* game for his own children.

Crowther describes the event in these terms: "I had been involved in a non-computer role-playing game called *Dungeons and Dragons* at the time, and also I had been actively exploring in caves—Mammoth Cave in Kentucky in particular. Suddenly, I got

---

*The example is from Weizenbaum's *Computer Power and Human Reason*.
**In his book *Computer Power and Human Reason*, for example, Weizenbaum quotes Carl Sagan: "In a period when more and more people in our society seem to be in need of psychiatric counseling, and when time sharing of computers is widespread, I can imagine the development of a network of computer psychotherapeutic terminals, something like arrays of large telephone booths, in which, for a few dollars a session, we would be able to talk with an attentive, tested, and largely non-directive psychotherapist."

involved in a divorce, and that left me a bit pulled apart in various ways. In particular I was missing my kids. Also the caving had stopped, because that had become awkward, so I decided I would fool around and write a program that was a re-creation in fantasy of my caving, and also would be a game for the kids, and perhaps had some aspects of the *Dungeons and Dragons* that I had been playing. My idea was that it would be a computer game that would not be intimidating to non-computer people, and that was one of the reasons why I made it so that the player directs the game with natural language input, instead of more standardized commands. My kids thought it was a lot of fun.''

That first *Adventure* game had no scoring. It was, basically: you are going out to explore a cave. You start on the surface, near an old building at the end of a road. You have to wander around. You have to find the cave and find the light and start exploring. As you go in deeper it starts getting more fanciful. There are problems and you have to be imaginative to find your way through. There's a snake you have to get past, and then you start running into trolls and giants and things. It becomes a bit of a fantasy, and a bit of a puzzle.

Crowther named his game, simply, *Adventure*. It aroused some minor interest at work, and occasionally colleagues tried it on the PDP–10. The company he worked for, however, happened to be connected to the ARPAnet, a computer network connecting all of the major computer research groups in the United States. This network might be compared to a large private phone system that has computers instead of telephones at the ends; people running the computers can send messages or entire programs to any other computer on the network, and any message or program can be stored in memory and called up at any time to any computer in the network. Crowther eventually put his *Adventure* game on the ARPAnet, and suddenly people working at some twenty major computer research centers all over the country were playing the game.

Enter Don Woods, at one of the centers connected to the ARPAnet. ''I was a student at Stanford University,'' Woods recalls, ''and I heard through the grapevine that someone had found this game on the medical center computer. So I hauled it over, and started playing it a little. It had some bugs in it, but it was an interesting idea. So I tried to figure out how to improve it. Of course, all I got on the network was just the game: the source code for the program wasn't accessible. But it did mention Will Crowther, and I sent messages all over the ARPAnet addressed to him. I got in touch with him that way, and he sent the source code. I cleaned it up and began expanding it, adding some of the trickier treasures, and possibly tripling the size of the game—with the help of a few of my friends, roommates, and classmates. After that, I figured I might as well put it back out on the ARPAnet. I did, and sent out a few messages to various sites around the country to get people interested. Then I left for a couple of weeks' vacation. Well, when I came back, Stanford was irritated with me. Their computer had been swamped with people connecting via the network just to play the game! I accumulated the comments that people had about the game, and then fixed up some bugs and added features, and eventually came up with the version that got spread around.''

Crowther's original version had about five treasures, according to Woods, who added ten more. "Some of the rooms, such as Bedquilt and the Swiss Cheese Room, were in Will's version, but didn't really have anything and so were tagged as 'under construction.' There were indeed some bugs, such as rooms you could get into and couldn't get out of. Things like that. So all of the stuff beyond Bedquilt, pretty much, was what I added. The entire Troll Bridge section was mine. The Soft Room, the Vase, the Oriental Room, and the Chasm and Waterfall and Witt's End. Will's version had this sign hanging in midair, just before you got to Bedquilt, which said 'Cave under construction. Proceed at your own risk.' I thought that was a nice sign, so I moved it off to the entrance to Witt's End, and just left it there as an annoyance to anyone who wandered past. Anyway, after I had finished that, I sent it out to MIT and various other places on the ARPAnet, and the requests for copies began pouring in. I offered people what help I could with that, and it just exploded from there.''

That's how Crowther and Woods describe the origin of the *Adventure* game. *Adventure* is no longer a single game, however: it is a genre, a type of game, with numerous variations, written in many different computer languages for hundreds of different kinds of computers. What precisely is an *Adventure*-style game? What distinguishes it from any other computer fantasy game?

The original *Adventure* was a narrative puzzle, with problems, traps, clues, and goals, based on a theme of cave exploration. Subsequent *Adventure* games have been based on different themes—wandering through an enchanted land, being stuck in a haunted house, or Count Dracula's castle, and so on. The distinctive features of *Adventure* games are the following: (1) they are puzzles; they progress through a series of problems, each of which has only one solution; (2) they unfold on the screen in the form of a narration; and (3) the player makes his or her moves in narrative style, with verbal (natural language) commands typed on the keyboard.

The commands have to do with three types of events—motion, examination, and action—and in terms of the imaginative structure of the game, commands are instructions to the player's "alter ego" or "character" who exists inside the works somewhere, probably just behind the front of the screen. "GO WEST," you type in. The character goes west, and suddenly a new scene is described on the screen: "YOU ARE NOW ON A LONG AND LONELY ROAD. TO THE RIGHT IS A CRAGGY MOUNTAIN. TO THE LEFT IS A DYING HORSE." After the description, the question, "WHAT DO YOU WISH TO DO NOW?" appears at the bottom of the screen. You type in "GO ROAD" (not entirely grammatical, but you're only allowed two-word commands). On the screen appears the following message: "UH-OH. THE ROAD HAS BEEN WASHED OUT IN BOTH DIRECTIONS. YOU CAN'T USE THE ROAD. WHAT DO YOU WISH TO DO NOW?"

You think about that for a while, then type in: "SCALE MOUNTAIN." The program doesn't recognize the word "scale," however (it contains appropriate responses for over a hundred verbal commands—assume "scale" isn't there), so it fakes comprehension by flashing up this standard response: "QUITE IMPOSSIBLE. WHAT DO YOU WISH TO DO NOW?" You're practiced enough in the game to recognize that the computer's "quite impossible" response may simply mean that your command wasn't in the computer's vocabulary, so you try rewording the same command: "CLIMB MOUNTAIN." On the screen it says, "YOU'D BETTER NOT. WITHOUT PROPER CLIMBING EQUIPMENT, YOUR CHANCES OF SURVIVAL ARE ONLY 15 PERCENT. WHAT DO YOU WISH TO DO NOW?" By this time, you're getting frustrated, perhaps even irritated by the constant prodding of that "WHAT DO YOU WISH TO DO NOW?" At last you remember the dying horse. You start thinking (a prerequisite to getting anywhere in the game). "What is the horse dying of?" you ask yourself, and you proceed to find out. You type in "EXAMINE HORSE," and the screen tells you, "THE HORSE LIES THERE, PANTING. HIS LEGS ARE THIN AS STICKS. HIS RIBS ARE PROTRUDING. FLIES BUZZ AROUND HIS DRY NOSTRILS. ON HIS SIDE LIES SOMETHING THAT LOOKS LIKE A MASS OF FEATHERS—A DEAD EAGLE PERHAPS? WHAT DO YOU WISH TO DO NOW?" "Feathers?" you ask yourself. But you decide the horse is dying of thirst. "WATER HORSE," you type in. "THE HORSE DOESN'T DRINK. WHAT DO YOU WISH TO DO NOW?" the computer says. "FEED HORSE," you type in. "YOU HAVE NO FOOD. WHAT DO YOU WISH TO DO NOW?" Well, that's it: you've had it. If you hadn't just put last week's paycheck into a disk drive for the computer, you'd certainly give it a swift kick. Instead, you type in: "HELP! HELP!" The computer responds: "TRY LOOKING IN YOUR INVENTORY." You type "INVENTORY" and on the screen you get a list of things in inventory, that is, the things you're carrying along on this adventure. The inventory includes a hatchet, two matches, and a canned ham. Canned ham! You call back the horse with a couple of commands on the keyboard, and you FEED HORSE—with what?—WITH HAM. Having done that, lo and behold, the horse stands up, and those feathery bags turn out to be wings. Pegasus! You hop on the horse and fly over the mountain . . . only to arrive at a new scene and a new problem.

The common criticism leveled at the *Adventure* games is that they are puzzles instead of games. Each problem has only one solution, and once the player has successfully completed an *Adventure* game, he or she is not likely to want to play it again—the solution is found, the mystery and challenge are gone. Ultimately the object of the game is to guess the designs of the programmer, and the means to achieve the solution are limited to a distinctly finite number of two-word commands.

While repeating some of the concepts and situations of the *Adventure* games, other styles of computerized exploration games have added several levels of complexity. Among other things, for example, the *Zork* series introduces elements of time and randomness into a highly complex and varied imaginary world that can be manipulated with relatively complex natural language instructions.

Zork began during spare moments, off-hours, and a summer vacation at the computer science laboratory of MIT in 1977. One of the authors of *Zork*, P. David Lebling, tells the following story about how *Zork* began: "Basically, what happened was that the Crowther and Woods *Adventure* game appeared on the MIT computers through ARPAnet, and it took the computer science department by storm. At some times during the day you would see half a dozen people playing *Adventure* and nobody else doing anything. We all played it through, and really enjoyed it—it's very hard to overestimate Crowther and Woods' contribution—but we were dissatisfied with some of the aspects of the game, such as the fact that the language commands were so simple. Our laboratory has been associated with a lot of work on the development of natural languages on computers, and so we thought we had some good ideas about that. It was partly a case of, 'Well, we can do better,' and partly just the sheer fun of writing something like that."

At the time, three of the four authors of *Zork*—Marc Blank, Tim Anderson, and Bruce Daniels—were graduate students, and Lebling was a staff member at the computer science laboratory. They started writing *Zork* in earnest after the end of the Spring term. Consequently, three of the four of them could spend full time on it for a while, and the game was written very quickly. "The first version took less than two weeks. This was never released, since it was just a small prototype to try things out. Since it was early in the Carter administration, this version had rooms like the Peanut

Room, and things like that, which have never seen the light of day. Anyway, it just got added to, and we played it amongst ourselves on the PDP–10, just for fun. Then one day, Marc Blank had the bright idea that *Zork* had advanced to the point where it could be programmed for small computers. We originally were quite skeptical, because the program was so big, but Marc just thought about it for a long time, and he said, 'You know, this is really a do-able thing.' He sat down and did some designing, and the rest is history—of course, we could only fit about half the original game on a microcomputer program, so we just cut it in half, and put out the two halves.'' The two halves of the original *Zork* (now available from Infocom for both the Apple and the TRS–80) are called *The Great Underground Empire, Part I*, and *The Wizard of Frobozz*.

In the world of *Zork*, time is a potent factor. Certain events, once begun, are automatically scheduled to end. Switch on a flashlight, but remember that the batteries will wear out. Activate a time bomb, but remember to leave the room.

In the world of *Zork*, much is unpredictable. During his progress through the maze, the character encounters a number of weird actors and villains—monsters, gnomes, a troll, a thief, a wizard, and a princess. The character may have to fight any of the villains. However, the outcome (appearing on the screen in the form of a running narration of the battle) will not be entirely predictable. The character can be killed, wounded, knocked out, or survive intact, according to a mathematical formula worked out by the computer, which takes into account the strength and skill of the villain and the character, the types of weapons they are using, and a randomizing factor. "Ever since the beginning of writing the game," explains Lebling, "there was a certain amount of randomness available. For instance, one of the standard things when a player does something stupid is to give out a random selection from a list of wise remarks, such as 'What a silly thing to do,' or 'Only fools try to do that,' and so forth. I think that the reason fighting was introduced was partly just from the sheer enjoyment of writing the code, and partly to introduce a certain enticing unpredictability into the game. You know that if you meet up with The Thief there is a probability he will fight you. If you fight The Troll, there is a probability he will win. There is a probability that it will take you thirty-seven moves to do it, or whatever the random number generator throws out."

In the world of *Zork*, objects (lamps, bottles, treasures, and so on) may have contents, weight, position, and other properties or qualities. A box may contain a candle, for instance. A treasure may be heavy or light. If it is heavy, the character may not be able to carry it, or he may have to drop something else in order to carry it. Any object may be in, on, or under, any other object. A bottle may be open or closed, a lamp may be on or off, and so on.

The complexity of the *Zork* world means that, if the player is going to give instructions in the form of typed English words (natural language instructions), the commands themselves will have to be in some complex form. In other words, the complex world of *Zork* requires a complex use of language. One of the distinctive things about the *Adventure* series was that the commands were in the form of English sentences—but only two-word sentences. But in *Zork*, it is not enough to type in "DROP BOX." A player needs to be more specific. For example: "PUT ONLY THE OPEN BOX UNDER THE TABLE."

In order for such a sentence to have any significant effect, the program has to be able to make sense out of it, and to know how to integrate the instructions with the *Zork* world. Basically, the *Zork* program is constructed to "understand" a large number of natural language instructions put in the form of imperative sentences. The program includes a vocabulary of over six hundred words, including one hundred verbs. When a command in English is typed into the computer, the program (by referring to its internal vocabulary and by noting the positions of words within sentences) divides the sentence into three meaningful areas: verb, direct object, and indirect object. Thus it quickly knows, with the above example, that some kind of BOX is to be PUT into some relation with the TABLE. Prepositions in the sentence are used to modify verbs, moreover, so that the program recognizes the special case of PUT UNDER. In the same way, objects are not acted upon until the modifiers are in place, so that the object is clearly specified: the open and only the open box.

According to Lebling: "The language recognition-subprogram is now in at least its fifth complete rewrite. The first one we wrote was very simple, not much better than the one in *Adventure*, that is to say a straight two-word parser. Then we said, 'Well, we can add indirect objects.' Then once we added indirect objects, it became necessary to add prepositions, and so forth. In fact, now we're working on a microcomputer *Zork* game that's a mystery, like Dashiell Hammett or Raymond Chandler, and it has adverbs in it along with everything else, so that you can do things 'carefully,' such as 'search a desk carefully,' and that sort of thing."

In the *Zork* and *Adventure* games, the main character of the narration is essentially you, the player. You are the one who steps, imaginatively, into the tube and lurks there behind the screen to discombobulate the dragon and bobulate the princess or prince. But there are a number of computerized role-playing games (some of them based upon noncomputer role-playing games such as *Traveler* and *Dungeons and Dragons*) in which the fun comes from entering the skin of a character not predictably similar to yours.* Likely as not, the main character will be vastly different—in intelligence, strength, endurance—from the player, and part of the interest of the game lies in this ability to take on the role of a vastly different person, just as the reader of a book may enjoy identifying with an extraordinary character. Additionally, much of the outcome depends precisely on the qualities of the character or characters playing.

In the *Dunjonquest* series, for instance (this includes *Morloc's Tower*, *The Temple of Apshai*, *Hellfire Warrior*, and *The Cliffs of Tyyr*, by Automated Simulations), the player imaginatively becomes a character with some combination of levels of six traits: dexterity, constitution, strength, ego, intelligence, and intuition. The computer assigns 16 possible values (from 3 to 18) for each of 6 traits, and thus there are 16 times itself 6 times, or 16,777,216 different possible characters in the game. In any battle between a character and a monster, the computer determines, using instructions on probability, whether the monster strikes with his teeth, or

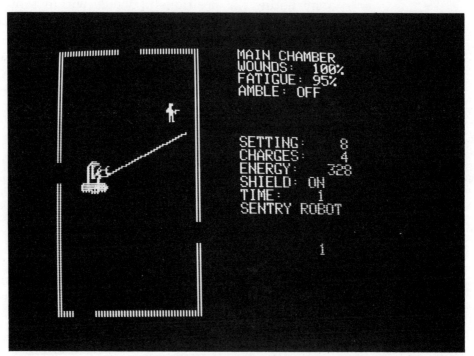

4. 11. In the main chamber, a sentry robot fires away at our tired and wounded character.
From *Rescue at Rigel*, by Automated Simulations

*The advent of computerized role-playing games was predicted by Arthur Clarke in his 1956 science fiction novel, *The City and the Stars*. Clarke describes a society of the future in which residents play computerized fantasy sagas. Players take roles in the sagas, and the computer provides direction and definition.

claws, or club, or bad breath. Similarly, the computer determines how often the character strikes the monster. Given those initial determinations by the computer, however, the player's tactics and choice of weapons, combined with the six traits of the character determine the results of any contest. A character with a low level of dexterity will have trouble hitting with the sword, and will be constantly swishing about both with the sword and the shield. If the character has a high level of strength, however, he or she can afford to wear heavy armor, wield a heavy sword, and—if successful—will dash off with lots of treasure. A character with a high level of constitution, will, among other things, be able to take many more blows (damage points), than a character with a low constitution.

4

These fantasy games are beginning to sound like standard written fiction. They have characters, including a main character that the player identifies with. They have a plot. And the natural language games have a limited narration. Of course, all games resemble written fiction in some basic ways: both games and fiction are designed to move the participant into fantasy and imaginative projection. But it is only with the advent of computerized fantasy games, making use of conversational subprograms, that language comes to have such a significant role.

Robert Lafore, a computer scientist who once wrote a series of novels about sailing, saw the *Eliza* program in operation one day, and decided he could combine his skills in programming with what he had learned as a fiction writer to produce a new art form he calls novels about sailing, saw the *Eliza* program in operation one day, stories existing on computer disk for home computers that use key word identification to provide a conversational interaction. The stories strongly resemble standard fiction: on the screen appears a standard written narration, dialogue, extensive descriptions, different characters, and so on. But this fiction takes advantage of its existence in a program by being *interactive*. The reader chooses the name of the main character, participates in the dialogue, and makes some decisions about where the story is going. If the story is a mystery, the reader participates in finding the solution. If the story is an adventure, the reader decides what kinds of risks he or she wants to take. Some decisions may be obvious. For example, in a seafaring adventure the reader, as captain of a ship, decides whether or not to attack an enemy vessel. Others are not so obvious. Decisions made early in the story may come back to haunt the reader when least expected. Attitudes of the interactive reader may alienate an important character, who later betrays him or her.

The author John Fowles included two separate endings in his novel, *The French Lieutenant's Woman*. Lafore's fictions similarly have multiple endings, as well as multiple middles and beginnings. An important difference, however, is that in Fowles' novel, the reader can examine both endings. In Lafore's fictions, the reader is never quite sure what the alternative endings are going to be.

But certainly the story of Robert Lafore and *Interactive Fiction* belongs in the earlier chapter on *Creation in Symbol*.

Selected Bibliography

Adams, Henry. *The Education of Henry Adams, an Autobiography*. Boston: Houghton Mifflin, 1961.

Ahl, David H. "Computer Games in Education." In *The Best of Computer Faires*, Vol. V. San Francisco: Computer Faire, 1980, pp. 39, 40.

Anderson, J. J. "Twenty Years of CAD/CAM." *Computer Graphics World*, January 1981, pp. 22–27.

Austin, Larry. Interview with John Cage and Lejaren Hiller. *Source—Music of the Avant Garde*, July 1968, pp. 10–19.

Austin, William. *Music in the 20th Century*. New York: W. W. Norton, 1966.

Babbage, Charles. *Passages from the Life of a Philosopher*. London: Longman, Green, Longman, Roberts, & Green, 1864.

Backus, John. *The Acoustical Foundations of Music*. New York: W. W. Norton, 1977.

Bailey, Richard W. "Automating Poetry." *Computers and Automation*, April 1970, pp. 10–13.

Bailey, Richard W. "Computer-assisted Poetry: The Writing Machine is for Everybody." In *Computers in the Humanities*, edited by J. L. Mitchell. Minneapolis: University of Minnesota Press, 1974.

Bailey, Richard W. *Computer Poems*. Drummond Island, Mich: Potagannissing Press, 1973.

Bateman, Wayne. *Introduction to Computer Music.* New York: John Wiley and Sons, 1980.

Beauchamp, J. W., and Von Foerster, eds. *Music by Computers.* New York: John Wiley and Sons, 1969.

Beaver, Paul, and Bernard Krause. *The Nonesuch Guide to Electronic Music.* New York: Nonesuch Records, 1968.

Beck, A. H. W. *Words and Waves.* New York: McGraw-Hill, 1967.

Beckwith, John, and Udo Kasemets. *The Modern Computer and His World.* Toronto: University of Toronto Press, 1961.

Begley, Sharon, and others. "The Creative Computers." *Newsweek,* July 1982, pp. 58–62.

Berger, John. *Ways of Seeing.* New York: Penguin, 1972.

Berliner, Hans. "Computer Backgammon." *Scientific American,* June 1980, pp. 64–70.

Bernstein, Alex, and Michael de V. Roberts. "Computer V. Chess-Player." *Scientific American,* June 1958, pp. 96–105.

Besant, C. B. *Computer-aided Design and Manufacture.* New York: Halstead Press, 1980.

Bornoff, Jack, ed. *Music Theatre in a Changing Society.* New York: UNESCO, 1968.

Borroff, Marie. "Computer as Poet." *Yale Alumni Magazine,* January 1971, pp. 22–25.

Borroff, Marie. "Creativity, Poetic Language, and the Computer." *Yale Review 60* (1971): 481–514.

Brand, Stewart. "Fanatic Life and Symbolic Death among the Computer Bums." *Two Cybernetic Frontiers.* New York: Random House, 1974, pp. 39–94.

Burke, James. *Connections.* Boston: Little, Brown, 1978.

Cage, John. *A Catalogue of Works.* New York: Henmar Press, 1962.

Cage, John. *M: Writings '67–'72.* Middletown, Conn.: Wesleyan University Press, 1969.

Cebulski, Frank. "Words as Art." *Artweek,* October 1981, pp. 1, 16.

Chadwick, Bruce. "The Furor Over Video Games." *Home Video,* July 1982.

Chapel, Lee. "Monster Combat." *Creative Computing,* February 1981, pp. 106–8.

Chasen, Sylvan H. *Geometric Principles and Procedures for Computer Graphics Applications.* Englewood Cliffs, N.J.: Prentice-Hall, 1978.

"Cheops Plays Chess." *Scientific American,* July 1976, p. 66.

Cook, William. *Plotto.* Ellis Publishing, 1928.

Coombs, D. H. "Poetry and the Machine." *Spirit* 36 (1969): 85–105.

Cope, David. *New Directions in Music—1950 to 1970.* Dubuque, Iowa: Wm. C. Brown Company, 1970.

Cross, Lowell. *A Bibliography of Electronic Music.* Toronto: University of Toronto Press, 1966.

David, Douglas. *Art in the Future, History/Prophecy of the Collaboration between Science, Technology and Art.* New York: Praeger, 1973.

Davies, Hugh, ed. *International Electronic Music Catalogue.* Cambridge, Mass.: MIT Press, 1967.

Demel, J., and others. *Computer Graphics.* College Station, Tex.: Creative Publishing, 1979.

Ditlea, Steve. "Inside Pac-Man." *Technology Illustrated,* August-September 1982, pp. 25–29.

Doliner, Irwin. "Word Processing Systems: Points to Consider." *Creative Computing,* May 1979, pp. 28–30.

Dyson, Freeman. *Disturbing the Universe.* New York: Harper & Row, 1979.

Eastman, C. M. "Through the Looking Glass: Why No Wonderland—Computer Applications to Architecture in the USA." *Computer-Aided Design,* July 1974, pp. 119–124.

Ehora, Theodore. "World Chess Champion Computer." *Creative Computing,* January 1979, pp. 134–36.

Eimert, Herbert. *Electronic Music.* Ottawa: National Research Council of Canada, 1956.

Evans, Christopher. *The Micro Millennium.* New York: Viking Press, 1979.

Ferrero di Roccaferrera, G. M., "Poetry by Computer." *Computers and Automation,* August 1969, pp. 34, 35.

Findler, Nicholas V. "Computer Poker." *Scientific American,* July 1978, pp. 144–51.

Forrester, Jay W. *World Dynamics.* Cambridge, Mass.: Wright-Allen, 1971.

Franke, Herbert W. *Computer Graphics—Computer Art,* translated by Gustav Metzger. London: Phaidon, 1971.

Freeman, H., ed. *Tutorial and Selected Readings in Interactive Computer Graphics.* Los Alamitos, Calif.: IEEE, 1980.

Freeman, Jon. "Character Variation in Role-Playing Games." *Byte,* December 1980, pp. 186–90.

Froehlich, Leopold. "Give Tchaikovsky the News." *Datamation,* October, 1980, pp. 130–140.

Gagne, Coles, and Tracy Caras, eds. *Soundpieces: Interviews with American Composers.* Metuchen, N.J.: Scarecrow Press, 1982.

Gilbert, I. S. "Modern Poetry Technique and the Machine." *Chicago Jewish Forum* 27 (1968): 119–122.

"Good Try." *Scientific American,* June 1977, pp. 56, 61.

Goran, Morris. *The Story of Fritz Haber.* Norman: University of Oklahoma Press, 1967.

Grady, Michael. "Micros Say the Darn'dest Things." *Microcomputing,* April 1981, pp. 92–96.

Graetz, J. M. "The Origin of Spacewar." *Creative Computing,* August 1981, pp. 56–67.

Greenberg, Clement. *Art and Culture*. Boston: Beacon Press, 1961.

Greenberg, D. P. "Computer Graphics in Architecture." *Scientific American*, May 1974, pp. 98–106.

Greeno, N. *Wordworks*. Ann Arbor, Mich.: The Author, 1973.

Griffiths, Paul. *A Concise History of Avant-Garde Music*. New York: Oxford University Press, 1978.

Hamilton, Clarence G. *Sound and Its Relation to Music*. Boston: Oliver Dilson, 1912.

Hassan, Ihab, ed. *Liberation: New Essays on the Humanities in Revolution*. Middletown, Conn.: Wesleyan University Press, 1971.

Henahan, Donal. "Are We Ready for Computer Operas?" *The New York Times*. July 25, 1982, pp. H15, 16.

Hiller, Lejaren. "Composing with Computers: A Progress Report," *Computer Music Journal*, Winter 1981, pp. 7–21.

Hiller, Lejaren, and L. M. Isaacson. "Computer Contata: A Study in Compositional Method." *Perspectives of New Music*, Vol. 13, no. 1, 1964.

Hiller, Lejaren. "Computer Music." *Scientific American*, December 1959.

Hiller, Lejaren, and L. M. Isaacson. *Experimental Music: Composition with an Electronic Computer*. New York: McGraw-Hill, 1959.

Hiller, Lejaren. "Music Composed with Computers—A Historical Survey." In *The Computer and Music*, edited by Harry Lincoln. Ithaca: Cornell University Press, 1970.

Hofstadter, Douglas R. *Gödel, Escher, Bach: An Eternal Golden Braid*. New York: Basic Books, 1979.

Hughes, Robert. *The Shock of the New*. New York: Alfred A. Knopf, 1981.

Hussey, James. "Inside Space Invaders." *Creative Computing*, June 1980, pp. 150, 151.

Informatique No. 13. IBM, 1975.

Johnson, Alastair. "Words as Images: Rediscovering Typographic Printmaking." *Print News*, August-September 1981.

Kahn, Martin. *Computer Imagery: A Coloring Book*. Los Angeles: Golden Triangle Distributors, 1981.

Kakutani, Michiko. "Exotic, Packaged Romances of Happiness Always and Forever." *San Francisco Examiner and Chronicle (This World)*, September 7, 1980, p. 38.

Kasson, John F. *Civilizing the Machine: Technology and Republican Values in American, 1776–1900*. New York: Grossman Publishers, 1976.

Kastner, Joseph. *A Species of Eternity*. New York: Alfred A. Knopf, 1977.

Kent, Ernest W. *The Brains of Men and Machines*. Peterborough, N.H.: Byte/ McGraw-Hill, 1981.

Kim, Scott. *Inversions: A Catalog of Calligraphic Cartwheels*. Peterborough, N.H.: Byte/ McGraw-Hill, 1981.

Kinnucan, Paul. "Solid Modelers Make the Scene." *High Technology*, July-August 1982, pp. 38–44.

Kirby, E. T., ed. *Total Theatre—A Critical Anthology.* New York: E. P. Dutton, 1969.

Kirby, Michael. *The Art of Time—Essays on the Avant-Garde.* New York: E. P. Dutton, 1969.

Kitching, A. "Antics—Graphic Animation by Computer." *Computers and Graphics,* Vol. 2, no. 4 (1977), pp. 219-223.

Klein, Sheldon, with John F. Aeschlimann, David F. Balsiger, Steven L. Converse, Claudine Court, Mark Foster, Robin Lao, John D. Oakley, and Joel Smith. "Automatic Novel Writing: A Status Report." In *Text Processing/ Text Verbarbeitung,* edited by Wolfgang Burghardt and Klaus Holker. New York: Walter de Gruyter, 1979, pp. 338-412.

Klein, Sheldon, with John F. Aeschlimann, Matthew A. Appelbaum, David F. Balsiger, Elizabeth J. Curtis, Mark Foster, S. David Kalish, Scott J. Kamin, Ying-Da Lee, Lynne A. Price, and David F. Salsieder. "Modeling Propp and Levi-Straus in a Metasymbolic Simulation System." In *Patterns in Oral Literature,* edited by H. Jason and D. Segal. The Hague: Mouton, 1977, pp. 141-222.

Klein, Sheldon, with David A. Ross, Mark S. Manasse, Johann Danos, M. S. Bickford, Walter A. Burt, and Kendall L. Jensen. "Revolt in Flatland: An Opera in Two-Dimensions." Presented at the Fifth International Conference on Computers and the Humanities. Ann Arbor: University of Michigan, 1981.

Kostelanetz, Richard, ed. *John Cage.* New York: Praeger, 1970.

Kostelanetz, Richard, ed. *Theatre of Mixed Means.* New York: Dial Press, 1968.

Kranz, Stewart. *Science and Technology and the Arts.* New York: Van Nostrand Reinhold, 1974.

Lang, Paul H., and N. Broder, eds. *Contemporary Music in Europe.* New York: G. Schirmer, 1965.

Leavitt, Ruth, ed. *Artist and Computer.* Morristown, N.J.: Creative Computing, 1976.

Leavitt, Ruth. "Computer Art." In *Encyclopedia of Computer Science,* edited by Anthony Ralston. New York: Van Nostrand Reinhold, 1982.

Lebling, P. David. "Zork and the Future of Computerized Fantasy Simulations." *Byte,* December 1980, pp. 172-82.

Lefkoff, Gerald, ed. *Computer Applications in Music.* Morgantown: West Virginia University Press, 1967.

Levine, Ronald D. "Supercomputers." *Scientific American,* January 1982, pp. 118-135.

Liddil, Bob. "On the Road to Adventure." *Byte,* December 1980, pp. 158-70.

Lincoln, Harry, ed. *The Computer and Music.* Ithaca: Cornell University Press, 1970.

Lomax, J. D. *Computers in the Creative Arts (A Studyguide).* Manchester: National Computing Centre, 1973.

Lorentzen, Bengt. *An Introduction to Electronic Music.* Rockville Center, N.Y.: Belwin Mills, 1970.

Lubar, David. "Fantasy Games (Part I)." *Creative Computing*, March 1981, pp. 32–34.

Lubar, David. "Fantasy Games (Part II)." *Creative Computing*, June, 1981, pp. 30–34.

Lusignan, Serge, and John S. North, eds. *Computing in the Humanities.* Waterloo, Ontario: University of Waterloo Press, 1977.

Machils, Joseph. *Introduction to Contemporary Music.* New York: W. W. Norton, 1961.

Machover, Carl. "A Brief Personal History of Computer Graphics." *Computer*, November 1978, pp. 38–45.

Machover, Carl. "A Guide to Sources of Information about Computer Graphics." *Centerline*, July 1981, pp. 10–14.

Machover, Carl, and Robert E. Blauth, eds. *The CAD/ CAM Handbook.* Bedford, Mass.: Computervision, 1980.

MacLow, J. "Poems." In *Stony Brook 3/4*, 1969, pp. 99–102.

Martellaro, John. "The Newest Sargon—2.5." *Byte*, January 1981, pp. 208–12.

Martellaro, John. "Sargon II: An Improved Chess-playing Program for the Apple II." *Byte*, December 1980, pp. 114–18.

Martin, J. *Design of Man-Computer Dialogues.* Englewood Cliffs, N.J.: Prentice-Hall, 1973.

Marx, Leo. *The Machine in the Garden: Technology and the Pastoral Ideal in America.* Oxford: Oxford University Press, 1964.

Mathews, Max, et al. *The Technology of Computer Music.* Cambridge, Mass.: The MIT Press, 1969.

McCauley, Carole Spearin. *Computers and Creativity.* New York: Praeger, 1974.

McKean, Kevin. "Computers, Fiction, and Poetry." *Byte*, July 1982, pp. 50–53.

McKenzie, A. E. E. *The Major Achievements of Science.* Vols. 1, 2. Cambridge: Cambridge University Press, 1960.

Meehan, James Richard. *The Metanovel: Writing Stories by Computer, Research Report #74.* New Haven, Conn.: Yale University (a dissertation), 1976.

Mendoza, E. "Computer Texts or High-Entropy Essays." In *Cybernetic Serendipity*, edited by Jasia Reichardt. New York: Frederick A. Praeger, 1969, pp. 58–62.

Milic, Louis T. *Erato.* Cleveland: The Cleveland State University Poetry Center: 1971.

Milic, Louis T. "The Possible Usefulness of Poetry Generation." In *The Computer in Literary and Linguistic Research*, edited by R. A. Wisbey. Cambridge: Cambridge University Press, 1971.

Milne, M. *Computer Graphics in Architecture and Design.* New Haven: Yale School of Architecture, 1969.

Mitchell, J. L., ed. *Computers in the Humanities.* Minneapolis: University of Minnesota Press, 1974.

Morris, J. "How to Write Poems with a Computer." *Michigan Quarterly Review* 6 (1967): 17–20.

Mumford, Lewis. *Technics and Civilization.* New York: Harcourt, Brace & World, 1963.

Murgio, M. P. *Communication Graphics.* New York: Van Nostrand Reinhold, 1969.

Myers, W. "Interactive Computer Graphics: Flying High (Part I)." *Computer*, July 1979, pp. 8–17.

Myers, W. "Interactive Computer Graphics: Flying High (Part II)." *Computer*, August 1979, pp. 52–67.

Negroponte, N., ed. *Computer Aids to Design and Architecture.* New York: Petrocelli-Charter, 1975.

Nelson, Harold. "A Stellar Trek." *Byte,* December 1980, pp. 78–82.

Nelson, Ted. "Interactive Literature." *Creative Computing*, February 1981, p. 42.

Nelson, Theodor H. *Computer Lib/Dream Machines.* The Author, 1974.

Nemerov, H. "Speculative Equations: Poems, Poets, Computers." *American Scholar* 36 (1966/67): 395–414.

Newman, W. M., and R. F. Sproull. *Principles of Interactive Computer Graphics.* New York: McGraw-Hill, 1979.

Norman, Colin. *The God That Limps: Science and Technology in the Eighties.* New York: W. W. Norton, 1981.

"N × P!" *Scientific American*, November 1974, pp. 52–54.

Ogg, Oscar. *The 26 Letters.* New York: Thomas Y. Crowell, 1971.

Ogle, James V. "How Computers Are Changing Life in the Soviet Bloc." *San Francisco Chronicle*, November 18, 1981, p. C-1; reprinted from the *Washington Post.*

O'Neill, Gerard K. *2081: A Hopeful View of the Future.* New York: Simon and Schuster, 1981.

Orwell, George. *1984.* New York: Harcourt, Brace, 1949.

Parslow, R. D., and R. E. Green, eds. *Advanced Computer Graphics: Economics, Techniques and Applications.* New York: Plenum Press, 1971.

Parslow, R. D., R. W. Prowse, and R. E. Green, eds. *Computer Graphics: Techniques and Applications.* New York: Plenum Press, 1969.

Peterson, Elmer. *Tristan Tzara: Dada and Surrational Theorist.* New Brunswick, N.J.: Rutgers University Press, 1971.

Pound, Ezra. *The ABC of Reading.* Norfolk, Conn.: New Directions.

Pournelle, Jerry. "A Writer Looks at Word Processors." *On Computing,* Summer 1980, pp. 83–87.

Press, Larry. "Word Processors: A Look at Four Popular Programs." *On Computing,* Summer 1980, pp. 38–52.

Prince, M. D. *Interactive Graphics for Computer-aided Design.* Reading, Mass.: Addison-Wesley, 1971.

Rager, Edward. "Scramble." *Microcomputing*, January 1981, pp. 78–80.

Reed, J. D. "Plugged-In Prose." *Time,* August 1981, pp. 68, 70.

Reichardt, Jasia. *The Computer and Art.* New York: Van Nostrand Reinhold, 1971.

Reichardt, Jasia, ed. *Cybernetics, Art and Ideas.* Greenwich, Conn.: New York Graphic Society, 1971.

Reichardt, Jasia, ed. *Cybernetic Serendipity: The Computer and the Arts.* New York: Frederick A. Praeger, 1969.

Reichardt, Jasia. *Robots: Fact, Fiction, and Prediction.* New York: Penguin, 1978.

Rosenboom, David. *Biofeedback in the Arts: Results of Early Experiments.* Vancouver: A. R. C. Publications, 1975.

Rothman, Milton A. "The Writer's Craft Transformed: Word Processing." *On Computing,* Winter 1980, pp. 60–62.

Russett, Robert, and Cecile Starr. *Experimental Animation: An Illustrated Anthology.* New York: Van Nostrand Reinhold, 1976.

Ryan, D. L. *Computer-aided Graphics and Design.* New York: Marcel Dekker, 1979.

Salzman, Eric. *Twentieth Century Music—An Introduction.* Englewood Cliffs, N.J.: Prentice-Hall, 1967.

Schillinger, Joseph. *The Mathematical Basis of the Arts.* New York: Philosophical Library, 1966.

Schwartz, Elliot, and Barney Childs, eds. *Contemporary Composers on Contemporary Music.* New York: Holt, Rinehart & Winston, 1967.

Scott, R. I. "The Mechanical Bard: Computer-composed Parodies of Modern Poetry." *West Coast Review* 4 (1969): 11–15.

Secord, Paul F. "Chess Programs for the TRS–80: An In-depth Evaluation." *On Computing,* Fall 1981, pp. 52–60.

Shannon, Claude E. "A Chess-playing Machine." *Scientific American,* February 1950, pp. 48–51.

Shea, D. "Poetry by Computer." *Avant-Garde,* September 1968, pp. 30–31.

Sherr, S. *Electronic Displays.* New York: Wiley-Interscience, 1979.

Shirley, R. "Poet and Program." *Bulletin of the Computer Arts Society* 25 (1972): 11.

Snow, Charles P. *The Two Cultures: A Second Look.* Cambridge: Cambridge University Press, 1964.

Sofer, Ken. "Art? Or Not Art?" *Datamation,* October 1981, pp. 118–127.

Speer, Rick, Bill Kovacs, and Ruth Kovacs. *An International Guide to Computer Animated Films.* Seattle: Animation Research, 1979.

Stevens, P., and R. I. Scott. "Mindlessly Mass-Producing Poetry by Computer, or a Multiple-Version Poem for all Canadian Places and Seasons?" *University of Windsor Review* 5 (1970): 27–34.

Strange, Allen. *Electronic Music: Systems, Techniques, and Controls.* Dubuque, Iowa: William C. Brown, 1972.

Strawn, John. "Digital Recording." *Contemporary Keyboard,* March 1981, pp. 16–20.

Strawn, John. "Digital Synthesis." *Contemporary Keyboard*, June 1981, pp. 18–22.

Stuckenschmidt, H. H. *Twentieth Century Music*. New York: McGraw-Hill, 1969.

Sutherland, Ivan E. "Computer Displays." *Scientific American*, June 1970, pp. 56–81.

Sutherland, Ivan E. *Sketchpad, a Man-Machine Graphical Communications System*. Cambridge, Mass.: Massachusetts Institute of Technology (a dissertation), 1963.

Swift, Jonathan. "Travels into Several Remote Nations of the World, By Lemuel Gulliver." *The Works of Jonathan Swift*. Vol. 1. London: Henry G. Bohn, 1843.

"Thinking Machine." *Scientific American*, October 1949, p. 29.

Thullier, Henry. *Gas in the Next War*. London: Geoffrey Bles, 1939.

Tomkins, Calvin. *The Bride and the Bachelors: The Heretical Courtship of Modern Art*. London: Weiderfled and Nicholson, 1965.

Trask, Maurice. *The Story of Cybernetics*. New York: E. P. Dutton, 1971.

Trilling, Lionel. *Beyond Culture: Essays on Literature and Learning*. New York: Harcourt Brace Jovanovich, 1965.

Von Neumann, John. *The Computer and the Brain*. New Haven: Yale University Press, 1958.

Waite, Mitchell. *Computer Graphics Primer*. Indianapolis: Howard W. Sams, 1979.

Weizenbaum, Joseph. *Computer Power and Human Reason: From Judgment to Calculation*. San Francisco: W. H. Freeman, 1976.

Wheatley, J. "The Computer as Poet." *Queen's Quarterly* 72 (1965): 105–120.

Whitney, John. *Digital Harmony: On the Complementarity of Music and Visual Art*. Peterborough, N.H.: Byte/ McGraw-Hill, 1980.

Wiener, Norbert. *Cybernetics, or Control and Communication in the Animal and the Machine*. New York: MIT Press, and John Wiley & Sons, 1961.

Wiener, Norbert. *God and Golem, Inc.: A Comment on Certain Points Where Cybernetics Impinges on Religion*. Cambridge: MIT Press, 1964.

Williams, Raymond. *Culture and Society 1780–1950*. Garden City: Doubleday, 1960.

Wulforst, Harry. *Breakthrough to the Computer Age*. New York: Charles Scribner's Sons, 1982.

Ziman, John. *The Force of Knowledge: The Scientific Dimension of Society*. Cambridge: Cambridge University Press, 1976.

Zobrist, Albert L., and Frederick R. Carlson, Jr. "An Advice-taking Chess Computer." *Scientific American*, June 1973, pp. 93–105.

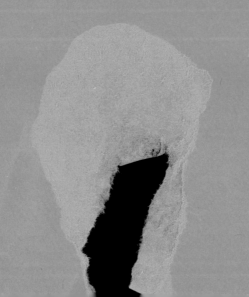